CHIANTI

To
Alessandro Boglione

Banker, bibliophile, historian

Who with grace and learning
rendered this book into his native tongue

also by Raymond Flower:

NAPOLEON TO NASSER: The Story of Modern Egypt

THE PALACE: A Profile of St Moritz

THE OLD SHIP: A Prospect of Brighton

RAFFLES: The Story of Singapore

YEAR OF THE TIGER

MEET YOU AT RAFFLES

MOTOR SPORTS: An Illustrated History

THE HISTORY OF SKIING AND OTHER WINTER SPORTS

THIS BUSINESS OF WRITING

CHIANTI, Storia e Cultura

with Michael Wynn Jones:

LLOYD'S OF LONDON: An Illustrated History

A HUNDRED YEARS OF MOTORING: An R.A.C. Social
    History of the Car

Editor, with Rene Burri and H.V. Morton:

IN SEARCH OF THE HOLY LAND

Forthcoming Titles:

PORTRAIT OF PENANG (with S. Cunyngham-Brown)

OUNDLE and The Evolution of Public Schools

CHIANTI
The Land, the People and the Wine

Raymond Flower

CHRISTOPHER HELM
London

© 1978 Raymond Flower
Revised edition 1988
Christopher Helm (Publishers) Ltd, Imperial House,
21-25 North Street, Bromley, Kent BR1 1SD

ISBN 0-7470-1011-0

A CIP catalogue record for this book is available
from the British Library

Cover photographs by Peter Flower
Cover designed by Kelly Chopard

Printed in Singapore by
Amsterdam Type Printers

CONTENTS

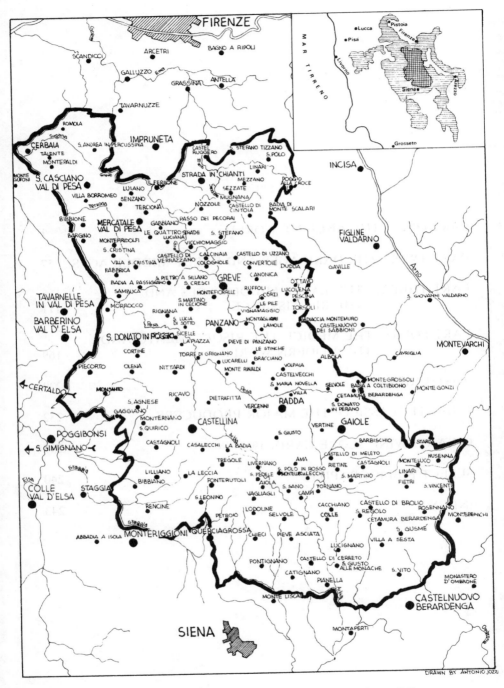

The area of Chianti Classico, as officially defined in 1932. The inset map shows all the areas of Tuscany that produce Chianti wine; dark shading – Chianti Classico; lighter shading – the other types of Chianti.

PART ONE: THE ANCIENT WORLD

ONE

It may dream a little less, it may be less rumbustious now. But were the old ghosts to return, they would not feel out of place. Amerigo Vespucci could still slip back to his house at Montefioralle. Machiavelli could still play *tric-trac* at the inn across the road; Michelangelo and Galilei would still recognise their farms above Grignano. And Monna Lisa Gherardini, would still smile with secret pleasure at the view from Vignamaggio — which Leonardo drew on the feast of the Madonna delle Neve in 1473.

This sense of continuity — the interweaving of present and past in a manicured landscape — is what grips you as you first drive into Chianti. 'The hills between Florence and Siena come as near to a poet's idea of gentlemanly country life as anywhere on earth,' mused Hugh Johnson in his *Atlas of Wine*. 'The blending of landscape and architecture and agriculture is ancient and profound. The villas, the cypresses, the vines and the woods compose pictures that could be Roman, Renaissance, Risorgimento . . . there is no way of telling.'

For, withdrawn and intact, and as beautiful as ever with its weathered contours, its villages and its farms, its churches and its hilltop castles, this is a land whose rhythms of change and growth have their roots in the deep pagan antiquity of the Etruscans or perhaps even earlier, maturing through generation after generation of dedicated toil. Here is a land whose equilibrium has been built up through an intimate link between man and the environment — whose charm and grace radiate over one with the same unconscious purity as a Sienese primitive.

It has always, I suppose, been a painter's country. In vain one scans the rag-bag of vocabulary for words that will do it justice. Indeed, whatever the season — under clouds the colour of oiled steel, or luminous against an enamelled blue sky — the beauty of these softly rounded hills, so exact in their perspectives, needs an Old Master's brush.

In Chianti we live in an historic present. We can, if we like, cloak reality with our fancies. And after all, why not? Yet I suspect that the Tuscans themselves — the lineal heirs of this ancient way of life —

may find the lingering afterglow less attractive than we do. The past, for their taste, is still too much with them: unchewable, as it were, in its structural harmonies. Why else, one wonders, would a village priest plaster over the massive stone walls of a *dugento* sacristy to disguise it as a modern 'villino'? Or our local carpenter, who handles antiques with the loving care of a renaissance artisan, rip the splendid fifteenth-century fireplace out of his sitting-room to install a sad little stove? Why, come to think of it, did the mason who so sensitively restored the stonework of my home, with such a precise feel for the texture of the materials, build a house for himself in steel and breeze blocks and fill it with plastic furniture of soul-smiting ugliness?

Open, frank, natural, spontaneous, warm-hearted — the Tuscans are realists rather than romantics, who (with a smile and a shrug) have amiably helped bankers, poets and even royalty to reconstruct the hilltop farmhouses that they themselves had abandoned. To them old stones are of less interest than south-facing slopes. And one really can't blame them. For, apart from all else, this is the area that produces Italy's most celebrated wines.

Chianti: it must be one of the most evocative words in the Italian language. Yet if to most people it simply means a straw-covered *fiasco* beside a plate of spaghetti, your dedicated wine-drinker will seek for the imprimatur of *Chianti Classico*: a black cock in a red and yellow circle. Because this is what counts. Plenty of pleasant wines that call themselves Chianti find their way around the world, bringing a whiff of Tuscany to Bali or Brazil. But it is only from the historic confines of Chianti itself that the great vintages come.

In the last decade or so, the hillsides have been bulldozed to make way for new industrialised vineyards, which now sprawl around the countryside like vast military cemeteries. Sometimes I wonder, rather sadly, if they are not changing the face of Chianti more than all the centuries that have passed. Perfection — the dusty elegance of the old Chiantigiana road curling through olives, ginestra and terraced vines, with glimpses of ivy-covered farmhouses, somehow more beautiful because of neglect — is so terribly vulnerable. But I daresay that they are inevitable. For us no less than the Etruscans, the Romans and the Renaissance, wine is the life-blood of this place. And when the prismatic evening light reveals a tailored landscape that could still be the backdrop to a Lorenzetti or a Ghirlandaio, it seems clear that the Tuscan soil, like the Tuscan spirit, has a genius for renewing itself, whatever may happen.

For the past fifteen years, I have enjoyed the hospitality of Chianti, and since it became my home I have been searching back into the complex tapestry of what has gone by. Thirty centuries is a long trip to take, yet if (as Lawrence Durrell once remarked) history is made up of the thoughts and actions of people who lived here before that seem to hang around the air, this private little corner is surely the right place to explore. After all, there are families in Chianti who can trace their names back to Etruscan days, and others who have owned the same land since the Middle Ages. Across the thickets of time, the essentials have changed so little that the young ladies of Boccaccio's *Decameron* would hardly raise an eyebrow if whisked 630 years forward from their villa near Fiesole to a contemporary *divertissement* in one of the smartly converted farmhouses on the Chianti social circuit.

TWO

It lies slap in the centre of Tuscany, this hill-girt little area, like a
foetus with a mountainous backbone, and if you were to make a
cross on the map from Sicily to the Austrian border and from
Brindisi to Aosta, the two arms would meet just over the middle of
Chianti. There was a time, geologists tell us, a million or so years
ago in the Pliocene Age, when the Mediterranean lapped against
these foothills, even if the sea is now over an hour's drive away.
There was a time, too (if the fossilised plants found near San Miniato
are any indication) when vines[1] grew wild on these uplands, before
there were any trees and long before man made his appearance.
Which, for a wine-producing zone, was not a bad start.

Then, like shadows across the softly moulded skyline, the first
nameless settlers moved in, sometime in the second millennium
before Christ, building their primitive dwellings at strategic, well-
watered points.[2] They were hunters rather than farmers, and each
family had its own roughly defined territory; but gradually, they
began to raise cattle and plant patches of grain. From around 1500
BC onwards, consistent traces of these Bronze Age people appear,
first on the high pasture land and later in the valleys as they moved
down and began to develop a village economy. ('The whole place is
congested with Bronze and Iron Age remains', commented Rik
Bronson, the Canadian archaeologist, as he idly picked up fragments
of incised grey-black *bucchero* here and there in my rose-garden.)
These early aborigines lived in round stud-and-mud huts with a
hearth in the middle — not unlike the pre-Punic structures still to be
seen in Sardinia — that were built behind protective walls along good
natural lines of defence. Remains of such enclosures have in fact
been discovered (above the rubbish dump at Panzano, for instance)
and the eager teams of students who turn up each July to spend a
hot month digging at sites like Cetamura and San Fedele are
beginning to put together a working picture of how these archaic
agrarian societies behaved.

But if the earliest inhabitants of Chianti were almost certainly a
branch of the Italic people — Indo-Europeans who spread through
the peninsula during the second millennium BC — they were joined,

sometime around 1200 BC, by a new wave of migrants who seem to have arrived by sea in Northern Italy and are known, rather tritely, as Villanovans (because the first evidence of them was unearthed at the village of Villanova, near Bologna). The fact that they buried the ashes of their dead in double-decker urns could point to a connection with the great urnfield cultures that flourished in Rumania from about 1600 BC onwards. However this is may be, the Villanovans were skilled workers, adept at producing bronze armour, *fibulae*, and swirled clay pots decorated in rather the same geometric style — with incised meanders, zig-zags, lozenges and so on — as the early Greeks had developed in Athens. But whereas the social structure of the earlier Italics had centred around the family unit, the Villanovans had a tribal culture.

Then, as archaeologists will tell you, a dramatic thing happened. The old, civilised world of the Orient suddenly burst into an exciting and dynamic new phase. The Assyrian Empire burgeoned out, along with the cities of Urartu, the new Chaldean and Lydian kingdoms, the independence movements, and the Saitic rule in Egypt. And before long this oriental renaissance had its impact on Italy. The Chaldeans established an advance post in Ischia, and the Greeks began colonising the south of the peninsula. Pioneers (such as Odysseus, if you like) sent tales back home that further up the coast they had discovered one of the richest mineral areas in the whole Mediterranean. Copper, iron, aluminium and perhaps even tin were there in abundance.

Soon, as Jacques Heurgon puts it, the country between the Apennines and the Tyrrhenian Sea was touched with the rays of a new sun. Populonia became the 'Pittsburgh of the Ancient World' and the mines both on Elba and in the Metalliferous mountains of Maremma galvanised the local economy much in the same way as the oil boom has done to the sheikhdoms of the Arabian Gulf today. For there is no doubt that the slag-heaps at Luni, the iron-ore chunks at Santa Severa, the magnetite at Blera, the remains of mines on the eastern part of Elba, to say nothing of the metal deposits around Tolfa and the zinc and tin just north of Siena all tend to bear out references in the literature of antiquity to a country filled with iron and copper. And almost abruptly, it would seem, this booming area, which hitherto had known a purely pastoral mode of life, became inhabited by a highly civilised people who spoke Etruscan, rather than an Indo-European tongue, and were known to the Romans as Tusci, Tyrrheni, or Etrusci, though their own name for themselves was *Rasenna*.

Most of the classical writers (who had access to sources that are now lost) took it for granted that the Etruscans had originated in Lydia. Seneca wrote: 'Tuscos Asia sibi vindicat' while Virgil, Ovid and Horace often called the Etruscans 'Lydians' in their poems. Herodotus, who was born in Asia Minor at a time when the Etruscans were still at the height of their power, relates that due to a famine (which probably meant pressure from the Assyrians) some of the Lydian population emigrated by sea with their goods and chattels; finally,

> after skirting the shores of many lands, they reached the land of the Umbrians. There they founded towns, in which they live to this day. But they changed their name of Lydians for another, derived from that of the son of the king who had led them.

Somewhat in contradiction to all this, Dionysius of Halicarnassus, a Greek historian who moved to Rome in 30 BC and became the leading member of an active circle of *literati*, was at pains to point out (possibly as a sop to Roman Imperial pride) that far from being a people who came from the East, the Etruscans were an indigenous race — a purely Italic phenomenon, in fact.

Whether indeed the Etruscans were part of Italy's oldest pre-Indo-European people who suddenly, like today's inhabitants of Kuwait, Qatar or Saudi Arabia, became enormously rich and powerful, or whether they were an oriental people who emigrated to Tuscany some time before or during the eighth century BC, is a question that still has the experts guessing. All the same, the conflicting views could very well be complementary. For, as likely as not, the Etruscan phenomenon came to life through a fusion of sophisticated Oriental immigrants with the native Italians, transforming what had been little more than a primitive, agricultural community into a highly cultured urban population.[3]

But regardless of how the Etruscans originated it is clear that they were the first non-Greeks in Western Europe to have adapted, or recreated, the brilliant civilisation of the East. Colourful, crowded and exciting it must all have been in the hilltop cities, each one a miniature universe of its own, that they built even beyond the boundaries of Tuscany, and which, once the sun finally set on the ancient world, were either incorporated — as at Arezzo, Cortona, Fiesole or Volterra — into a medieval and finally a modern town, or in other cases, such as Vulci, Roselle and Populonia, were simply abandoned to remain, as Logan Pearsall Smith evocatively put it, like so many empty sea-shells on the shores of time. Since they left no literature, we cannot hear what tongue they spoke in. But from the effigies on their funerary urns, and above all from the brilliantly painted scenes in the tombs of Tarquinia, or Chiusi or Orvieto, we can see their faces — those slanting eyebrows and brooding, enigmatic smiles that turn up, hundreds of years later, in so many Florentine paintings, and can still be spotted, every now and then, in any Chianti village.

Theirs was an archaic society that maintained, in the manner of the East, a system of master and slaves, *domini* and *servi*, with a well-defined gulf between privilege and impotence. Although no one has determined the dominant twelve of the Duodecim Populi Etruriae (which seem to have shuffled around, like the committee of a club) the kings — or *lucomons* — in each of these city-states were elected from the aristocracy of the founder, colonising families. Lavishly stage-managed, with a pomp and circumstance that was copied later by Imperial Rome, the ceremony of magistrature revolved around them: one visualises the dream-like figure of the *lucomon*, grave on his cerule state throne, flanked by twelve lictors carrying the *fasces* to symbolise their coercive power. (This was a bundle of rods with an axe in the middle, which was invented, according to Cato, at Vetulonia, where a copy of the fasces was found in the seventh-century BC tomb of the Lictor.) The army commander wore a bright red mantle, while other dignitaries had sumptuously embroidered togas, those of the senators being bordered in purple.

They loved a show. No people in antiquity, indeed, were more obsessed with rites than these early Tuscans. Their celebrated rules, embodied in the *Disciplina Etrusca*, with its Libri Archerontici, Haruspucini, Fulgurales, Rituales and so on, which laid down a complicated system of regulations and taboos, had close similarities to the divinatory science of the Assyrians and the Hittites. For as they saw it, the natural order of existence flowed from the elemental powers of nature. Life and death were one, and the subsistence of the community, no less than that of the individual, was part of a natural, pre-ordained rhythm. And so, in the belief that any transgression of an earthly law was a sacrilege, and that everything in the world was predestined, the whole machinery of state and all its legislature rested squarely on religious doctrine — on the traditions of a revealed religion, administered by priests who were trained in the esoteric arts of divination. Both Pliny and Seneca described how, during thunderstorms (of which there are some beauties around here) the Etruscan *Fulguriatores*, carefully dividing the sky up into sixteen separate parts from the cardinal points, could interpret the omens from each flash of lightning according to where it occurred; while *Haruspices*, the corner of their mantles pulled spookily over their heads, made predictions from the study of livers and entrails of freshly slaughtered animals. There were other augurs, too, who spelt out the future from the flights of birds and from any unusual occurrence that could be considered as a manifestation of the will of the gods. For, if nothing else, the Etruscans believed in the survival of man, in one form or another, after death; so that much of their art, like that of Pharaotic Egypt, especially their funereal offerings, sprang from a desire to assure the prolongation, as comfortably as possible, of life beyond the grave. Their tombs, furnished with everything they could possibly need (including household utensils) were almost replicas of the houses of the living.

Carved out of rock all over Tuscany, these tombs enable us to peer back across the centuries and get a hint of the sparkling Mediterranean life-style there enjoyed. For, paradoxically enough, along with their preoccupation with the supernatural and the grim piety which invested every object with a hidden significance (Arnobius, writing in late antiquity, called Etruria the ancestress of all superstition), they had a pullulating, pagan zest for life. The tomb murals at Tarquinia, depicting banquets, dances and athletic contests, suggest a daily round of lives joyfully dedicated to ease and luxury. There, elegantly if scantily clad, are men and women basking in the *dolce vita* with quite as much gusto (and rather more style) as any of the Beautiful People in Italy today. A flute player seems to be jiving as he blows his double pipes; dancers whirl round, their fingertips touching, in something suspiciously like a fandango, a girl at a feast throws her arms round the neck of her lover, a slave winks knowingly that he is fetching more wine. Elsewhere, two naked athletes wrestle and boys fish from a rowing boat while another dives into the sea. There is a great sense of liberation, as D.H. Lawrence noted. But in other murals there is a touch of cruelty, too: a man with his head in a sack being attacked by a molassan mastiff, and, at Caere, the decapitation of Medusa. For if they had a gift for pleasure, they also had a taste for violence (the Etruscans invented gladiatorial fights). And as you stand in the little vaulted tombs and study the scenes of merriment intermingled with such grisly undertones, permeated above all with the symbolism of death, you are inclined to wonder whether this does not find echoes today, and is not a clue to that special Italian genius that periodically breaks out, like the sun from behind the Tuscan clouds, in the Romans, the Renaissance, and the Risorgimento.

Possibly, as many people have suspected, an historical empathy emanates from the Tuscan soil. Michelangelo believed, so Vasari tells us, that his talents were due to 'the lively and subtle air one breathes in Arezzo'. Raymond Bloch once substituted an Etruscan head on Donatello's St George and found the similarity quite striking, while, as Jacques Heurgon noted, the angels of death on the cinerary urn of Arruns Volumnius at Perugia might equally well be guarding a tomb of the Medici. For, if one thinks of it (and it *is* a striking thought) this same region of central Italy has twice — under the Etruscans and during the Florentine Renaissance — been a spark point of our Western civilisation.

NOTES

1. When they were first discovered in 1858, these fossilised vines were thought to be of the *ausoniae* species. But on further investigation, they were ascribed to *vitis vinifera*.

2. On the hilltops between the Greve and Pesa rivers, archaeologists have found stone tools which can be ascribed to the so-called 'aurignacian' culture, which attests to the presence of man here in the Paleolithic epoch — much earlier, in fact, than the Bronze and Iron Ages. (Indeed, one such artefact was picked up on the golf course at Grignano.)

3. Sir Gavin de Beer made a study based on the frequency of blood groups in Tuscany, and discovered that the distribution of blood groups in central Tuscany, including Chianti, was similar to those in certain parts of Anatolia (cf. Scullard, *Etruscan Cities and Rome*).

THREE

And the fact is that some of their old rituals and taboos survived practically until the twentieth century. Indeed, as he wandered around Tuscany less than a hundred years ago, Charles Leland, the American anthropologist, was astonished how many of the country folk still clung to fragments of the old, pre-Christian faith, tending to identify their religious feelings in an intimate fashion with everyday domestic events. Out of the village priest's earshot, the old gods retained their grip, and to keep on the safe side of them, good, church-going *contadini,* when they passed a grove or a rock where such *folletti* or spirits were thought to dwell, would surreptitiously leave a coin or some small gift to please them, as a sort of double insurance, one might say. Woodcutters and charcoal-burners made sly little offerings to Silvanus, the spirit of the woods; and to stay in the good graces of Palo (the Pales of the Romans, and the god of agriculture) a farmer, when planting corn or working the vines, would light some straw and jump over it, incanting, 'Lo spirito Palo/ sarà quello/ che mi farà/la buona fortuna.'

Aplu, none other than our old friend Apollo, who appears on so many Etruscan vases and mirrors, was the guiding force for hunters, and quite liable to play tricks on them if they didn't look out. In the middle of the night he would pull off the bedclothes and then sit on their chests. But if his help was invoked with the appropriate saying ('Aplu, Aplu, Aplu/ io ti prego di darmi/ Fortuna e talento' — and so on) they could be sure of coming home with a full bag. Aplu was also the spirit of music, and according to Aelian (a Greek rhetorician who lived in the third century AD) Etruscan hunters used to catch game with the help of music. He tells us:

A skilful flautist takes up position and plays the purest and most harmonious melody . . . in the silence and the calm the sound easily reaches the peaks of the hills, the valleys and the woods, and finds its way into the animals' lairs. When the sound comes to their ears . . . they are overcome by the irresistible pleasure of the music, and . . . as if drawn by some charm, they are forced to approach and the power of the melody makes them fall into the nets, the victims of music.

There is no record of modern *cacciatori* using the same ploy, but then transistor radios would hardly have the same fascination as the flute. Yet smile as one may at these old wives' tales (and most of my *contadini* friends do), you will still hear it said that the upper reaches of our little stream, the Cerchiaio, are full of *fantasmi*, and not so long ago the old myth was trotted out, with hardly a chuckle or a blush, by the local mechanic, as he tuned the carburettor settings of a Maserati coupé. When out hunting, he says, his father and some cronies dossed down in a deserted farmhouse up the valley called Garbina (which etymologically, at least, has Etruscan origins) and in the middle of the night, with much scuffling and banging, the blankets were tugged off them and they felt an almost intolerable pressure on their breasts. So presumably Aplu was still in business, although my brother and his family, who now live in the place, have never experienced such nocturnal excitements. Perhaps electricity and central heating have finally been a match for the old spirit's pranks, just as, one sadly suspects, the jovial Etruscan spirit of the vineyards, Fufluns (the Bacchus of the Romans) who had an eye for the girls and would ensure a good vintage if suitably placated, has finally been banished by the bulldozers as they flatten out the traditional terraced vines to make industrial vineyards. But that, of course, is another story.

FOUR

For if northern Etruria corresponded roughly with the wine-growing area of Tuscany today, it did not take long for the Etruscans to discover the charms of the hilly region that has traditionally become known as Chianti *storico* — the three communes of Radda, Castellina and Gaiole which, in medieval times, formed the Lega del Chianti. Castellina in Chianti may now cluster hugger-mugger around its massive crenelated *rocca*, built by order of the Florentine government in 1400 after the older fortified village had been sacked by the Sienese in 1397, but its original location was half a mile or so away, on the site of an Etruscan settlement called Salinvolpe. The old Etruscan walls can still be seen, under a tangle of ivy and blackberry bushes, in the grounds of a farm called Poggio al Vento, now owned by the *Rector Magnificus* of Siena University, who has a splendid, if windswept view over successive lines of foothills as far as San Gimignano, and can still, if he feels inclined, draw water from an eighty-foot-deep Etruscan well. And a little way apart, on a neighbouring hillock, is the sixth-century BC hypogeum.

Thanks to Shakespeare's contemporary, a pugnacious Scot of whom it was said that 'not a day passed that he did not use either his fists or his sword', we possess a description of how it was discovered. Thomas Dempster sounds a flamboyant figure (a contemporary reports that when a young officer of the French king's horse guards made a pass at his wife, 'he caused his breeches to be let down, a lusty fellow to horse him, and whipped him soundly in a full school') but he was also an internationally known scholar, a professor of civil law at Pisa University, and arguably the founder of modern Etruscology. For, in between feuding and teaching, Dempster managed to gather all the facts and theories to be found in ancient texts and produce a massive seven-tomed work which, although it went unpublished for over a century, nevertheless became the starting-point for subsequent Etruscologists.

In presenting Dempter's *capolavoro* for its belated publication in 1724, Filippo Buonarroti (a kinsman of Michelangelo, who figures in the registers of S. Giorgio a Grignano as the owner of the artist's *torre* and farms) gives details of how the necropolis at Salinvolpe was brought to light.

According to Buonarroti, on 29 January 1507, when digging the earth to plant vines, the local *contadini* accidentally broke through the vault. He quotes the contemporary report verbatim:

A repulsive stench came out of the tomb. It was shaped like a cross, one arm of which was 20 braccia (or about 40 feet) long, six feet wide and ten feet high. This part was empty, but to the left was a large chamber full of cinerary urns containing the ashes of ordinary people, *gente di bassa mano*, whereas in the right-hand chamber were the coffins of the nobles. A queen's apparel was laid out on a table; a silver mirror on a decorated pedestal, a silver clothes stand, and a jar which had a golden cicada inside it and four more golden cicadas on each corner; a woman white as alabaster to the waist with a golden necklace; a copper vase with a lid like those that barbers use, containing drawers full of rings. We found precious stones and quantities of silver leaves which were subsequently sold in Siena, and I spoke to the jeweller who bought them. I saw likewise a sculptured funereal statue of a woman with a bowl in her hand; her name was engraved on it in Etruscan letters: and many others urns with cinders still in them; all these were in a chamber built without cement (the customary form of Etruscan construction) of large overlaid stones that joined to form a vault. . .

The discovery of a royal tomb dating back to the sixth century BC gives one the impression, if nothing else, that Salinvolpe was a place of some consequence. It may, of course, have been simply the country domain, or *latifundia*, of a *lucomon*. But a scattering of Cyclopean stones over a wide area of the surrounding countryside, and a network of Etruscan roads along the crests of the Chianti hills suggest that the Etruscans must have been here in force. The farmhouses along the ancient highway between Salinvolpe and Cetamura — a fourth-century BC site now being excavated by the University of Florence — bear names that are clearly of Etruscan derivation, such as Vercenni, Vistarenni, Rofina, Garbina and Vecine (where a particularly ugly Mussolini-era house was built on the probable location of the Etruscan dwelling). Further to the east, what is more, towards Brolio, a number of Etruscan and Roman tombs have been found, and a whole string of other place names, such as Nusenna, Rosennano, Adine, Avane and Avenano, all testify to the Etruscan presence. I remember, indeed, after trudging over the early site at Poggio la Petraia on the crest of the hills overlooking the Val d'Arno, now a tangle of weeds and inhabited only by a few sheep, how Mario del Chiaro of the University of California at Santa Barbara remarked, with a sweep of his hand as we gazed southwards from Cetamura towards Gaiole and the valleys dotted with Ricasoli farms: 'If you look over there, you can see just what it was like when the Etruscans were here.'

Maybe he was right: one cannot really tell. But it does seem likely that when the mists of pre-history began to clear over these Tuscan hills, they disclosed a prosperous agricultural scene built up by the seafaring traders from the coast who, by the sixth century BC, had achieved a sort of hegemony over much of the Italian peninsula from Naples to the Alps. The Etruscans had an eye for a good site. They liked, whenever possible, to build their settlements high up, like eagles' nests, on a couple of hills separated by a ravine. On one would be the painted wooden houses and gilded temple, glowing with colour in the bright Italian sun, and in the other an underground stone necropolis, designed to contain the dead for ever. Salinvolpe followed this pattern, indeed the mound in which the hypogeum is built has a distinctly man-made look about it. The four tombs in the form of a cross are faced with squared-off stones that jut progressively out towards the top to form a sort of vaulted roof, similar to those found at Populonia,[1] which may give a clue to the provenance of the people whose burial place it was. The boundaries of Volterra, traditionally allied to Populonia, are supposed to have reached as far as the river Pesa, with Grignano as its most easterly strongpoint, and certainly some Volterra coins were discovered in another important third-century BC tomb unearthed at Malacéna, not far from the railway station at Castellina Scalo. Its contents were apparently intact, and among a quantity of alabaster and stone cinerary urns, bronzes and painted vases was one with the inscription: 'MI: CAPRA: CALISNÁS LARTHAL: ŠEPÚS: ARNTHALISLA: CURSNIALX.'

Usually, as it happens, the countryside belonged to the territory of one city or another, but even after the Romans had appropriated most of Tuscany from the Etruscans in the course of the third century BC, it is difficult to specify hard and fast boundaries. Since so much of the evidence depends on individual discoveries, one can only conjecture. At San Donato a Citille, for instance, on the hills between the Pesa and Greve rivers, a tomb inscription dating from the middle of the Roman period mentions the tribe of Scaptia, who controlled the area around Florence. So perhaps the old boundary between the territory of Volterra, or Velathri as the Etruscans called their city (then four times as large as it is now, and surrounded by impressive stone walls) and that of Faesulae (modern Fiesole), the Etruscan city that pre-dated Florence, divided Chianti in those days along roughly the same line as the modern boundary between the provinces of Florence and Siena. At all events, the land that slopes down from modern Panzano to the Pesa river is ideally suited to the heavy cultivation of vines, olives and corn, and there is no reason to doubt that it was put to as good use two and a half thousand years ago as it is now.[2]

Filippo Buonarroti, who could look out on the whole area from his *torre* across the Pesa, says that an inscribed Etruscan stele was discovered around 1700 AD at a farm called Mura a Sala, and before long was used, by the same people who found it, in the construction of some unidentified building. So, given the likelihood that this useful piece of evidence is now propping up the beams of some local farmhouse, it seems reasonable to assume that there was an Etruscan settlement somewhere near Panzano, particularly as the remains of a tomb, hitherto held to be the grave of the first Christian evangelist in these parts, S. Eufrosino of Panfilia, appears to be of a much earlier construction. The precise site of the Roman settlement also presents something of a question-mark, and does not necessarily coincide exactly with its Etruscan forerunner or its medieval successor. Early medieval documents in the Passignano archives refer to the local parish as San Leolino a Flacciano, and it is only in 1103 that we come across the first document referring to it as 'Plebem Sancti Leolini sitam in Panzano cum Curte'. Etymologically, of course, both Panzano (the fundus of Pantius) and Flacciano (the fundus of Flaccus) betray their Roman origins; but bearing in mind the better agricultural setting and the proximity of the old Etruscan site, it seems likely that the more important Roman settlement was at the latter — now only traceable to a farmhouse called Felciano on the old road connecting Panzano and San Leolino, and some little distance from Mura a Sala. It was probably the overriding insecurity of the later tenth and eleventh centuries that led the Firidolfi family to build their castle on the site of the old Pagus Pantianus which, through its formidable position, was easier to defend than Flacciano. From that point on, Panzano became the main centre of habitation in the area, as it remains today.

All too often, of course, it is difficult to differentiate between the Etruscan and the Roman. After all, three of Rome's own seven hills were named after Etruscan families: Palatinus from Palanius, Palla; Velius from Vel, Velni, Vellanius, Velus; Caelius from Caile. And we have precious little evidence, so far, about the origins of either Florence, where the Etruscan site was up the hill at Faesulae, or, indeed, of Siena. Tradition would have that Siena was founded by Senius, the son of Remus, who brought with him from Rome the *Lupa* which still remains the city's badge. (In the inevitable sacrifices that attended the city's inauguration, we are told, a dense black smoke rose from the altar of Apollo, while a pure white one was given off from Diana's — in commemoration of which the *Balzana*, the black and white shield of the commune, was created.) But in reality its genesis is rather less definitive. In his book *Rome in Etruria and Umbria*, William Harris connects Roman Saena with the Etruscan Saenius, who, according to Sallust, was a Roman senator in 63 BC, and whose son had some relationship to Oufentina, the tribe of Siena. But this does not rule out the possibility that there were other Saenii beforehand: indeed Siena was referred to as a Roman 'Socius' in 241 BC and again in 91 BC.

For all this, we know that after a struggle lasting over a century and a half, the Romans finally completed the conquest of Etruria, whose main cities had become *foederati* by 246 BC — much in the same way, one suspects, as the Iron Curtain states are satellites of the Soviet Union today. With a wary eye on their loyalty (and also to guard what was in effect the Roman frontier with the Gauls) the Romans kept a hefty garrison in the area: in 190 BC, for instance, Praetor P. Iunius Brutus had at his disposal in Etruria a Roman legion along with 10,000 infantry and 4,000 cavalry. What with one thing and another, the process of latinisation was in full swing before the towns were destroyed and the countryside turned into a desert by the ruinous civil struggle that preceded the downfall of the Republic. In the Social War itself, most of the Etruscan cities sided with Marius; and when, after prolonged and vicious fighting, Volterra finally fell after a two-year siege in 82 BC, it shared the same fate as Fiesole, Arezzo and Siena. Sulla planted colonies in each place, and ruthlessly suppressed the local language and customs. Even so, a spark of independence remained. Tacitus records, in fact, that anti-government feeling is nothing new in Siena, which cocked a snook of its own at the Senate in 70 AD:

> A complaint had been made by Manlius Patruinus to the effect that he had been roughly handled in the town of Sena by a rowdy mob, and indeed at the bidding of the local officials. Nor, it seemed, had the outrage stopped there. He had been cornered by a throng of groaning and wailing townsfolk who celebrated a mock funeral under his nose and hurled insults and abuse at the senate as a whole. The accused were summoned to appear, and after a hearing, convicted and punished. In addition, a senatorial decree was passed warning the common people of Sena to behave (*Histories*, IV, 45).

Faint, perhaps, may have been the echoes of all this bloodshed and unrest in the pastoral fastness of Chianti. Yet we know that it was

the scene of some fighting (the decapitated skeletons found at
S. Fedele tell a tale of their own) and that, demographically speaking, the Romans made themselves felt in the area. Their habit of
giving farms the personal name of the owner with the suffix '-anus'
ensured that, once included in the census rolls, the label stuck, if
nothing else. A good many have survived, right up until now: Vitigli-
ano, for instance, which stems from Vitellianus, the farm of Vitellius;
Bracciano, once Braccianus from Braccius, and so on. Very often, of
course, the newcomers may have simply taken over the Etruscan
settlements and Romanised them. It has been suggested, for example,
that Sicelle may have derived from the Etruscan 'Secnes', taking a
diminutive form 'Secin(u)las' and becoming Sicelle today. Complicated though this may seem, it is confirmed by the name of the stream
that runs just below, the Argenna, whose denomination derived quite
feasibly from the Etruscan personal name 'Arcnal' and was latinised
to Arginna.

How peaceful this Roman incursion can have been is uncertain.
During the years from the outset of the Social War in 90 BC to the
Battle of Actium in 31 BC, Italy was the scene of proscriptions,
confiscations, devastation and casualties in one civil war after another. Sulla had to demobilise no less than 23 legions, and ultimately
managed to secure land from over 10 colonies for some 120,000
men, involving large-scale social and economic upheavals that may
have spilt over into Chianti as well. Certainly two marble plaques,
discovered in the process of demolishing an old wall in the priest's
house at S. Marcellino, give more than a hint of coercion. The one
states that Tiberius Claudius Glyptus acquired his property by
Decurian decree; the other records the gratitude of two freedmen,
Secundino and Pereliano, to their former masters, the Flavia family.
Which may have meant the grant of some real estate. For, if one
recalls, Virgil only too vividly described, in the Ninth Eclogue, what
happened when disbanded armies were put on the land:

> *Lycidas*: Where are you footing it, Moeris? To Town? This
>   trackway leads there.
> *Moeris*: Oh Lycidas, that I should have lived to see an outsider
> Take over my little farm — a thing I never feared —
> And tell me, 'You're dispossessed, you old tenants, you've got to
>   go.'
> We're down and out. And look how chance turns the tables on
>   us —
> These are *his* goats (rot them!) you see me taking to market.
>   *Lycidas*: Can this be true? I heard that all the land, from the
>   place where

That spur with its gentle slope juts out from the recessive
Hill-line, as far as the water and the old beech trees with
Their shattered tops — all this had been saved by Menalcas'
   poetry.
Moeris: So you heard. That rumour did get about. But poems
Stand no more chance, where the claims of soldiers are invol-
   ved,
Than do the prophetic doves if an eagle swoops upon them.

Whatever their inception, the archaeological finds near the parish
church of S. Marcellino — including columns of valuable marble and
Corinthian capitals, as well as a necropolis dating from the second or
third century AD unearthed in the farm of Castellare — all go to
show that there must have been a prosperous Roman settlement in
the region around Cacchiano, the 'Pagus Caculanus'. Yet potentially
the most positive evidence of the Roman presence in these parts is
the recent suggestion that the Cassia — the most important Roman
highway linking Rome with the north — may have passed right
through the centre of Chianti, thereby drawing this area into the
hurly-burly of imperial activities. The medieval copy of a Roman
road map known as the 'Peutingerian table' gives the itinerary of the
Cassia from Chiusi to Florence, indicating the various staging posts
on the way. The assumption has always been that it ran down the
valley of the Arno. But now Dr Alfredo Moroni, of the Gregorian
University at the Vatican, armed with a good deal of local knowledge,
has argued that from Rapolano it led via the Colonna di Grillo and
Castelnuovo Berardenga to a spot known as Valcortese where it
crossed the highway from Siena to Arezzo. Here, it seems, there was
a colony of Greek traders (26 of whose names have survived in
Florentine inscriptions from the Roman period) and here too was an
inn for travellers known as 'Ad Graecos'.
   The next stretch of the Cassia is mentioned in a medieval document (Gli Estimi di Cerreto, dated 1320 and now in the Siena state
archives) which, according to Moroni's reconstruction, ran through a
number of places — Ponticelli, Petrosa, Sexta, Ghinicciano, Tisciano,
La Petrose, Campo Asinelli, Vinitaio, Bucciaglie, Poggiolo, Ponte
Renzo, Pozzolo and Lo Spedale — to Pievasciata, a distance of 12
Roman miles or 17 kilometres. At Pievasciata was another hospice,
known as 'Ad Ioglandem', presumably after an adjacent walnut tree.
(Sciata itself comes from *aesculus*, or oak, and certainly there are
plenty in the neighbourhood.) The route then followed the ridge of
hills to Vagliagli and Fonterutoli, from whence it proceeded along
roughly the same line as the present Chiantigiana road up to Castellina — which, incidentally, was described as the 'strata de Castillione'

in a document from Coltibuono dated 1078.

According to Dr Moroni's reading of the Peutingerian map, the next *mansio* or hostel was 10 miles after Ioglandem and called 'Bituriha' — very likely a copyist's error, which should have read 'Viturina'. This would identify it with 'La Massa Veternensis apud Tuscos' that Ammiano Marcellino concluded was Castellina. At any rate the distance is correct, and one can well imagine the relief of travellers at the sight of food and lodging after a tough haul over the hills. The 'hotel' itself, designated on the map with two towers like a Michelin guide, would almost certainly have been on the southeast slopes near Salinvolpe, where traces of Roman buildings have been found.

After this welcome halt, the Cassia continued northwards, as the Chiantigiana still does, down to Grignano, the Ager Janii, where it crossed the River Pesa by a bridge of which traces still remain, and after skirting the Pieve of San Leolino and the settlements at Panzano, proceeded along the crest of the hill via San Martino a Cecione to S. Pietro a Sillano. Here, according to the map, another hostel, 'Ad Aquileia', was encountered, 14 miles from Bituriha, which would throw some light on why the earliest Chianti documents, dating from 884, were concerned with this particular spot, as we shall see.

Finally, the last stretch to Florence ran through S. Fabiano, S. Stefano a Campoli, Mercatale, S. Cecilia a Decimo and Tavarnuzze (ad Tabernas). All of this ties up quite neatly with the indications given in the Peutingerian map, and is an attractive item, when one considers that the route through Chianti was by far the most direct. For all its ups and downs, it would have meant a considerable saving in distance over the more roundabout way up the Val d'Arno or the Val d'Elsa. But whether it was the main Cassia or not, the old highway through Chianti remained in use for many centuries. We know from the records that the Emperor Otto III came down it on a trip from Pavia to Rome, and while resting at Fonterutoli issued an edict in favour of the Church of Arezzo. Henry VII camped at Cerreto in 1313, and Sir John Hawkwood, when passing through, took Castelnuovo della Berardenga in 1382. In 1446 King Alfonso of Aragon trundled along it on his way to Milan, and Charles VIII came down in the opposite direction with 6,000 Swiss lancers half a century later. It was the route chosen by Charles V of Bourbon in 1527 when heading to sack Rome. And there were so many others who brought a momentary gleam of fame to these tucked-away valleys.[3]

At all events, the roads that crossed Chianti contributed to its prosperity from Roman times on, and I like to fancy that the cobbled drive up to my own place here, whose Latin name still figures in the church documents of S. Lorenzo a Grignano as 'Ad Agrum Janii', may once have led to the Roman *fundus* that is thought to have existed on this spot (though visitors who bump up it simply complain that it is more suited to the suspension of a horse than a car).

Certainly it is fun to have one's grass-roots so close to the ancients, and to be able to wander up the hill, as I often do, and root around the *tegole* of a Roman habitation that are still strewn around the field. But it does little enough to help one visualise the life that was led within these precincts. What the Romans left behind enables us to reach certain limited and cautious conclusions about how they lived. It enables us to say, without any danger of contradiction, that the Romans were here — which is more than historians would concede a few years ago. Yet one cannot help feeling — without disrespect of the archaeologists and the valuable ground-work that they have done — that rather than scratch around the site, let us say, of Pliny's villa at Tifernum for bits of his roof, there is more to be gained by reading his own elegant and detailed account of the place as he knew it. After all, the whole splendid backdrop, from the amphitheatre of hills to the Tiber flowing by, is still just as it was (allowing, of course, for a factory or two), and the Marchese Cappelletti's *seicento* mansion that has now supplanted Pliny's sumptuous colonnades still retains a whiff of the old patrician life.

So let us turn from the fragmentary remains of Roman life here and listen, through the words of their writers, to what the Romans themselves have to say about it all.

NOTES

1. The structure of the vaults of the Castellina tumulus bears resemblance — if I am not wrong — also to the tombs of Quinto Fiorentino (La Montaguola and La Mula).

2. Professor Enzo Mazzeschi of Siena University has shown how the Celtic tribes under Brennus swept through this part of Chianti in 400-390 BC from the Adriatic coast, accompanied by their women and children and cattle, before attacking Rome. He believes that the *castelliere* of S. Fedele was built at this period as a fortress in which the agricultural community could take refuge against such invasions. (*Cronache d'Archeolologia Senese*, 1976, pp. 34-55.)

3. From the tenth century onwards, travellers going to and from Rome tended to follow the Val d'Elsa route through Empoli and Poggibonsi known as the *Francigena* which can be traced in detail from Sigeric's itinerary as early as 990-994. The growing importance of Florence in the thirteenth century also channelled a good deal of traffic through San Casciano — San Donato — Castellina and Siena. But although the modern Cassia runs from Florence to Siena via Poggibonsi, it has little connection with the Roman Cassia.

FIVE

Rural life reassured them: it touched the roots of their feeling. Consider that passage, so full of tenderness for the colourful aspects of his native land, in which Virgil enshrined the nostalgia that so many Romans felt for the countryside:

> Then let the country charm me, the rivers that channel its valleys
> Then may I love its forest and stream, and let fame go hang

> *(Georgics*, II, 485-6)

Horace, reacting against the rat race of Rome in the first century BC, exclaimed: 'Why should I change my Sabine dale for the greater burden of wealth?' (*Odes*, III, 1). While Juvenal, reflecting how the splendour of Rome's public buildings disguised the squalor and unpleasantness of its private dwellings, crammed together in dark narrow alleys and subject to disease, fire, or simply collapsing, asked:

> Who, at cool Praeneste, or Volsinii, amidst leafy trees, was ever afraid of his house falling down? . . . But here we inhabit a city propped up for the most part by slats: for that is how the landlord patches up a crack in the old wall, bidding the inmates sleep in ease under the ruin that hangs over their heads.

He concluded, with some warmth, 'No, no. I must live where there is no fire, and the night is free from alarms' (III, 190-8). Varro, who was at pains to prove that country life was not only preferable, but also more logical, argued:

> For Divine Nature made the country, but man's skills the towns; and all the arts were discovered in Greece, 'tis said, within the space of a thousand years, but there never was a time when there were in the world no fields that could be cultivated . . . [Wherefore] Our ancestors with good reason sent their citizens back from the towns to the land, for in peace they were fed by the rustic Romans, and in war they were defended by them (III,1, 4-5).

23

Many voiced the belief that Rome's greatness and strength stemmed from her rural background. Cato, for instance, observed that the farming classes supplied the bravest and sturdiest soldiers, while Livy repeated a cherished old tradition that Cincinnatus was called from the plough to dictatorship in 458 BC to save the Roman army besieged by the Aequians on Mount Algidus, and once the job was successfully done, immediately went back to his three-acre farm. (Columella has similar stories about Gaius Fabricus, Consul of 282 and 278 BC, who brought about the evacuation of Italy by King Pyrrhus of Epirus, and Curius Dentatus, Consul of 290 and 275 BC, who after a string of conquests over the Samnites, the Sabines, the Lucanians and Pyrrhus as well, is said to have refused all share of the booty and simply retired to the country. And then, of course, there was the tale of Scipio Africanus who worked his own fields after being driven from public life.)

But if the countryside seemed more pleasant than the splendours of Rome, no one suggested that rural life was Arcadian bliss. Virgil, for his part, was an advocate of the need for hard work. 'Let not the earth be lazy!' he warned, and certainly the Oebalian garden that his Corycian veteran had created from a wilderness enabled the old man to return home at night to a table heaped with 'dainties he never had to buy'. Yet, if the truth be told, many of those who took to the countryside were little more than absentee landlords, divorced from the day-to-day working of the fields — rather like the foreigners and Milanese industrialists who have bought up estates in Chianti during the last few years as an agreeable investment, and have only a passing interest in the running of their farms. Pliny's letter to Venator could quite easily have been written today:

> As for me, at this very moment I am gathering in the grape harvest which is poor, but better than I had expected; if you call it 'gathering' to pick an occasional grape, look at the press, taste the fermenting wine in the vat and pay a surprise visit to the servants I brought from the city (IX, 20).

Most of our sources, as it happens, were concerned with the running of large estates. Cato's *De Agri Cultura*, written in the middle of the second century BC, dealt mainly with what we would now call investment farming, and the owning of extensive plantations run by slave labour. Significantly, the first two chapters of his book give some sound, practical advice to anyone interested in buying a property. He cautions:

> When you are thinking of acquiring a farm, keep in mind these

points, that you be not over-eager in buying, nor spare your pains in examining, and that you consider it not sufficient to go over it once. However often you go, a good piece of land will please you more at each visit . . . Go in and keep your eyes open, so that you may be able to find your way out (I, 1-2).

Once the estate has been bought, though, he insists on the importance of good management, expounding as meticulously as any modern lawyer about various types of contracts, on how money should be spent and the farm books kept, and giving clear-cut duties and responsibilities for each member of the staff.

His excellent advice would be valid today — with the difference, of course, that slaves featured so largely. In fact Cato is remembered not only for his implacable hatred of Carthage ('Delenda Carthago') but for a particularly tough attitude towards slaves. Fortunately Varro, whose *De Re Rustica* was published in 37 BC, when he was 80 years old, expressed a more humane view that probably reflected the customs of the time. It also gives an insight into labour relations on a country estate:

The slaves should not be timid nor yet of too high spirit. Those set over them ought to know how to read and write and should have received some slight education; they should be of good character and older than the labourers . . . for the latter obey them more readily than they do younger men. In addition to this, the one quality necessary in an overseer is *practical skill in farm work*; for his duty is not merely to give orders, but to *set an example*, that those under him may imitate as he works, and realize that his superior position is not without cause, but is the result of a superior knowledge. Nor must an overseer be allowed to enforce his orders by the whip rather than by words, provided that the same result can be obtained equally well by the latter. It is well not to have too many slaves of the same tribe, for this is a principal cause of quarrels in the household.

You should quicken the interest of the overseers by means of rewards, and should see that they have something of their own, and women slaves to live with them and bear their children; for this makes them steadier and more attached to the estate. The slaves from Epirus are a good case in point, for owing to these family ties, they are of better repute and fetch a greater price than others. The goodwill of the overseers you should win by an occasional mark of esteem; and you ought to discuss too with the best of the labourers the farm work that is to be done; for where this is the case, their sense of inferiority is lessened, and they feel that they are held in some account by their master. Their enthusiasm for work is increased by treatment more generous than usual, by better food and clothing, by occasional exemption from work, or the permission to graze a beast of their own on the farm, and by other privileges of the same kind — so that any who have been given too hard a task or too severe a punishment may thus be consoled, and their goodwill and kindly feeling towards the master be restored.

Columella, himself a landowner (whose work appeared in the first century AD), commented that he did not regret having held slaves, but admitted to 'chatting rather familiarly' with those in the country. He explained,

> When I perceived that their unending toil was lightened by such friendliness on the part of the master, I would even jest with them at times and allow them to jest more freely. Nowadays I make it a practice to call them into consultation on any new work, as if they were more experienced, and to discover by this means what sort of ability is possessed by each of them, and how intelligent he is. Furthermore, I observe that they are more willing to set about a piece of work on which they think that their opinions have been asked and their advice followed (I, viii, 15).

For all such broad-minded and rational talk, both Varro and Columella believed in the use of the whip if words should fail. Nor did the notion that a rustic slave was part of the farm stock (distinct from implements and animals only in so far as he was endowed with speech) really die out with Cato, who made no bones about what should be done in the interest of efficiency: 'Sell worn-out oxen, blemished cattle and sheep, wool, hides, an ancient wagon, old tools, an old or sickly slave, and whatever else is superfluous' (II, 7).

Even for a free man, there was a stigma about the offering of service, for work on the land or indeed anywhere else; in fact hired labour was placed on exactly the same footing on a farm as slave labour — though perhaps treated with rather more suspicion and mistrust. Cicero summed it up when he remarked: 'Unbecoming to a gentleman, too, and vulgar are the means of livelihood of all hired workmen, whose labour, not their professional skill, we purchase; the very wages they receive are a symbol of their servitude' (*De Off.*, 1.42.150).

Be this as it may, while Columella and Varro dwelt on the theoretical side of the Roman improving landlord, Pliny the Younger showed it actually happening. He seems to have been the first to recognise the problems of absentee landlordism, and the necessity of being on the spot to deal with such problems as arose. In fact, when begging leave of absence from his senatorial duties in Rome to build a temple at Città di Castello, he confessed to the Emperor Trajan:

> I should fail in sincerity if I concealed from your kindness the fact that my personal affairs will benefit very much. The farms I own in the district bring in more than 400,000 sesterces, and I cannot postpone letting them, especially as the new tenants should be there to see to the pruning of the vines, and this must be done soon. Moreover, the series of bad harvests we have had are forcing me to consider reducing rents, and I cannot calculate these *unless I am on the spot* (X, 8).

If senatorial duties prevented Pliny from spending as much time as he would have liked at his estate on the borders of Tuscany and Umbria, when he did get there it was not really much of a respite from the hubbub of Rome, as he grumbles in a letter to Pompeius Falco:

> I took refuge in Tuscany to be free to do as I liked, but even there it has been impossible. I am beset on all sides by the peasants with their petitions full of complaints, and these I read rather more unwillingly than my own writings, which I really have no wish to read either (IX, 15).

To give him his due, Pliny never pretended to be a farmer. All the same, he was obviously concerned with the welfare of his tenants, and tried (rather smugly at times) to find practical solutions to the problems that arose:

> Other people visit their estates to come away richer than before, but I go only to return the poorer. I had sold my grape harvest to the dealers, who were eager to buy, when the price quoted was tempting and the prospects seemed good. Their hopes were frustrated. It would have been quite simple to have given them all the same rebate, but hardly fair; and I hold the view that one of the most important things in life is to practise justice in private as in public life, in small matters as in great, and to apply it to one's own affairs no less than to other people's ... Accordingly, I returned to every one 1/8th the sum he had spent ... Then I made a special provision for those who had invested very large sums in their purchase, since they had been of greater service to me, and

theirs the greater loss. I therefore allowed everyone whose purchases had cost him more than 10,000 sesterces $^1/_{10}$th of anything he had spent over the 10,000, in addition to the original $^1/_8$th, which was a sort of general grant . . . My system . . . has cost me a lot, but it has been worth it. The whole district is praising the novelty of my rebate and the way in which it was carried out; and the people I classified and graded, instead of measuring all with the same rod . . . have departed feeling obliged to me in proportion to their honest worth (VIII, 2).

More significantly still, writing to Valerius Paulinus, he discusses a form of share-cropping that clearly anticipated (though was not directly related to) the *mezzadria* system which has lasted up to the present in Tuscany:

I shall have to stay here to arrange for letting my farms on long leases, and I shall have to adopt a new system for this. During the past five years, despite the large reductions I have made in rents, the arrears have increased, and as a result most of my tenants have lost interest in reducing their debt because they have no hope of being able to pay off the whole; they even seize and consume the produce of the land, in the belief that they will gain nothing themselves by conserving it. I must therefore face this growing evil and find a remedy for it. One way would be to let the farms not for a money rent but for a fixed share of the produce, and then make some of my servants overseers to keep a watch on the harvest. There is certainly no more just return than what is won from the soil, climate and seasons, but this method requires strict honesty, keen eyes and many pairs of hands. However, I must make the experiment and try all possible changes of remedy for an obstinate complaint (IX, 37).

Such sources as survive give the impression that the large estates or *latifundia* were progressively threatening the survival of peasant farmers; and as impersonal agriculture replaced personal attachment, one senses a poignant ring about Virgil's advice to 'admire a large estate if you like, but farm a small one'. And yet, to tell the truth, we have no definite evidence about the size of holdings in the early Roman days. Legend has it that Romulus gave each Roman citizen two *iugera* apiece, which was later increased to four or even seven *iugera*; and this tradition seems to have continued at least to the third century BC. Indeed, M. Curius Dentatus (who played a major role in the conquest of central and southern Italy) is said to have remarked that anyone who was not content with seven *iugera* was a dangerous man. But by the second century BC the 100-*iugera* slave-run plantations began to appear, and once farming had turned into a business, size became important. According to Cato, at least 240 *iugera* were necessary to make an olive plantation pay, although 100 *iugera* were sufficient for a vineyard. (1 iugerum = 2/3 acre)

For all this, the peasant proprietor remained the backbone of the agrarian economy of Rome, and the source of military strength during the centuries of conquest that made her the most important state in Italy. And some of the old notions of self-sufficiency lingered on in industrial farming. Cato, for one, insisted that the basic needs of the farm should be produced on the spot — such as vine-props from poplar stakes, baskets from reeds and willows, grain and wine for the workers, beans and lupins for the animals, and manure — which was only common sense, after all. Yet if a certain amount of guessing is still needed to fill in the picture, specialists like White (in *Roman Farming*) have suggested that subsistence level could be achieved by less than 100 days' work, out of a total in the Roman calendar of about 250 (there were even more holidays then than in present-day Italy, it seems). All of which meant that the peasant proprietor was capable of cultivating a good deal more land than was necessary for bare subsistence — although for the first four centuries of the Roman Republic he was a part-time soldier as well.

Certainly the long-drawn-out war with Hannibal interfered with farming and caused widespread devastation of the land, and although Laelius (in 140 BC) and the Gracchi brothers (Tiberius in 133 BC and Gaius in 123-122 BC) did their best to restore the peasant farmers to their old prosperity, the Social Wars in the first century BC hardly improved the lot of the small-holder. Many of the disbanded soldiers who had been granted land proved to be incapable of farming, and simply sold out to the large landowners. Both war and provincial administration, what is more, offered plenty of scope for pickings and filled the pockets of Senators and *equites*, who promptly bought land as a safe and attractive investment.

This invasion of the countryside by big capital had inevitable results. As the *latifundia* got bigger, the *pauerculi*, or small independent proprietors, declined. They never disappeared altogether, but Appian, rather sadly, left a description of their plight:

> The result [of taking over large areas of land and renting them out] was the opposite of their intentions. The rich seized most of the unoccupied land. Circumstances made them confident that no one would deprive them of it, and so they acquired the land surrounding their own, and all the small farms owned by poor men, partly by purchase, partly by force, until they were farming wide

plains instead of estates. They used slaves to till the land, and raise the stock, so that they should not be mobilised to serve in war, not being of free birth; also the possession of slaves brought great profit to their owners, since slaves, being immune from war service, multiplied with impunity. Consequently the ruling class accumulated all the wealth for themselves, and the slave population filled the country. While the real Italian population decreased terribly, worn out by poverty, taxation, and military service. And when there was a respite from these things, they found themselves unemployed, because the land was owned by rich men who used slaves instead of freemen on their farms (*Bell. Civ.*, I, 7).

SIX

Strabo, in his *Geography*, described the coastline of Tuscany as 'unhealthy', and although the Etruscans had reclaimed much of the low-lying Maremma with their drainage systems, it seems again to have become abandoned in Roman times. 'What can I do,' asks Varro's Fundanius, 'to prevent disease if I should inherit a farm in swampland?' To which the answer was uncompromising: 'Sell it for the highest cash price, or if you can't sell it, abandon it.' And so, bearing in mind that Columella's candid advice was 'to move back a considerable distance from the sea rather than a short way, since the intermediate space is filled with heavier air' (I, v, 6), it is not unreasonable to suppose that the hilly region of Chianti, traversed as it probably was by the main highway from Rome to the north, must have been as desirable an area to settle in for the Romans as it is for us today.

The question of locality was certainly a matter of concern to them, and much of the advice given has a familiar ring about it. Discussing the purchase of a property, for instance, Cato recommends that one should 'notice how the neighbours keep up their places; if the district is good, they should be well kept' (I, 2), and that ideally it 'should be among those farms which do not often change owners — where those who have sold farms are sorry to have done so' (I, 4). If Varro was inclined to concentrate on the general conditions of the neighbourhood, he nevertheless made a point of warning against certain plantations next door which, he thought, might be damaging to one's own crops (such as oak groves or walnut trees on the boundaries that were said to be harmful to the cultivation of olives). More essential still was to be safe from brigands, and to have access both to a local market and a good source of labour and supplies. Cato believed in being close to 'a good and much travelled road', although our old friend Columella was not unaware of the hazards that this might involve 'through the depredations of passing travellers, and the constant entertainment of those who turn in for lodging' (I, V, 7) — a sentiment, I might add, that will readily be endorsed by those of us whose Chianti hide-outs are all too accessible to acquaintances who drop in unannounced.

Next in importance was the position of the farmhouse. Cato wrote that 'it should have a good climate and not be subject to storms . . . if possible it should lie at the foot of a mountain and face south' (I, 2-4). Needless to say, all were agreed on the necessity of having a steady supply of water, not only for drinking, but for irrigation as well. Columella insists:

> Let there be a never-failing spring either within the steading or brought in from outside . . . if running water is wanting, make a search for a well close by, to be not too deep for hoisting the water, and not too brackish or bitter in taste. If this too fails, and if scant hope of veins of water compels it, have large cisterns built for people and ponds for cattle; this rain water is after all most suitable to the body's health, and is regarded as uncommonly good if it is conveyed through earthen pipes into a covered cistern (I, v, 1-2).

Which, incidentally, is the same sort of advice that old hands hasten to proffer to newcomers today.

The houses themselves focused round a single living room shared by all and sundry — the precursor, one suspects, of the *tablinum* in classical Roman town houses, and which has certainly been preserved down the centuries in Tuscany, where the business of living is still carried on in a central *cucina*: you have only to walk into any Chianti farmhouse to see that this is so. (There may also be a formal dining-room, housing the pride of the family's possessions, kept tightly shut up and used once or twice a year.) And usually the steading was built around a yard, enclosed by walls or a hedge, with rows of cells for slaves and livestock, until with the growth of the big *latifundia* country living became far more elaborate. The plan of the villa Sambuca, discovered north-west of Veii, in southern Etruria, shows what a working farm looked like, whereas Pliny's description of his villa at Tifernum (*Letters*, V, 6) which takes the reader through colonnades and suites of rooms, baths, a ball court and a riding ground, quite apart from formal and informal gardens and flower beds, box hedges, lawns, trees and fountains, exemplies the magnificence that rich Romans lavished on their country estates — a splendour that was recaptured in some of the superb Renaissance villas, such as Catiguano, Vignamaggio and Uzzano, that were destined to spring up, some fifteen centuries later, in the choice spots of Chianti.

For it is a pretty sure bet that when the boom for Italian wine started in the second century BC (hitherto the local products had been overshadowed, it will be remembered, by Greek vintages) the big wine-producing *latifundia* must have spread into Chianti, where viticulture had been practised for centuries by the Etruscans. Virgil, after all, referred to them in the Aeneid as *Oenotrians* (165) and the legendary offer by Mezentius to help the Rutuli against the Latins for the price of all the wine in the territory of Latium, recounted by Varro, is a clear indication of the importance that the grape played in their lives. In 154 BC Cato placed the profit from wine at the top of his list, as against wheat in sixth place; and although vineyards were the most expensive form of farming, the high cash return that they yielded prompted farmers to plant more and more land with vines. Towards the end of the first century BC, in fact, over-production brought a dramatic fall in prices, which, from figures given by Petronius, have been estimated at 35 per cent in relation to the price of wheat during the years 100 BC to 65 AD. (Whereas the ratio of wheat to wine was 1:2.72 in 100 BC, by 65 AD it had fallen to 1:0.72, and this in a period of continuous inflation.)

It was the old story of overdoing things that shows signs of being repeated by the big industrial vineyards today. Admittedly the Romans preferred sweet southern wines such as Falernian to the dry vintages of Tuscany. Yet it is no mere speculation to say that in the early days of the Empire the countryside of Chianti, or *Clantum*, must have been covered with vineyards and dotted with villas and farmhouses just as it is now. Indeed, as I look out of my study window down the valley of the Pesa, tracing in my mind the old highway that led over the hills to Florence, it needs little effort of the imagination to visualise the *cinquecento* villa of Santa Lucia amid its vineyards a mile or two away as an impressive *latifundia*, and the little stone farmhouses as Roman *pagi*. Repeated historical earthquakes may have dashed down the buildings and engulfed the place time and time again, yet so little has changed. After all, the outer furnishings of the ancient world are still here — quiet, folded-away *alberese* valleys, the vines, the olives, the oxen; the cross-hatched red-tiled roofs, the Rafaelesque clouds, the nightingales and the fireflies; the oak woods bisected by splashing rivulets. Etruscans, Romans, Florentines of the Renaissance, and now ourselves: who can doubt that we have all shared the same calm happiness and bounty?

SEVEN

> . . . Drown the cups
> as custom of Postumia
> tighter than the bursting grape
> ordains
>   but keep the water jug
> boon of the straight-faced
>   far hence
> No friend of wine
> The Bacchus here is neat.

The original codex of Catullus' poems was in a shocking state when discovered in Verona at the end of the thirteenth century because (so tradition says) it was wedging up a wine barrel. But it is a clue to the Roman attitude about wine, just as the status of the vine itself is stressed by a sculpture of a centurion carrying a vine rod as a symbol of his authority (Pliny tells us, in fact, that it was the somewhat dubious privilege of the Roman soldier to be flogged with a vine cane, whereas auxiliaries had to put up with anything that was handy.) Decoratively, too, the vine was often found in Roman friezes and in early Christian art — such as the catacomb frescoes and the limestone bas-reliefs in the Fayoum — which is not so much of a paradox, really, since the one stemmed from Jesus as the 'True Vine', and the other from the Roman glorification of Bacchus. In any case, it all goes to illustrate the importance of the vine in the daily life of antiquity.

For there is no doubt that by the first century BC and perhaps even earlier, wine had become the staple drink of all Italians — though, despite what Catullus says, it was almost always diluted with water, just as the *contadini* in Chianti still do. The quality, moreover, was carefully controlled by an official taster known as 'Vini Boni Arbitoratus', who had legal access to the wine three days before it left the grower's cellar. It had to be sold in a cask of exactly 41 urns, and be neither vinegary nor oily — 'neque aceat, neque muceat'. The merchant was entitled to a warranty in the form of an oath from the producer that the wine had been properly made (though what he

34

then did to it before selling it to the housewife is quite another matter).

Certainly the growth of guilds during the later Empire enabled the wine merchants to organise a monopoly which inevitably led to a good deal of price-rigging. In fact Diocletian found it necessary to fix maximum prices for wine in 301 AD and even to threaten the nationalisation of wine-producing if his decree was disregarded. Under it, top-quality southern vintages such as Sabine, Setian, Sorrentan and Falernian fetched 30 deniers per sextarius (which was about a litre); ordinary wine was fixed at 8 deniers when new and between 16 to 24 deniers when fully matured. Since 30 deniers was the price of two chickens, or two and a half litres of olive oil, it sounds as if wine was generally more expensive for the Romans than for the modern Italians.

While their preference was for red, white wine was also quite common, as the third century AD wine cellar discovered at Marcena, in the *comune* of Subiano, shows: two big vats, still capable of containing liquid, and sloping uniformly towards a stone cavity in the centre, were found to have been used for storing red and white wine respectively. In Tuscany (where the predominance of red Chianti now tends to overshadow the excellent white vintages from the Val di Chiana, the Vernaccia of San Gimignano, and the very drinkable white wines made from Trebbiano and Malvasia grapes in Chianti Classico itself) there is no reason to suppose that both red and white wines were not drunk in similar quantities to what is produced today. Though admittedly they did not attract very favourable comment from Latin authors. Martial decries them, and only in Pliny the Elder are there any serious references:

> The 'bee-vine' [probably Muscatel] is so called because bees are specially fond of it. It has two varieties, which also are covered with down in their young state; the difference between them is that the one ripens more quickly than the other, although the latter also ripens fast. These vines do not object to cold situations, and nevertheless no others rot more quickly from rain. The wines made from them are sweet at first but acquire roughness in the course of years. In Tuscany this vine flourishes more than any others (*Natural History*, XIV, 24).

In the Val d'Ombrone, near Montalcino, a good Moscadello is still made today. Pliny goes on to describe some of the other Tuscan wines:

> Among the vines of Tuscany, that of Todi [which is hardly in

Tuscany anyway] is a special variety, and also they have special names, a vine at Florence being called a Sopina and some at Arezzo 'mole-vine', 'seasonal vine', and 'crossed vine'. The mole vine has black grapes and makes a white must; the seasonal vine is a deceptive plant, giving more admirable wine the larger crop of grapes it bears and. remarkably enough, coming to the end of its fertility and good quality simultaneously; the crossed vine has black grapes and makes a wine that does not keep a long time at all, although its grape keeps a very long time; and it is gathered a fortnight later than any other variety, bearing a large crop of grapes but only good for eating. The leaves of this vine, like those of the wild vine, turn a blood-red colour before they drop off. This also happens with other vines and is a sign of very poor quality (*Natural History*, XIV, 36-7).

The only other references he makes are to Pisa, which 'rejoices in the vine of Paros', and to Luna which 'among the remaining wines . . . carries off the palm of Tuscany', though Villfranchi, writing in his *Oenologia Toscana* in the eighteenth century, recalls the tradition that 'vino fiorentino' was mentioned in a pamphlet attributed to Cyprian of Carthage in the third century AD, describing a smart dinner at which the guests, togged out as Biblical figures, each sponsored a different wine. Rachel, it seems, gave her support to Vinum Florentinum.

If drinking tastes change (both Italians and French, after all, have recently acquired a taste for whisky), it is a pity that the Roman preference for the sugary vintages of the south led them to turn up their noses at the lighter, more acidulous wines of Tuscany that are now so highly regarded. In fact, since they tended to scent their wines with iris roots as well as Greek hay, fragrant pitch fennel and saffron, the only direct link that we can reasonably establish between the wines produced on the slopes of Chianti in Roman days and today's offerings is the characteristic smell of iris — a plant widely grown around here — in the bouquet of Chianti Classico.

And yet so many of the problems and procedures were the same. Laying down a vineyard involved a large capital outlay, and the subsidies now offered to growers under the framework of the EEC were anticipated by the Emperor Nerva (and extended by Trajan, Marcus Aurelius and Septimus Severus before being halted by Diocletian) who made state help available through a series of treasury loans to farmers: these, basically, amounted to one-twelfth of the value of the land at an interest rate of 5 per cent per annum which was paid to the local township. Varro makes it clear, moreover, that there was a great deal of money to be made in wine, not least for the investor who could both purchase and develop his land, for planting vines was a sure way of increasing its value:

> it is also true that the efforts which by culture makes land more beautiful, not only increase as a rule the return from it — as for example when vineyards and olive plantations are laid down in regular order — but also render it *more saleable*, and *add to the value* of the farm (I, iv, 2).

In fact, a document from the later Empire period quotes a rental of three solidi per arura for a vineyard against one solidus for mere arable land.

Needless to say, this did not pass unnoticed by the fiscal authorities. Since the greatest part of the national income came from agriculture, there is no doubt that taxation hit the farmer (especially the small one) very hard, and the land tax, relied on by the Praetorian prefecture — the most important financial ministry which supplied all the major needs of the administration — was assessed not only on land, but on farm stock and the rural population as well. The actual tax on vineyards varied on the nature of the land, the number of bearing vines growing on it, and the income from the vintages of the last ten years. Even so, says Columella, any wine producers 'who combine painstaking care with scientific knowledge ... will easily outdo in the increase of their ancestral estates all those who hold fast to their hay and pot-herbs' (III, iii, 7).

EIGHT

Let all be spaced out in alleys of perfect symmetry
Not merely so that their vistas may charm a frivolous mind
But because only thus can earth supply impartial
Vigour to all, and the growing boughs have room to extend.

(Georgics, II, 284-7.)

So wrote Virgil, and whatever else may have happened to mankind in the meantime, the techniques of wine-making have hardly changed. Orange Fiat tractors may have replaced the white oxen of Tuscany during the last few years, but otherwise the methods used by farmers today are similar to those of their Roman predecessors. After all, the natural tendency of the vine is to grow prolifically, running to wood and leaf and producing surface rootlets, which sap the plant's strength and prevent the grapes from maturing; so that operations such as pruning, moulding, tying, trimming and manuring have always been necessary to ensure a good vintage. 'There are three natural impulses in a vine,' said the Roman proverb, 'One which makes it sprout, another which makes it blossom, and the third which makes it ripen.' Similarly, it was generally held that three diggings were necessary each year: the 'ablaqueatio' in late autumn to cut off surface roots and enable the air to penetrate the earth; a second digging in May when the shoots were trimmed, and finally the 'pulveratio' in summer to break the clods into finer earth.

The same routine is still carried out, and the vine-dresser's tool described by Columella, the *falx vinitoria* with its blade and beak, its paring edge for smoothing, its pointed projection for gouging and its tiny axe-blade for striking was only superseded by the secateur a century ago, and is even now very much in evidence; while in my own little vineyard the *zappa* and the *ubbidiente* are still being used for turning and weeding the earth in exactly the same way as the Romans did.

Those changes that have occurred — such as the standardisation of vine supports — may be more economical but are unattractive to the eye: to comply with some bureaucratic requirement (and draw the state subsidy) all the big Chianti vineyards are now held up by white concrete posts; though happily enough some of the smaller ones (including my own) have retained their age-old means of support,[1] either from individual wooden posts, or more characteristically, on other trees. And nothing, really, could be more attractive. Horace speaks of the husbandman 'wedding the full grown vine to the tall poplar'; Columella of 'mating' the elms with vines (in Chianti fruit trees are often used as well), and Catullus tops them all with a delightful little verse:

> No fickle lusts
>   no rooting between
>   other sheets —
> your husband will lie
>   only in the valley of your breasts
> a 'hero' caught in your arms
>   as the grape-pole
> caught in the twisting vine.

(61)

Ecologically, too, the Romans could teach us a thing or two. For whereas most of the fertilising is nowadays artificial, they were quite aware that at least three of the four elements necessary for a healthy vine — nitrogen, phosphorous and potassium — are present in all animal excrement, and that animal manure supplies abundant humus and a rich assortment of bacteria and fungi as well. Even so, inorganic fertiliser was not unheard of in the ancient world. Nitrum[2] was found in natural deposits (especially in Egypt) and there are frequent references to its use in fruit and vegetable cultivation to improve both tenderness and flavour. Virgil, for one, recommends soaking seeds in it to make them germinate quicker. On the subject of manure, in fact, the Romans had a good deal to say. Best of all, they reckoned, was the dung from pigeons, blackbirds and thrushes; but human excrement was also considered useful: Varro suggested that the slaves' privies should be sited in the manure heap, and Columella believed that six-months'-old urine should be applied to young shoots. 'There is nothing', he says, 'that makes them bear more abundantly.'

Plant sickness is another matter that brings the modern farmer very close to the ancients. Their tendency to personify plants (for instance Virgil's 'happy branches' and 'precocious corn crop' or even Jesus' punishment of the fig-tree) had something of the tenderness of a kinsman to his sick friend, and just as human diseases were attributed to sidereal causes, so also the stars were blamed when a plant began to wither. Inevitably, too, they were faced with the same agricultural problems. The danger of frost, for instance, was none the less real for a Roman farmer, and on any frosty night in Chianti you can still see *contadini* following the age-old remedy prescribed by Mago, Columella and Pliny, of lighting straw in the vineyards to create a thin layer of smoke between the vines and the sky and so prevent radiation of the ground heat upwards.

In contrast, the only chemical pesticide we hear of in the farmer's cupboard is Cato's sulphur and bitumen mixture which he burnt as a fumigant against caterpillars and other harmful insects. (Other ancient advice was for a menstruating woman to walk in the vineyard in bare feet and unbraided hair.) But the one single yet deadly threat from which every modern European vine is protected, whereas its ancient equivalent was not, is *phylloxera* — an epidemic of which nearly wiped out Europe's entire vine collection in the 1880s. Nowadays there is not a cultivated vine growing in the whole of Europe that is not grafted to an American root, which is immune to the danger. But it may be that Columella's faith in Mother Nature, 'who has established an equable law of fertility for all green things even as for human beings and other living creatures', was considered by his contemporaries to be sufficient protection against this particular evil.

To be sure, the most colourful period of the wine-producer's year has always been the *vendemmia*, which sees the transition of grape to wine. Virgil sang in the *Georgics:*

Come, Lord of the wine-press, everything here is lavish,
By your largesse, for you the fields aflower and laden
With vines of autumn, the vintage foams in vats overflowing —
Come then, Lord of the wine-press, pull off your boots and paddle
Bare-legged with me and dye your shins purple in the grape-juice!

For all that has ever been necessary to turn grape-juice into wine is the simple and natural process of fermentation — basically the chemical change of sugar into alcohol and carbon dioxide — which is brought about by the yeast and micro-organisms living in the grape-skins. These, in fact, need only to have the skin broken to go to work on the sugar which comprises about 30 per cent of the pulp inside the grape. And unless the reaction is restrained by some physical means, it will normally continue until all the sugar is converted to alcohol, or until the alcohol level is high enough to overcome the yeast. Some southern vines are able to produce grapes with sufficient sugar in them for this to happen naturally; but whereas the Greeks found it difficult to arrest fermentation completely (with the result that their wine had to be drunk within three or four years at the most) the Romans took elaborate steps to do so. Even if their native Italian wines were normally drunk within four years, some took as much as ten to fifteen to mature, a process which could be accelerated by raising the alcohol level to anaesthetise the yeast (now sometimes achieved by the use of sugar). In the absence of sugar, the Romans had various methods of increasing the sweet content of the 'must'. The use of honey is referred to in the *Geoponika* (VII, 25, 66) and by Palladius (XI, 17), and very often the must was heated (Palladius XI, 4 and Columella XII, 19). Another common way was to concentrate the sugar content in the grapes by leaving them to over-ripen on the vine, or by hanging them up to dry in the sun — both of which methods are still used in the process of making Vin Santo in Chianti.

As Cato warns: 'See that the grapes are not gathered until they are thoroughly ripe and dry, that the wine may not lose its reputation;' the question of ripeness was all-important and Columella dealt with the matter at some length:

> Some people have thought that the time for the vintage has come when they have seen that some part of the grapes is becoming green, others when they have noticed that the grapes are highly coloured and transparent; still others when they have observed that the tendrils and foliage are falling. All these signs are deceptive . . . and it is better to do what we do and to consider the natural ripeness in itself. There is natural ripeness if the grapestones which are hidden in the berries, when you press them out, are already dusky in colour and in some cases almost black; for nothing can give colour to the grapestones except nature's own ripeness, especially as they are situated in the middle of the berries, so that they are protected from the sun and wind, and the moisture itself does not allow them to be ripened prematurely or to turn to a dusky colour except by a natural process of their own (XI, ii, 67-9).

Each farmer no doubt had his own ideas about this and set about the vintage according to his private rule of thumb. Even so, Varro's description of a Roman *vendemmia* is not so very different from what happens today:

> The vintage should begin when the grapes are ripe; and you must choose the variety of grapes and the part of the vineyard with which to begin. For the early grapes, and the hybrids, the so-called black, ripen much earlier and so must be gathered sooner; and the

part of the plantation and the vineyard which is sunnier should have its vines stripped first. At the vintage the careful farmer not only gathers but selects his grapes; he gathers for drinking and selects for eating. So those gathered are carried to the wine-yard, thence to go into the empty jar; those selected are carried to a separate basket, to be placed then in small pots and thrust into jars filled with wine dregs, while others are plunged into the pond in a jar sealed with pitch, and still others go up to their place in the larder. When the grapes have been trodden, the stalks and skins should be placed under the press, so that whatever must remains in them may be pressed out into the same vat. When the flow ceases under the press, some people trim around the edges of the mass and press again; this second pressing is called circumsicium and the juice is kept separate because it tastes of the knife. The pressed grape-skins are turned into jars and water is added; this liquid is called lora, from the fact that the skins are washed (lota), and it is issued to the labourers in winter instead of wine (1, liv).

Surprisingly enough, the only picture we have of grape-treading in the classical world comes to us through pottery decoration. While Cato describes in detail how to build wine-presses, it is solely in the *Geoponika*, written by Cassianus Bassus in the sixth or seventh century, that the age-old element of treading survives in words:

Those who are in charge of the larger baskets . . . must pick out the leaves and any sour grapes or wizened clusters. Those who tread must pick out anything that has been missed by those in charge of the baskets; for the leaves, if pressed with the grapes render the wine rougher and more apt to spoil; and great damage is done by grapes that are dry and sour. Those who are charged with this task must immediately press with their feet the grapes that are thrown into the vats, and having equally trodden all the grape-stones, they must pick up the kernels, so that most of the liquor may run into the channel . . . The men that tread must get into the press having scrupulously cleaned their feet, and none of them must eat or drink while in the press, nor must they climb in and out frequently. If they have to leave the press they must not go in bare feet. The men that tread must also be fully clad, and have their girdles on, on account of the violent sweating. It is also proper to have the press fumigated, either with frankincense or some other sweet odour.

Varro insists that the must, once casked, should not be brought out while it is still fermenting, and that, once become wine, it should

1. An early Etruscan bronze (in the Villa Giulia at Rome) of farmers ploughing: both oxen and yolk can still be seen in Chianti today.

2. The white oxen of Chianti, barely changed since Etruscan times. Here, at Terciona, they are taking the *tinello*, or wine-vat, strapped on a cart down to the vineyard for the grape-harvest. The decorations on their heads are to celebrate the *vendemmia*, and keep off the flies.

3. (Top left) The fourth century mosaic in the Church of S. Constanza at Rome depicts vintage scenes similar to those that take place in Chianti each October: picking the grapes and hauling them on an oxen-drawn cart to the cellar where they are trampled by foot.

4. (Bottom left) Part of a fourth century (?) copy of a Roman military road map, known as the Peutingarian table. The full map extends from Britain to India and because of its disproportionate length (nearly 20 feet by only 9 inches in width) is curiously foreshortened. The section illustrated here shows the North Sea at the top and the coast of Africa at the bottom with the boot of Italy stretching out to the right. The Cassia highway between Chiusi (*Chusio*) and Florence (*Florentia Tuscorum*) is featured south of the Appenine range. According to Dr Alfredo Moroni's theory, *Bituriha* corresponds to Castellina in Chianti.

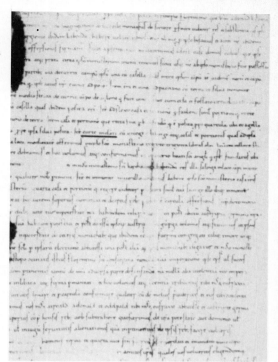

5. (Top right) A twelfth century copy in the Florence State Archives of a parchment dated 14 July 790, which contains the first known reference to Chianti. The Deed, a donation to the monastery of S. Bartolomeo a Ripoli, mentions an estate in Chianti (*curte in Clanti*).

6. (Bottom right) The Badia di Passignano, built in 890 (though its origins may go back to the fourth century) in whose archives were to be found many of the early Chianti documents.

6a. Among the frescoes in the Badia di
Passignano (actually in the Church of
S. Biagio) is this *Resurrezione* by
Domenico Ghirlandaio.

6b. Part of a fresco in the Badia di
Passignano depicting the life of S.
Benedetto by Filippo Filipelli.

be left to mature in its own way. But before it went into the casks there were various additives which could be mixed in if desired. Indeed the custom of 'governo' which is so characteristic of Chianti wine today — that is, specially selected and over-ripe grapes that are partially crushed and thrown in with the fermenting must to give the wine more life, as well as helping the fermentation — can be compared with the Roman habit of adding, in Cato's prescription 'a 40th part of must boiled down from untrodden grapes, or a pound and a half of salt, to the culleus' (120 gallons), the object in both cases being to inject an extra bit of sparkle. To counter over-acidity the Romans used crushed marble or pulverised resin, which meant stirring the must frequently during the initial period. Finally, comments Pliny, 'We add colouring agents to colour our wines and give them more body (XIV, 25).

Once the *vendemmia* had been concluded on a wave of libations and offerings to Bacchus, the casual labour left the vineyards and the proprietor settled down to his books. Equipment was cleaned and put away, and the wine was left to its own devices in the cellar with a parting word from Cato: 'Have the jars wiped off twice a day, and see that you provide each jar with its own brush to wipe off the edges. Thirty days after the gathering, if the fermentation is complete, seal the jars; if you wish to draw the wine from the lees this will be the best time to do it' (26).

The positioning of the cellar was important, of course. Columella remarks that it should be on the north side of the house, 'for that exposure is coolest and least humid'. Moreover, it should be 'far removed from the baths, oven, dunghill and other filthy places which give off a foul odour, and no less so from cisterns and running water, from which is derived a moisture that spoils the wine' (I, vi, 11). Varro recommends two schemes for the storage of wine: the newly pressed juice could be run off into the *cella vinaria* either along a sloping paved tunnel into a vat, or into a series of large pottery containers set deep into the ground — although since the containers were liable to break under the pressure of strong fermentation, the former was preferable. His general rule was that

> When it is a year old it is brought out for consumption. If however it belongs to the class of grape which quickly turns acid, you must consume or sell it before the next vintage. There are some kinds of wine, though . . . which are more valuable when you bring them out, the more years you keep them in the cellar (I, LXV).

Nor were they any less anxious than their modern counterparts to maintain a standard of genuineness. Cato, for instance, outlines the procedure for tasting before the wine was sold, and also describes a method 'to determine whether a wine has been watered or not. Make a vessel of ivy wood and put some of the wine you think contains water in it. If it does contain water, the wine will soak through and the water remain, for an ivy vessel will not hold wine'(III).

Nevertheless, there were plenty of ways of treating wine. Cato tells us how 'to make a sharp wine mild and sweet' with vetchflour and boiled must (109), or 'to remove bad odour from wine' (110) and 'impart a sweet aroma' (113). While Columella, who devotes no less than ten chapters to the subject, favours boiled-down must, liquid pitch, 'Allobrogian' and 'Nemeturican' pitch and even salt water. Some of his recipes, in fact, would make a *maître de Ché*'s eyes pop, when confronted with such concoctions as 'Horehound' and 'Wormwood'; 'Squill' wine and vinegar, 'Squeezed' must or 'Greek-like' wine; myrtle, raisin and 'thin after' wines; mead and fruit syrup. For just as every cook has his favourite seasoning, be it salt and pepper, garlic or herbs or even Earl Grey tea, so the Romans loved to titivate their products:

. . . baskets of violets bring
And balsam, with black privet mixed, entwined
With marjoram and clustering saffron-flowers.
Sprinkle these blossoms with the unmixed wine
Of Bacchus, for with wine are perfumes seasoned.

(Columella, X, 11, 299-303)

NOTES

1. According to Emilio Sereni ('Storia del Paesaggio agrario Italiano'), the practice of supporting rings on poplars and fruit trees dates from Etruscan times.
2. Nitrate of soda?

NINE

But wine was not all that this land had to offer them. For amongst the large industrialised *vigneti* that now sprawl over so much of Chianti can still be seen, as I have said, some of the old-style vineyards in which the vines are interspersed with olive trees, with corn growing between the rows. And although not everyone may realise it, this system of intercultivation is a direct legacy from the ancient world.

In their thrifty way, the Romans believed in making the best use of the soil, and planned each farm with an astute eye to yield. Thus since olives normally give a full crop only every other year, they divided each grove into separate parts, producing fruit in alternate seasons; moreover, by spacing the trees at intervals of between forty to sixty feet to allow room for corn, they were able to ensure, as Columella put it, that

> when the ground underneath has not been sown with a crop, the tree is putting forth its shoots; when the ground is full of sown crops, the tree is bearing fruit, so that the olive grove gives an equal return every year (V, 9, 12).

Nor may my *contadini* friends be aware, as they quote the old Tuscan proverb with a knowing smile, that the old sage had put it down in writing some nineteen centuries ago: 'He who ploughs the olive-grove, asks it for fruit; he who manures it, begs for fruit; he who lops it, forces it to give fruit.'

Since the small green olives of Chianti are prized for their strong, pungent oil, there is no reason to doubt that the Romans cultivated them as widely as we do today. After all, the olive was more important to them in many ways than the grape. It was needed not only for cooking, but also for illumination and anointing the skin — 'a lubricant for the outside as well as the inside of the owner's body', as Varro says, 'following him to the baths and the gymnasium'.

Agreeably enough, his prescription for the olive harvest is still valid today:

Such olives as you can reach by hand from the ground, or from ladders are better pulled than shaken from the tree; for those that have been struck lose flesh and give less oil. Those picked by hand are better if gathered with the bare fingers, not pincers, for the hardness of the latter not only nips the berries, but barks the branches as well and leaves them unprotected against the frost. Those branches that cannot be reached by hand should be beaten with a reed rather than a pole, for a heavy blow demands a doctor. The man who beats must not strike directly, for often an olive so struck carries a green shoot away with it from the branch, in which case the fruit of the next year is lost (I, LV, 1-3).

And of course every family had its vegetable patch, or *orto*, which Pliny described as the poor man's farm. For vegetables were an important part of the Roman diet, supplementing a sort of porridge made from unhusked 'far' or 'emma' that was unsuitable for baking bread, and which was only replaced by wheat much later on. Additionally, beans of various kinds, together with turnips, carrots and radishes as well as peas, cabbage and lettuce, formed the bulk of their food, at least in the country. As time went by, meat appeared more frequently on the menu, but there is little evidence that livestock was reared for the table. In fact Apicius' cookery book devotes only ten lines to beef and veal combined, against a niggardly three pages on pork.

Admittedly, dinner at Trimalchio's was a different matter, to be sure. For *hors d'oeuvres*, along with different sorts of olives, hot sausages, grilled damsons and pomegranate seeds, there were dormice rolled in honey and poppy seed, followed by a succession of entrées that included wild boar, sucking pigs and boiled calf. Commenting on the skills of the Roman chef, Petronius remarked ironically:

If you want it, he will make you a fish out of a sow's belly, a wood pigeon out of bacon, a turtle dove out of ham, and a chicken out of a knuckle of pork. There could not be a more versatile fellow.

Or a more versatile animal, come to think of it. But such splendours were, in the main, restricted to Roman banqueting. The country folk in Chianti, while no doubt following Columella's recipes for pickling fruit and vegetables, salting pork or preparing mustard, would like him have been 'abundantly satisfied with such things as may, without great expense, fall to the lot of those living a simple, rural life' (XII, XLV, 1).

For alongside the kitchen gardens were the orchards, providing nuts and fruit, where marvellous things were done with grafting: Columella himself managed to get six different types of grape on a single vine.

But perhaps the biggest change in the countryside was the gradual disappearance of forests. Widespread over-cutting by both Etruscans and Romans had already turned them into a hallowed memory by Virgil's day, when large tracts of wooded shrubland already characterised the Tuscan landscape.

Much of the timber was used for shipbuilding and for the smelting of iron ore. Livy's record of the gifts sent by the Etruscan cities to help Scipio's expeditionary force against Carthage in 205 BC included fir for ships from Perusia, Clusium and Rusellae, and interior marine fittings from Volterrae. But wood was also needed for heating. As the historian A. H. M. Jones has pointed out, 'under the Roman Empire, the innumerable baths must have contributed to deforestation by their immense consumption of fuel, mostly saplings.'

Strabo, moreover, tells how the timber resources of Pisa were being used 'upon the buildings at Rome, and also at the villas, now that people are devising palaces of Persian magnificence'. What with one thing and another, in fact, Tuscany seems to have been a main source of constructional materials, that were transported along the coast by sea or, if their destination was Rome, down the Tiber to the capital. Which lends weight to the belief that, far from being 'depleted and unwanted' as some historians have suggested, the area continued to be prosperous in Imperial times, when such fine buildings as the Augustan theatre at Volterra and the walls, towers and theatre at Florence were built.

In the geographical centre of this activity, one can visualise the trains of pack animals wending their way through Chianti, 'usually made up by traders', notes Varro, 'who use pannier-carrying donkeys to take oil or wine, and grain, or other merchandise'. Clearly the Romans raised livestock as working animals rather than for food. In his list of 'proper equipment' for an olive plantation of 240 *iugera*, Cato prescribed three yoke of oxen along with three pack-asses to carry manure, two draft donkeys and one for milk. Donkeys were sometimes used for ploughing, where the soil was light, but mostly for transportation. Horses, on the other hand, were restricted to the cavalry, to chariot racing, and as playthings for the rich. Their only role on the farm was as sires or dams to jennies or jack-asses, and for the breeding of mules and hinnies.

Sheep, on the other hand (says Columella) were 'of prime importance . . . as our chief protection against extreme cold, and to provide us with a generous supply of coverings for our bodies (VII, 2). They also gave milk and cheese, 'which are important articles of diet for both country folk and for persons of taste'. The same could be said of goats (apart from their bewildering ability to graze on almost anything). Their milk was drunk fresh and made into a variety of cheeses; it is agreeable to reflect, as you sink your teeth into a succulent *pecorino* or some fresh *ricotta* that they are direct descendants of the Roman products which were made in exactly the same way.

Tailing the list came swine (which Pliny called the stupidest of animals, although one of his favourite recipes was 'Trojan Pig', consisting of a pig's stomach stuffed with sausages, roast chicken, eggs and vegetables), and if pigs were kept, it was essentially for pork. The Emperor made a free issue of gammon, which meant that Roman butchers were for a while distributing some 20,000 lbs of it a day. Even so, there was one way in which the pig really came into its own, and that was for sacrifices.

Varro has his own explanation for this:

> The pig is called in Greek hys, formerly thys, from the verb thyein, to sacrifice: for when men first sacrificed animals they began apparently with the race of pigs. Traces of this remain in the sacrifice of a pig at the initiation in the Eleusinian mysteries, the killing of one at the initiation of peace when a treaty is struck; and in the fact that at the beginning of a wedding among the ancient princes and exalted personages of *Etruria*, the newly made husband and wife, at their union first sacrifice a pig. The ancient latins too . . . seem to have had the same custom; for the women of our country, especially nurses, call that part which in girls distinguishes their sex, 'porcus', the Greek women, choiron [pig], meaning that the term is a worthy symbol of marriage. The race of pigs is, they say, a gift of nature designed to grace the banquet, and so life was given them, just as salt is, to keep their flesh good (II, IV, 9-10).

A bit far-fetched, maybe; yet, who knows, when the modern Chianti peasant grunts 'Porca Madonna!' to express surprise or dismay, he may unconsciously be harking back to the countless moments in the life of his forebears that called for sacrifice. And, etymology apart, each occasion had its own special ritual. An offering had to be made for the oxen 'when the pear-trees bloom'. Before tilling the ground there was a formula to be followed, and a slightly modified one if a grove was to be thinned. To purify a piece of ground required a different procedure, and if it happened that the steading should be hit by lightning, an expiatory prayer had to be offered. But by far the most important were the spring and autumn feasts. As Virgil says:

Above all, worship the gods, paying your yearly tribute
To the Corn-goddess — a sacrifice on the cheerful grass
Just as the close of winter, when spring has cleared the sky.
Oh then the lambs are fat, then are wines most mellow,
Sweet then is sleep, and rich on mountains lie the shadows.
Let all your labouring men worship the Corn-goddess:
For her let the honeycomb be steeped in milk and mild wine,
The mascot led three times round the young crops — a victim
Feted by all your fellows accompanying it in a body:
Let them call her into their houses
With a shout, and let nobody lay his sickle to the ripe corn
Till in her honour he's placed on his head a wreath of oak leaves
And danced impromptu dances and sung the harvester's hymn.

(*Georgics*, I, 338-50)

Cato describes the sacrifice of the *porca praecidanea* to be made to Ceres before harvest, accompanied by the offering of prayers, little cakes, incense and wine to Jupiter, Juno, and the two-headed Janus. No one is more superstitious than a farmer, and time and time again the old religious beliefs, *la vecchia religione* of the ancients, still crop up in their tenets today.

Of the moon, for instance, Varro wrote:

Certain farm operations are better done under a waxing moon, some under a waning moon, such as the cutting of corn or timber. Why, said Agrasius, I practise these precepts not only when shearing sheep, but in my hair even (following my father in this) for fear of growing bald if I cut it when the moon is waxing. Said Agrius: In what season has the moon four periods and what influence has such a division on farming? Did you never hear in the country, answered Tremelius, the expression 'on the eighth day before the moon begins to increase' or wane? And that of those things which need to be done when the moon is waxing some are yet better done after than before the eighth day before full moon? And whatever things it was good to do when the moon was waning were better done when that luminary had the least light? (1, XXXVII, 1-3).

While Cato warned: 'Do not touch timber except in the dark of the moon or in its last phase. The best time to take out timber which you dig up or fell is during the seven days following the full moon' (XXXVII, 4).

Manuring, says Columella, should be done under a waning moon, 'for this frees the crops from weeds', and likewise the picking of grapes and the transfer of wine from the vat. Pliny the Elder insists that the storage jars 'must not be opened at mid-winter except on a fine day, and not when a south wind is blowing or at a full moon' (XIV, 135).

Old wives' tales these may be, to be sure, but whatever one may say, they still linger on. Few modern wine-growers, in truth, would be bold enough to move wine when the moon is waxing, and I am sure that Alvaro, my factotum, would be horrified if I even dared to suggest such a thing.

TEN

Over an idle breakfast one sunny morning, I flipped through the pages of Pliny to see what he had to say about the weather in those parts. With some satisfaction (though not, one would have thought, much poetic inspiration) he described the summer climate at Tifernum as 'temperate and breezy', and went on to observe: 'Hence the number of elderly people living there — you can see the grandfathers and great grandfathers of people who have reached their own manhood, and hear stories and tales of the past, so that a visit here is like a return to another age' (V, 6). In his day, it seems that the Tuscan countryside was full of retired folk, to say nothing of rich people taking a breather from the city. *La villeggiatura in campagna* has always been popular in Italy, and we may be sure that the Romans spent the hot months in Chianti, just as so many city-dwellers do now. By retreating to his country villa (to quote J. P. V. D. Balsden) the wealthy Roman

> shed the townsman and enjoyed the life that his ancestors had led, entertaining the guests, hunting, meeting tenants, going round his estate with his bailiff, enjoying every moment of it and complaining . . . that his days were so full that it would be a relief to return to his work in Rome.

Certainly this is the impression that one gets from Pliny, and very agreeable it must have been, too. His villa at Tifernum (on the borders of Tuscany and Umbria, but near enough to set a pattern for Chianti) was clearly much more of a retreat than the lavish seaside house at Laurentum: it seems to have been *de rigueur* among top Romans to have places both in the country and at the seaside, and even today my smart Florentine neighbours spend July in Chianti and August at Forte dei Marmi or Port' Ercole. And while Pliny took an intelligent interest in the administration of his estate, he nevertheless did so in the same rather dilettante fashion that many of us (let us honestly admit) still indulge in, though rather less grandly. To his friend Pompeius Falco, for instance, we find him writing:

I do take a horse sometimes and play the part of the proprietor, but only to the extent of riding round part of the estate for exercise. Don't drop your habit of sending me the city news while I am rusticating here! (IX, 15).

Rusticating, as he calls it, was an almost perfect form of escape. Pliny usually woke around sunrise, but, as he says, 'My shutters remained closed, for in the stillness and darkness I feel myself surprisingly detached from any distractions and left to myself in freedom' (IX, 36). And once he got up, his routine was a smooth one. During the morning he attended to his affairs, from time to time calling in a secretary to dictate his thoughts. After a siesta he would go for a walk or a drive, and perhaps read a speech or two before having a massage and a bath, and then dinner. In the evening he listened to a comedy or some music. In a similar way, one suspects, the days spun elegantly by in such patrician villas as I daresay existed (though I cannot pinpoint them on the map) in Chianti at that time.

When it comes to hunting, though, we are on surer ground. Much of Tuscany was still wooded, as 44 per cent of Chianti still is, and there are countless references to hunts in the later texts. Varro spoke of a game reserve of 40 *iugera* near Tarquinia, and larger ones at Statonia and elsewhere; while nearer home, Rutilius described how, when delayed by a storm at Pisa, he and his party made good use of their time:

The respite from our voyage we spend in the neighbouring forests, delighted to exercise our limbs in the pursuit of game. Our innkeeper supplies the implements for the chase, and hounds trained to discover a strongly scented lair. By means of an ambush, and the snare of wide-meshed nets, a boar, though terrifying in the flash of his tusks, is overthrown and falls — such a large one as Meleager of the strong shoulders might dread to approach, such a one as would slacken the joints of Hercules. Then mid the echoing hills leap the notes of the bugle-horn, and singing makes the booty light in carrying back (*De Reditu Suo*).

Boar-hunting is still popular in this area, and the tradition of *la caccia* for game of all descriptions (including even the tiniest of songbirds) is so strong in these parts that some derivationists, presumably following the alliterative sound of the chase, maintain their declension of the Latin verb for 'to make a loud noise', against all grammatical rules, as clango, clangere, clanxi, *Chianti*. Maybe this is the origin of the name, but S. Pieri's suggestion that it comes from the Etruscan 'Clante' seems rather more plausible. In any case, one may be sure that on feast days the hunting fraternity were out in force.

And staggering, what is more, was the number of holidays. If in pre-Sullan times only 59 days in the year were devoted to state-paid holiday spectacles, by 354 AD there were no less than 159 days of games in a ludicrous total of 200 official holidays each year. Even in Juvenal's period we find him complaining that 'the public has long since cast off its cares; the people that once bestowed commands, consulships, legions and all else, now meddles no more, and wants only two things, panem et circenses.' (X, 77-81).

Seneca echoed this contempt in a passage which might have been written today:

People set out on a journey with no particular object in view. They wander down the coast. In a purposeless way they go by sea, they go by land, always wishing they were doing something else.

'Let us go to Campania.'

'No, smart resorts are a bore. Rough country is the thing to see.'

'Let us go to Brutium and see the ranches in Lucania.'

Once in the bush they must find a nice resort; after the extensive tedium of these uncultivated districts, something civilized is needed for their cultured gaze to feed on.

'Let us go to Taranto. People are always talking about its harbour and its splended winter climate . . . '

'No, let us go back to Rome.'

It seems a lifetime since they last heard the applause and the din of the games.

'It might be rather nice, too, to see somebody killed.'

But men like Juvenal and Seneca were wasting their breath. That permissiveness had become the order of the day is shown in a blatant inscription, which to our ears may have a *déjà vu* sound:

Balnea, vina, venus corrumpunt corpora nostra sed vitam faciunt.
(C.I.L., VI, 15258)

Baths, wine and women may corrupt our bodies, but they are the essence of life.

All this junketing had its effect on rural life, too, and Columella spent a whole chapter listing what could and could not be done on feast days. It was forbidden, for instance, to wash sheep for the good of the fleece, except as a curative measure, or to shear them. Nor might the vintage be gathered in, unless a puppy had been sacrificed. But for some reason it was lawful to cut torches, dip

candles, clear out and clean fish ponds, cisterns and ditches, and
to make cheese. Even animals were controlled by legislation. Cato
stipulated that 'oxen may be yoked on feast days only for these
purposes: to haul firewood, bean-stalks, and grain for storing'. Yet
there were no holidays for mules, horses or donkeys, 'except the
family festivals' (CXXX, viii).

If the record of the Italian people covers a span of some 27
centuries, the Roman state occupies more than ten of them, and for
something like 700 years the ancient Romans controlled the area of
Chianti. Over so long a period, changes were bound to occur, even
if the old seasonal routines struggled tirelessly on. Already in the
high period of Augustus, Varro and Columella were full of disgruntled murmurings about the state of agriculture, and there is
little doubt that the rot set in during the later years of the Empire.
Contemporary sources have tended to ascribe this to over-heavy taxation, and plainly the Imperial government was more concerned that
taxes should be paid than that the land should be cultivated. A decree of Aurelian, renewed by Constantine, ordered that local councils
should be responsible for the taxes of deserted lands in their territories. Even so, in 395 AD Honorius had to write off 528,042
iugera in the Campania as abandoned.

Shortage of manpower and insecurity caused by the Germanic
invasions no doubt played their part in this decline. But the root
cause seems to have been the overall inefficiency of the central
government. An example of the long and tortuous ways of the
Roman bureaucracy in the late second century is given by Jones:

> The farmers who have leased the imperial estates at Saepinum
> complain to Septimianus, the assistant officer in the Treasury,
> that the local magistrates are not using the law to protect their
> flocks. Septimianus has written to the magistrates 'again and
> again'; they take no notice. Accordingly, Septimianus refers the
> matter to his superior, Cosmus, chief fiscal minister, who sends
> papers to the Praetorian prefects who had power over local mag-
> istrates. And so the final letter is: 'From Bassaeus Rufus and
> Macrinius Vindex, praetorian prefects to the magistrates of
> Saepium. We send a copy of a letter received from Cosmus. We
> warn you to stop injuring the men who have leased the estate,
> and thus inflicting a loss on the Treasury: otherwise we shall
> inquire and punish.'

Perhaps it was all inevitable. From power to luxury, from luxury
to flippancy, and from flippancy to plain incompetence, the
Romans slipped; until finally the Empire of the West, which in its

prime had encompassed some 120 million people in an area of 2½ million square miles, was no longer a match for the tough barbarian tribes from over the Alps.

Which meant, among other things, a new epoch for Chianti.

PART TWO: THE DARK AGES AND EARLY MIDDLE AGES

ONE

Men are we, and must grieve when even the Shade
Of that which once was great is passed away. (Wordsworth)

It was, as we know, a painful and protracted decline. Rome was sacked in 410 AD by Alaric's Visigoths, and again in 455 by the Vandals under Genseric. In the end what remained of Pax Romana retreated to Byzantium (renamed Constantinople after the Emperor Constantine) when the Gothic general Odoacer came jackhammering down the peninsula, packed the last Roman Emperor in the West off to a villa at Naples on 28 August 476 (exactly 1500 years ago as I write these lines), and set himself up as the effective ruler of Italy.

It was not until thirteen years later that the eastern Emperor (only too uncomfortably aware that he was himself a sitting target for the Germanic armies that were mustering in Dalmatia) was able to head their leader Theoderic off in the direction of Italy with the argument that, as an Imperial *foederatus,* he should win back the territory that had been lost to the Empire. Patently this was an invitation to scavenge, but at least the danger to Constantinople was averted. In any event, Odoacer held out at Ravenna for two and a half years before finally agreeing to set up what, on the face of it, was to be a joint Gothic rule. And as things turned out, he was right to have resisted his besieging compatriot so long. For at the banquet to celebrate this consolidation of Nordic interests he was suddenly set upon by Theoderic, whose sword (so the story goes) met with little resistance. 'The wretch cannot have had a bone in his body,' was Theoderic's tart comment as he put in back in its scabbard.

Yet by all accounts, Theoderic's subsequent rule did succeed in giving the peninsula a much-needed breathing space. Clearly the object of his expedition was simply a land-grab, and over the next few years some 250,000 Ostrogoths, spilling into the countryside like water from an overflowing bucket, were turned into Italian farmers, apparently with a minimum of fuss. Theoderic endowed them with a third of the land they had invaded, but from what one gathers this metamorphosis was so smoothly carried out that the

Bishop of Pavia wrote cheerfully to Liberius (a Roman senator who
had been entrusted with the job) that 'you have enriched countless
hordes of the Goths with generous grants of land, and yet the
Romans have hardly felt it.' For the fact is that these Germanic
migrants who had surged in first as unwelcome guests and then as
opportunist conquerors had little or no experience of administration
and were only too glad to be able to make use of the Roman bureaucratic machine, cumbersome though it was. Theoderic's own secretary was a Roman, Cassiodorus — who was at pains to justify the
process by pointing out that the parcelling up of real estate not only
promoted a new sense of harmony between the two races, but also
consolidated the tenure of the land.

For a good thirty years, in fact, Italy seems to have basked in an
unexpected glow of prosperity. 'So great was the happiness that even
wayfarers were at peace,' wrote a contemporary chronicler,

> He [Theoderic] did no wrong. He governed the two nations,
> Goths and Romans, and although he himself belonged to the Arian
> sect, yet he attempted nothing aginst the Catholic faith . . . mer-
> chants from the various provinces flocked to him, for so good
> was the order he maintained that if anyone wished to leave gold
> or silver on his country estate, it was considered as safe as within
> a walled town . . . throughout the whole of Italy, Theoderic made
> no gates for any city, and what gates there were to the cities
> were never closed. Anyone with business to transact could do it
> at any time of night as safely as by day.

Sycophantic stuff, one may feel; but an edict tabulated by the
faithful Cassiodorus tends to confirm that Theoderic was an enlightened ruler. It runs:

> The king detests the oppression of the unfortunate, and encour-
> ages them to make their complaints to him. He has heard that
> powerful houses are failing to pay their share of the taxes, and
> that a larger sum in consequence is being exacted from the 'tennes'.
> To amputate such wickedness for the future, the letter last pre-
> ceding has been addressed to the Senate, and the 'possessores
> sive curiales' are now invited to state their grievances fully and
> frankly or else for ever after hold their peace and cultivate a habit
> of patience.

What effect this edict actually had is open to doubt, but the fact
that it was issued at all is remarkable, and perhaps there is some
reason for suggesting that an Ostrogothic renaissance, however short-

lived, may have flowered — even if in reality it was probably achieved by cultured Romans such as Cassiodorus, Boethius and Symmachus — to say nothing of Benedict, who founded the Benedictine Order, and whose influence was felt later.

All the same, Theoderic sprang from barbarian stock, and the local gods can hardly have been expected to be entirely on his side. In 531, during the month of September, a comet was seen ·for a full twenty days in the western quarter, shooting its rays northwards. Eight days later, with the sun in Capricorn, another larger comet, with its head in the East and its tail in the West, apparently became visible for no less than 40 days. While the impact of such celestial manifestations on the sixth-century mind can only by imagined, there is no doubt that subsequent events presaged neither Arcadian peace nor Eldoradian prosperity.

On the contrary, the decades of fighting that resulted from the Byzantine invasion under Belisarius after Theoderic's death had devastating effects throughout most of the country, including Chianti. Writing in 556, Pope Pelagius described the general distress:

> the Italian fields have been so ravaged that no one can restore them ... there is such poverty and destitution in this city [Rome] that we cannot look without grief and anguish of heart upon men whom we know to be meritorious and born to an honourable disposition.

What is more, these wars paved the way for yet a further invasion, this time by the Lombards.

By origin Scandinavians who had been on the move for several hundred years, this warrior race had already annihilated the Heruli on the plains of Hungary and the Gepidae in Pannonia before crossing the Alps in 567 in their unending search for food. Whether or not there was any truth in the rumour that they had been encouraged to come south by Narses in a fit of pique at his recall to Constantinople by the Empress Sophia, these long-bearded 'Longobardi' encountered very little resistance in the north of Italy where only Venice, Ravenna and Genoa remained independent for any length of time. Paul the Deacon explains that 'The Romans had . . . no courage to resist, because the pestilence which had occurred at the time of Narses had destroyed very many.' Nor did it take the Lombards long to discover the charms of Tuscany. Three years after their initial inrush, in 570, Chianti and the greater part of Tuscany were incorporated into the Lombard kingdom.

From all accounts there must have been a considerable influx of these raggety, disputatious newcomers into the choice spots of this enchanting landscape, at the expense of the established Roman and Gothic landowners, most of whom they murdered in the process. T.H. Hodgkin has written:

> Everything about them, even for many years after they had entered upon the sacred soil of Italy, speaks of mere savage delight in bloodshed, and the rudest forms of sensual indulgence. They are the anarchists of the Völkerwandrung, whose delight is only in destruction and who seem incapable of culture. Yet this is the race from which, in the fullness of time, under the transmuting power of the old Italian civilisation, were to spring Anselm and Leufranc, Hildebrand and Dante Alighieri.

To which might be added that whereas the invasions of the Ostrogoths had been initiated by Imperial *foederati* as a definite mission, no such tenuous legality could be claimed by the Lombards. They were in Italy as birds of prey in search for food. And in contrast to the Ostrogoths who had at least followed a policy of coexistence, fitting themselves peacefully into the countryside, the Lombards grouped themselves into the fortified safety of hilltop castles, well apart from the old settlements, and ruled the land as a warrior class, exacting a third of the produce of the land as their tribute.

They did so, moreover, with a strain of barbarity that curdles the blood. It is said that Alboin (who led their invasion) seized the king of the Gepidaes' daughter as his bride and forced her to drink a nuptial toast from the skull of her own father which he had fashioned into a goblet. So spookily, in fact, do saints and symbols jostle through their chronicles, and so readily to hand was the jewel-encrusted dagger, that it comes as little surprise to find that she was soon able to take her revenge. Nor was it by accident that Alboin's successor, Cleph, was disposed of a few months later by one of his dukes.

Indeed, during the ten-year interregnum that followed, the dukes were able to build up an independent authority which they fought tooth and nail later to maintain. A patchwork of some 36 dukedoms spread over the kingdom, each virtually autonomous in its own dominion, and subject only to the nominal control of the king's *gastald*, who acted as a central tax-collector and kept as often as not a tactfully blind eye on the ambitions of these magnates. Farwald in Spoleto and Totto in Benevento, for instance, entrenched themselves so powerfully in their semi-independent states that the later Lombard kings were hard put to control them.

And yet gradually one senses the Italian landscape putting its nymph's arms around even the toughest of these hard men, and by the middle of the seventh century some semblance of order had returned to the land. To Wallace Hadrill, the famous Edict of Rothair was an indication of quieter times:

> It appeared in the same year as a Life of St. Columban by Jonas of Bobbio. The two constitute a modest renaissance for Lombard Italy. The Edict, for all its barbarism, is law-giving such as the Romans would have understood, while the Life, written in a monastery, is no very polished performance. Both are evidence of more settled times, and are a kind of admission that the barbarians knew that they had come to their journey's end; for Italy there was no advance and no retreat; and terms were being arrived at with Roman civilization in all its respects, legal, ecclesiastical, artistic, commercial.

Much of the Edict, to be sure, was Roman in style; but there were some intriguingly barbaric traits, such as the principle of Wergild, which aimed at restricting blood feuds by codifying a monetary value on life and limb: thus the price payable for murdering an 'aldins' (a half-free Italian) was 60 solidi, that for a leading swineherd 50 solidi, while his underlings were worth only 25. A 'rustic slave under the farm labourer', finally, was valued at 15 solidi. A similar tariff was drawn up for wounds: breaking any of the bones of the head cost 12 solidi, and 'the broken bones are to be counted thus; that one bone shall be found large enough to make an audible sound when thrown against a shield at twelve feet distance on the road.'

The kings, too, were gradually regaining their power. Agilulf won back most of the Po valley, and Rothair conquered Liguria, while the famous Liutprand (helped no doubt by the Iconoclast controversy that had split the Empire) took Bologna and the Pentapolis, and thus threatened Ravenna itself in 727.

Yet while the Imperial exarch hung on for dear life to hold Constantinople's last foothold in the West, the motley fragments of the old Empire were shakily held together, as they had been since the days of Gregory I, by the Pope. Such papal power as there was stemmed mainly from the fact that in the shifting kaleidoscope of Italian affairs at the end of the sixth century there was no other source of order or salvation. 'The condition of this country does not forbode the end of the world,' Pope Gregory had written glumly, 'it realizes it.' And indeed his personal achievement in using the resources of the Church for the relief of the people was outstanding.

By the middle of the eighth century the position of the Papacy was legitimised by a notorious document, all too often denounced as a fraud, that has been the justification of the Papacy's temporal power ever since. Whether or not the Donations of Constantine was in fact, as is often alleged, a gift to Pope Sylvester in return for his cure for leprosy, it bequeathed what remained of the Roman Empire of the West to the Pope. 'Wherefore,' runs the vital clause, somewhat floridly:

> That the pontifical crown may not grow too cheap, but may be adorned with glory and influence even beyond the dignity of the earthly empire, Lo! we hand over and relinquish our palace, the city of Rome, and all the provinces, places and cities of Italy and the Western regions, to the most blessed pontiff and universal pope, Sylvester. and we ordain that they shall be governed by him and his successors, and we grant that they shall remain under the authority of the Holy Roman Church.

Suspect though this document may be, it was nevertheless the basis for all the future claims by the Papacy for political rule in the West.

But no one could doubt that volcanic forces were again rumbling beneath the landscape that had already enshrined so many dreams in the ancient world, and which in the eighth century was again enmeshed in a complex web of political cross-currents. The Lombards, the Pope, the Emperor of the East, the Exarch and the Archbishop of Ravenna were all hatching their private plans for supremacy (and by the same token their personal insurances against extinction). In 753, thirteen years after making a fruitless appeal to the Franks for help, but now faced with a direct threat from Ainstulf who was already in control of Ravenna, Pope Stephen II took his courage in his hands and set out over the Alps in dead of winter for King Pepin's court at Ponthion. There between the Vicar of Christ and the illiterate king who had consolidated his rule over north-east Spain, France, the Low Countries, Germany and Austria, an epic bargain was struck. The Pope anointed Pepin and his sons Charles and Carloman not only as kings of the Franks, but also as Patricians of the Romans. Pepin, in return, promised to champion the papal cause, and in his famous Donation recognised the Pope as sovereign of the Exarchate, sovereign of the Pentapolis, and 'Ducatus Romae'.

This invitation to the Franks to invade Italy — which is what Stephen's journey really amounted to — brought about yet another shift in the peninsula's all too turbulent history. For it meant Rome's final break with Constantinople in favour of a *mariage de convenance* with north-west Europe. This was consummated on Christmas Day of 800, when Charlemagne, wearing a white 'chlamys' over his giant frame, and the sandals of a roman patrician, crawled up the steps of St Peter's on his hands and knees to be crowned Emperor by Pope Leo III. Thus came into being that curious anomaly, the Holy Roman Empire. It was to last, in titular form at least, for a thousand years.

TWO

With a dash of romanticism (but some distortion of historical fact) the great Florentine chronicler, Villani, records that his city was completely destroyed by Totila, King of the Ostrogoths, only to be resurrected some centuries later by no less a person than Charlemagne himself. But archaeologists have established that the Roman walls remained intact until the twelfth century when, due to the rapid expansion of the city, they were replaced by the ampler medieval circle of fortifications.

Likewise, they have shown that many of the Roman buildings, which had been virtually abandoned, were incorporated into medieval constructions when Florence revived during the early Middle Ages.

Totila, it is true, had fought a famous battle at the Val di Mugello, north of the city in 542. But he did not destroy the place 'stone by stone', as Villani suggests. As the Lombards swept into Tuscany, they established their headquarters in Lucca, neglecting both Fiesole and Florence, which consequently declined in importance. Florence was not destroyed. It simply vegetated as a sleepy and impoverished little agrarian centre.

In the hills and valleys of Chianti, just to the south, the country life went on as it always had done, but in the place of the fine Roman country houses with their well cultivated estates, the watch-towers and castles of the Lombard barons sprang up at strategic defensive points dominating the river crossings and the valleys — such as Montegrossoli, Panzano, Radda, Monterinaldi and Grignano. And where husbandry declined, nature took over, scrub oak invading once cultivated fields, until a large proportion of the area was covered with tangled and almost impenetrable woods in which the rough buccaneering feudal barons held their hunts.

Some existing buildings, mainly religious, can be dated from this far-off period of early Germanic occupation. But they throw little light on this dark, undocumented period, all the same. The landscape of Chianti was surely then characterised, as it is today, by a perennial freshness, a perpetual springtime even as autumn shades into winter. For if the period between 400 and 700 AD was one of waste and depopulation, it was also a time of self-sufficiency. And it is not difficult to believe that the air of remote rusticity — exemplified by the cheerful voices of *contadini* calling down from the hills as they plough the slopes or bring in the harvest with their milk-white Chiana oxen, while the old women sit placidly in a doorway, plaiting or sewing — was always present. In mill houses, rebuilt half a dozen times on the same traditional pattern (and which today are being converted into smart weekend retreats) the water from the Arbia, the Pesa and the Greve was channelled into millponds and powered the threshing stones, while in the *fornaci, mattoni* were cooked and peat stacked, just as Lorenzo Ruffoli still does below Radda. Dark the political scene may have been, causing peasants to store their harvests within the massive protective walls of the feudal strongholds, and cluster their own meagre dwellings around the walls for safety's sake, trudging miles each dawn to the fields from which they scratched a bare existence; but fruit and wine and oil there certainly were, and as spring drew on, the constellations of fireflies, the rattle of the cicadas and the singing of the nightingales were less challenged by the noise of the hunt (the 'clangum' of the baronial chases that Repetti suggested was the origin of the word Chianti) than the racket of bulldozers carving out *vigneti* today, or helicopters spraying the vines.

Poor but Arcadian this land must have been when the first evangelists of Christianity brought their message of piety and faith. Radiated outwards from the towns, the gospel was conveyed into Chianti by such martyr figures as Vincenzo of Cortona; Marcellino of Monterongriffoli; Ansano of Siena; Donato and Lorentino of Arezzo. Our own local saint is S. Eufrosino of Pamphilia: he is said to have set off down the Cassia 'pieno di fervore', and, after passing through Siena, spent some time at Castellina. Then, after crossing the Pesa, he settled himself down a mile or so away, just beyond the boundaries of my land, below the Roman site of Flacciano, now the Pieve di Panzano: 'In Pamphilia Episcopo primo latente . . . longeva aetate . . . mox apud Panzanum vetustatis Etrusci Pagum,' says the record.

Once Constantine had made Christianity the official religion of the Roman state, first baptisteries and then sanctuaries, known as Pieves, sprang up in populated areas. The earliest recorded church in Chianti seems to have been S. Cresci a Montefioralle, above Greve, which dates from 365 AD, and was named after a martyr called Cursicus. But both S. Felice in Avano and S. Marcellino in Chianti are very early constructions, and there is reason to believe that the parish church of Castellina originated in the fifth century. Known then as S. Salvatore all' Arbia, it was erected at the source of the river Arbia, just down the hill from the old Etruscan site of Salinvolpe and presumably adjacent to the Roman habitation of Bituriha, a kilometre or so from the present *comune*. The name 'Monastero' given to a farm until recently owned by the church, traces its origin, in fact, to a very early monastery, probably Benedictine, that was situated at the north-west of the original church building, and it would seem likely that this modest little place, a farm since 1478, previously formed part of the monastery. The stonework certainly gives the impression of being either Lombard or Romanesque, and in all probability the structure dates back to the eighth century — which is not bad going for a farmhouse.[1]

From the Ricasoli archives we know, moreover, that in 770 Geremia de' Firidolfi da Monte Grossoli erected an oratorio at Coltibuono, where two and a half centuries later the lovely Badia was to be built, and since the Firidolfis — predecessors of the great Ricasoli family who figure increasingly in the history of Chianti — had added the name to their own, it can safely be assumed that the formidable Castello di Monte Grossoli dominating the pass leading from the Val d'Arno into Chianti had been constructed by this noted Lombard family even earlier than this.

The Lombards, if nothing else, were devout converts to Christianity, and tended to build churches within their castles or just outside them. Sadly enough, most the documents dealing with the period before the millennium were lost, some centuries ago, in a fire that destroyed the archives of the Archbishopric of Fiesole, under whose spiritual jurisdiction much of Chianti fell. We are deprived, therefore, of many vital documents which might have thrown light on the magnates who thrived in the area, if only through the donations they made to the Church.

But we do know that the boundaries of Chianti were a bone of contention. Sometime around the fourth century, in the first flush of Christian triumph, the earliest episcopal territories were marked out. Those of the bishoprics of Florence and Fiesole with Siena ran midway across Chianti from a point just north of Poggibonsi: along the Cerchiaio stream as far as Grignano and then down to the south of Radda, with a bulge as far as Pianella where they met up with the diocese of Arezzo. And here was the trouble. The tomb of Siena's patron saint, S. Ansano, erected on the spot at which he had been martyred only 15 kilometres from the city, fell under the jurisdiction of the Bishop of Arezzo, although politically it was within the boundaries of Siena.

According to tradition, Ansano was a Roman patrician who brought the doctrine of Christianity to Siena and was martyred during the persecution of Diocletian. He is said to have met secretly with his converts in the vaults of what subsequently became the Spedale, and to have been imprisoned in an old tower known as La Rocchetta (which probably formed part of the early castle) before being beheaded and buried in the little country church of S. Maria in Pacina.

At any rate, some four centuries later, in 711, the Bishop of Arezzo, when doing the rounds of his diocese, stayed at the church and (the Sienese suspected) was about to make off with the sacred relics. Led by their *gastald*, they rushed to the defence of the saint's bones, and in the clash that followed, the *gastald* was killed. 'Wherefore,' says the Aretine chronicler,

> The whole people of Siena became enraged against Bishop Lupertianus and put him to flight; and they obliged Adeodatus, Bishop of Siena, who was a cousin of Godipert, the judge whom the Aretines had slain, to hold that parish whethèr he would or not for one year; and there outrageously and against the canons of our church he consecrated three altars and two priests.

Both the Pope and the Lombard king were called in to mediate the dispute which, once submitted to judgement, embraced not only the place of Ansano's martyrdom but also all the parishes in the Sienese political territory — eighteen to be precise, with three monasteries — which were incorporated in the diocese of Arezzo. In due course, after a bench of bishops had declared against Siena, King Liutprand gave judgement in favour of the Bishop of Arezzo (15 October 715). Yet even though Charlemagne and Leo III reconfirmed this judgement in 801, the Sienese continued doggedly to appeal (and were in fact given satisfaction by Pope Leo IV in 853).

With this celebrated law case, which dragged on for five hundred years (until 1224 when the Pope finally delivered judgement in favour of Arezzo) Chianti entered recorded history. But that is about as much as one can say. When, a little later, Charlemagne set up the *Regnum Italiae* for his young son Pepin, it meant that each town again became the centre of the surrounding territory with an official called a count in charge of the *contado*. In theory, therefore, Chianti should have come under the control of Florence and Siena. But as it turned out, Charlemagne's successors were too feeble to get their orders carried out by the great nobles surrounding them, and even less in the scattered communities of such a large empire. The remoteness of their control played into the hands of both the landed aristocracy and the local Church dignitaries. As Imperial power weakened, the offices of Marchio, Count and Viscount became family prerogatives, along with the lands they controlled. By settling on their country estates, the nobles left the control of the towns to the bishops, who themselves became feudal magnates.

In Tuscany the Margrave, while prudently paying lip-service to the Emperor, turned Chianti and its surrounding territory into virtually a sub-kingdom, and the lesser landowners, aware that they were no longer protected by the Emperor, hastened to submit themselves to his authority. Which in substance meant that they and their vassals would follow him clankingly into the field. Big fleas had lesser fleas: this, after all, was the hey-day of the feudal nobility. And because, with all this, it was also a time of religious zeal, the fashion of founding and endowing monasteries grew — whose abbots, in their turn, became ecclesiastic landlords. The Badias of Passignano, Coltibuono, Monte Scalari and Monte Muro date from this period. And it is from them that we get the first documentary evidence about Chianti.

NOTE

1. The matter is dealt with in detail in the 'Campione dell' Archivio segreto del Monte Comune di Firenze', no. 5948.

THREE

Take the second door into the Uffizi (the first leads into the Gallery itself), ascend the lofty *pietra serena* staircase, and you will find on your right the state archives of Florence. Ask the girl behind the desk for the Passignano and Coltibuono registers, and with no more ado than a charming smile she will produce the nuts and bolts of the early medieval world for your inspection.

It may come as a surprise, on examining them, to discover that many of the oldest documents in this establishment deal not with Florence, but with Chianti. The first dates back to 11 March 884, in what is styled 'the fourth year of Empire of Charles the Fat', and concerns the sale of two 'sorti masserizia', the one at Ravanziano, in the parish of S. Pietro a Sillano, and the other at Materno, in the parish of S. Cecilia. (For these two pieces of real estate, a price of 30 soldi was paid.)

It is only one of many others. But it makes one scratch one's head. For, however anarchic life may have been in the tenth century, here are a whole series of day-to-day documents drawn up by notaries who used very much the same legal terminology as they still do today. In one, executed at the Castello di Vicchio near Greve in September 957, a concession is granted to 'renovate, work and improve' some land in the valley 'dove si dice Silquilo' in the parish of S. Pietro a Sillano again; in another of October 965 the monks of the monastery of S. Michele a Passignano lease six plots of land in their neighbourhood; in yet another, signed at the Castello di Fundegnano in 981, a certain Gottifredo, known as Gottizio, the son of the late Adolino, sold some land at Montacunni and Montacenno. The following year a farm called Scopeto in the parish of S. Leolino a Flacciano changed hands — which strikes a familiar note, since the same little property below Panzano is once again, I am told, on the market today.

Yet not all the contracts involved buying and selling. There are hints of long-dead squabbles in the deed enacted in February 985, for instance, whereby Pietro, the son of the late Teudo (known as Teuzio), promises not to molest Favolfo (the son of the late Rinaldo) in his enjoyment of the house and other items sold to him at Trecolla, in the parish of S. Pietro a Sillano. And along with these ordinary folk we also come across some of the aristocracy. In 989 at the Castello d'Elci in the territory of Volterra, the contessa Willa, who describes herself as the daughter of the late Landolf and widow of Count Rudolf, the son of Rudolf, sold, with the consent of her son Ildebrand, an estate (*una intera Sorte e bene*) at Pisignaulo (Pisignano?) in the parish of S. Stefano a Campoli, for the price of 50 soldi.

So even a feudal dowager was not above selling some property now and then — though to do so, she needed the approval of her son. Yet this lady should not be confused with the famous Countess Willa who, in 978 (eight years after her son Ugo assumed office as Margrave of Tuscany) founded the celebrated Badia in Florence at the spot on which it still stands today, and endowed it, among others, with estates at Radda, Vertine and Brolio. For this too she must have needed filial agreement, and indeed the Marchese Ugo — who donated further vast properties to his mother's foundation in 998 — is actually credited as the founder of the Badia, where an annual memorial service has been held on the day of his death, 21 December, without interruption for close on a thousand years.

Ugo was a chivalrous warrior, we are told. But what really endeared him to Florentines was that he moved his headquarters from Lucca to Florence. Because of his munificence he came to be regarded as the city's first hero, and was accorded an affectionate place in Paradise by Dante himself. Yet one cannot help remembering that the millennium was expected to see the end of the world (or alternatively the resurrection of Our Lord) and as doomsday approached there were many who agonisingly sought to ensure the salvation of their souls. *Il Gran Barone* was growing old (he died in 1001) and had no heirs, so the generous distribution of his wealth on 25 July 998 to the Badia and to the monastery he had himself founded at S. Michele a Marturi in the valley of the Elsa (among which featured properties at Monte Luco a Lecchi, Fonterutoli, Ligliano, Cispiano, Pietrafitta and Grignano) may possibly have been prompted by thoughts of the impending apocalypse.

There are echoes of this anxiety in our little parchment scrolls. In December 999, for instance, a certain Everard (who, though a Lombard, was at pains to explain that as a priest he practised Roman law) hastened to sell his property, presumably preferring to face his maker with cash rather than fixed assets. Yet Walberto, the Abbot of Passignano, seems to have been untroubled by such considerations as the millennium approached. In one notarial act we find him receiving a donation from a man named Teudegrimo 'for the good of his soul', and in another leasing out farms and vineyards at places called Elsato and Spanpagliannala. And hardly had the fateful day passed uneventfully by than in January 1000 he leased out on a *concessione a livello* some land at Rignano and at the crossroads at Sillano to Adolfo, the son of the late Taiberto, with the written obligation that the leaseholder would build a house on the property within the space of a year.

From this time onwards, the contracts multiply. But what caught my eye (understandably, perhaps, since it is now my home) was the number of deeds enacted at the Castello di Grignano in the Val di Pesa. There are, in fact, more parchments drawn up at Grignano than at any other place, and they enable us to retrace the genealogy, at least, of the family whose possession it was for a century or more. Since such documentation is rare enough, in all conscience, and virtually non-existent elsewhere for eleventh-century Chianti, it seems worth while to glance at it more closely.

FOUR

Ad Agrum Janii, they called it originally, after the twin-headed god of the gateways. And, capping a hill at the confluence of three valleys to command the narrow hump-backed bridge over the gorge where the River Pesa was joined by the Cerchiaio, the castello was a strategic point for any landed lord who was set on exacting tolls from traffic moving up and down the old Cassia highway, to say nothing of those travelling east-west along the road from S. Donato and the Val d'Elsa to Radda, Gaiole and the Val d'Arno. Just when it had first been built, on the site of the old roman 'fundus', no one can tell.[1] But soon after Otto I had set his seal on the feudal revolution by formally enfeoffing the territorial magnates with their lands late in the tenth century, the name Grignano begins to appear. It was mentioned in 998, and a document dated 1016 shows that the place was owned by the brothers Gottifredo and Gottizio, who controlled much of the surrounding countryside from this stronghold and Monte Rinaldi (itself named after a Lombard predecessor, Reinhart) just up the river. Themselves the sons of Gottifredo, alias Gottizio (who seems to have featured in the Passignano land deed of 981) they appear to have been among the most prominent Lombard figures in Chianti.[2] And from what remains of its original foundations, one can guess that their castle at Grignano, built of cut grey *alberese* limestone quarried in the neighbourhood, with six-foot-wide walls enclosing the whole top of the hill, must have been a daunting sight to any passer-by.

But apart from collecting tolls on behalf of their *padroni*, the inhabitants were kept busy on the land, and a further document, drawn up at Grignano on St Valentine's Day 1023, gives a glimpse of more homely, agricultural pursuits. Let us try and reconstruct the scene.

Since no one has left a record of the weather on that day, we will assume that it was cold and sunny, as it so often is in Chianti at this time of the year. There would have been a heavy ground frost, especially in the fields where the Cerchiaio runs into the Pesa, but just before half past eight the sun would have appeared over the hill to the south, dispersing the mists which swirled around the massive grey walls of the castello. First the *cassero* and then the watch towers would light up, and a few minutes later the humbler brick and wood dwellings of the peasants which clustered beneath the walls on the southern slope.

For farmers, February tends to be a quiet time, so the peasants would have been out in the fields chopping firewood or perhaps sowing some late crops — barley, for instance, in the fields towards Montanino — while the womenfolk did their washing down by the bridge and shouted to others who were baking pasta in the communal oven. Quite a few of the villagers would be working in the kiln just below the castle walls baking the same large, flat terracotta bricks that had been used since the early Iron Age days when a Villanovan settlement had first sprung up in this strategic, well-watered spot. Others would have been making flour in the mill on the river. The *gastald* would have been up in the tower on the look-out for approaching travellers.

On this February morning he would have spotted a party of donkeys as it crossed the bluff to the north, coming from the direction of Passignano. But when he recognised the notary Ranieri and his assistants he would have hastened to open the gates and welcome them in. For there was business to be done. Shortly afterwards, Gottifredo and his rather grander retinue would have galloped up from the other direction, bringing with him, quite possibly, his young son Landolfo.

In the main vaulted hall of the castello one visualises them all sitting down to *pranzo* at a long trestle table in front of a great charcoal brazier. Fat black cauldrons would be bubbling, and wild boar and pheasants roasting on a spit. Nor, one imagines, would there have been any shortage of wooden jars containing the 'rutilante' wine from the estate, known in those days as 'Vermiglio'. Before the meal they would probably have heard mass in the parish church of S. Lorenzo a Grignano just outside the castle walls, and the parroco and the *gastald* would be sitting with Gottifredo and the lawyer on high-backed chairs at one end of the table, while the villagers clustered on benches along the sides. The talk would have been about country matters: the weather, the hunting, and the work going on at the farms. Perhaps the notary Ranieri would have had some gossip about neighbouring magnates such as the young Tegrimo and his wife Purpurella at Rencine, and the conversation would have turned to the latest developments in the quarrel between the monks of Marturi and the new Margrave. (Bonifacio I had sequestrated the possessions of the Badia di Marturi near Poggibonsi which had been bequeathed to them by Ugo, and had occupied the monastery with his troops and his concubines, provoking a *cause célèbre* that lasted for over fifty years.)

In due course they would have moved over to another smaller table, and the serving women would have brought over the wine while the lawyer's assistants prepared the parchment and the quills. There they would have been joined by three of the villagers (and probably their wives as well) and the discussion would have turned to the business to be transacted: the transfer of a lease *a livello* above the castle from Benedetto (who held it from Giorgio) to Gherardo, against a yearly rental of six silver denari, payable in December.

Using a formula virtually identical to that followed in contracts even today, the notary would have begun writing in an elegant but spindly Latin script on a roll of parchment three inches wide by nearly a foot long, which broadened towards the bottom.

In nomine Domini nostri Iesu Christi. Anno ab incarnatione eous vigesimo tertio post mille et anno imperii Henrici Imperateris Augusti none, mense Februarius, Indictione VI. Be it known that we, Benedetto the son of Alberga; Giorgio the son of the late Meringo; and Gherardo the son of the late Gherardo, have agreed
. . .

A lengthy screed followed, setting out the location of the vineyard, the details of the lease, the method of payment and entry into possession. Finally, with a sigh, the lawyer wrote: 'Done in Grignano under the jurisdiction of Florence' and each of the contracting parties signed his name with a cross. Gottifredo likewise signified his approval with a cross, and Ranieri completed the document with his signature as notary.

The business concluded, one imagines that a final glass of wine was drunk before the party dispersed, and the notary and Gottifredo went on their separate ways.

Doubtless they would have been surprised to be told, as they rode back home — the notary along the winding *maremmana* road up past Grignano di Setto (now known as La Piazza), Sicille and San Donato, and the Lombard noble over the Roman bridge towards Monte Rinaldi — that nearly a thousand years later someone would sit down at Grignano in roughly the same spot, with the document they had just drawn up in front of him, and conjure up this very trivial transaction in a book on Chianti. They would have been even more surprised to think that this parchment, now lodged in the state archives at Florence, would be exhibited at the inaugural festival of Chianti Classico wines at Greve in 1970 as one of the earliest existing documents dealing with a vineyard in Chianti. Although the Castello di Grignano was destroyed and rebuilt at least twice in the centuries that followed, the vineyard at Calcinaia that can be seen from its windows remains much as it must have been in 1023. Or, come to think of it, in Etruscan and Roman times as well.

So perhaps it is not entirely fanciful to view the whole turbulent history of Chianti as the background to vineyards such as this.

NOTES

1. The castle itself is first referred to in a document in the Passignano archives, dated 1002, as 'Grignano gundicaria florentina', but according to S. Pieri the name of Grignano derives from 'Fundus Agrinianus' (*Toponomastica della valle dell'Arno*, p. 112).

2. The Gottizi family from Monte Rinaldi and Grignano were also known as 'del castello in Chianti' (Della Rena, Serie, 23).

FIVE

In November 1043 Gottifredo's son, now known as the noble Landolfo, married Aldina degli Ubaldini — a good match, one would say, since the bride's family headed the aristocratic *consorteria* of Mugello. In the marriage settlement, or *morgengabe*, Landolfo legally made over to his wife one quarter of his possessions in Chianti, listing farms and church livings at S. Maria Novella; S. Marcellino; S. Pietro a Avenano near Gaiole; S. Leolino a Flacciano; Ricavo, including the church of S. Stefano; as well as the castle and manor of Monte Rinaldi, but explicitly excluding (for some reason that must remain unknown) the castle of Grignano. Since the marriage settlement also covered extensive property in the Mugello, including the castles of Luco and Rifredi, along with a house and land in Florence, it gives an idea of how widespread the estates of a territorial noble in the eleventh century could be.

The wording of the deed, moreover (which is quoted in Appendix 3) indicates that these possessions were allodial — that is, the absolute property of their owner, and not subject to any service or acknowledgement to any superior. Indeed, whereas forests and pasture land had earlier been the prerogative of the Crown or the Margrave, it is clear that Aldina was to share her husband's dominium over many of the rivers, pastures, fens and woodlands of central Chianti. This meant the fishing and hunting rights, along with the entitlement to cut wood and graze cattle.

Thirty-nine years later, in 1082, by a further document drawn up in the castle of Monte Rinaldi, Landolfo and Aldina jointly made over their possessions at Monte Rinaldi and Grignano to their daughters Zabulina and Gasdia, and their granddaughter Parenza. Furthermore, in February 1085, Landolfo's brother Gottizio and his wife Cunizza sold their share of the property in Chianti, including the rights on Monte Rinaldi and Grignano, to a certain Tagido for the sum of 200 lire, and at the same time made important donations to the Camaldolesian order through the medium of Bishop Ranieri of Florence. Subsequently, in 1101, Zabulina, Gasdia and Parenza made over their inheritance to the Camaldolesian convent of S. Pietro a Luco that had been founded by their parents, and of which their aunt, Cunizza, was the first mother superior (followed by her daughter Beatrice). This donation was reconfirmed in a *placito* pronounced in October 1105 by the famous margrave of Tuscany, Matilda.

All of which suggests a large and united family who believed in good works and a precise handling of their affairs. And yet we know tantalisingly little about these people whose names have been preserved in their legal documents. From some fifty parchments in the state archives, it has been possible to trace the genealogy,[1] and to see that their ramifications spread into the Casentino and even down as far as Pistoia. In all probability they were a clan who, like the Firidolfi, successfully built up a feudal *dominium* in Chianti which was ultimately eroded through the extinction, perhaps on the battle-field, of their male successors.

At all events the Gottizi (as Davidsohn calls them) and the Firi-dolfi appear to have been the two most prominent families in Chianti during the eleventh century. It was a period when, as the power of the crown decreased, the fortunes of the landed nobles were rising. They were, in fact, the German *Grundherrschaft* who, as trusted followers of the Emperor, had been granted the right to build castles, which became their power centres. Often, in rural districts such as Chianti, the castle was built around an existing open village (known as a *villa*), and it usually entailed both rights and obligations as well: the right, for instance, to levy tolls on transit over the neighbouring roads and bridges (which had to be maintained) and to exploit the local mills. Moreover the tradition of 'albergaria' meant that when the lord and his retinue were in residence they were entitled to a free provision of supplies for themselves and their horses (which was often quite a burden on the inhabitants). But there was also the responsibility to have the walls properly guarded and to ensure that cattle and provisions were protected in time of war, as well as the obligation to raise troops when required by the Emperor.

All these matters were strictly regulated and created a complex relationship between the lord and the population, especially as a fief was not infrequently shared with other nobles. Each castle had its own story and its own juridical peculiarities, but in substance each one was a political unit and a 'business' concession. And so the actual stones and mortar were less important than the prerogatives that they conferred. A castle was a fortified village, not just the dwelling of a *signore*, and he might not actually own all the buildings within it. But he exercised his power over the locality through his representa-tive, the *gastald*, who resided in the *cassero*.

If, therefore, the Gottizi and the Firidolfi spent their lives exploit-ing their estates and building up private territorial fiefs, it would be wrong to dismiss them as local brigands engaged in wars and vendettas and stealing from passers-by. As part of the *feudalità* they followed the customs of the period which included the ideals of chivalry and religious belief. Yet these upper-class Italianised Germans whose lives spanned the eleventh century undoubtedly lived in a turbulent arms-bearing age, in which the townsmen and even the lesser nobility were already becoming impatient of depending on the caprice and wilfulness of their overbearing masters. The margrave Bonifacio of Canossa, appointed ruler of Tuscany in 1026 by the Emperor Conrad, was a grasping, iron-fisted lord who steadily increased his already enormous possessions in north and central Italy at the expense of both the clergy and the lesser nobility. Nor, for that matter, was the Church any better. Bishops and abbots, disregarding their vows, bribed their way to office, and had families for which they provided by robbing the ecclesiastic domains. 'The very sentiment of religion', comments Ferdinand Schevill, 'was threatened with complete disintegration by the spectacle of the great clerical titularies shamelessly wallowing in the black morass of a degrading materialism.'

Yet there were signs of an agricultural revival. Whereas the donation by the marchesa Willa to the Badia in 978 described anything between one-third and five-eighths of the land as uncultivated, the frequent contracts *a livello*, that is to say, on long leases, that we come across during the eleventh century show that the peasants were beginning to stir in their own right, and certainly the price of land was rising steadily.

What is more, a religious revival was getting under way. An early, John-the-Baptist figure called Romuald preached so furiously against the corruption of the Church throughout the Tuscan countryside that he is said to have won over the marchesa Willa herself and persuaded her to found the Badia as a retreat for holy men. Later, Giovanni Gualberti, the son of a small Chianti nobleman in the Pesa valley, gave up his feudal life to become a monk, and was soon haranguing people at the *mercato vecchio* in Florence against the shortcomings of his superiors. When, understandably, they clamped down on his activities, he escaped with some kindred souls to Vallombrosa, where he created a new order which rapidly spread and made itself felt throughout Italy.

But the reform of the Church was really consummated by a Tuscan monk named Hildebrand. After a long period in Rome studying the means whereby the Papacy could not only be freed from non-clerical influences (such as that of the Emperor) but also become more truly Christian, and as such the authoritative focal point for all believers, he produced the blueprint for a new electoral system. His idea, which has lasted more or less unchanged until now, was that the Pope should be elected by the college of cardinals. But when Hildebrand himself became Pope, and as Gregory VII enacted his whole reform programme into law, the stage was set for an out-and-out conflict with the Emperor.

For, well disposed though he was towards the Church, Henry IV could see that should the bishops and abbots no longer be nominated by himself, he would cease to be sovereign. So his response was immediate: he deposed the Pope. To which Gregory replied in kind by excommunicating the Emperor. The battle for supremacy between the two claimants to the power of ancient Rome was on. And what was of particular interest to our friends in Chianti was that it was brought dramatically to a climax by Matilda, the margrave of Tuscany.

One of the greatest 'women's lib' figures of medieval times, Matilda dominated the Tuscan scene for nearly half a century (from 1069 to 1115) in such feudal style that her vassals were expected to address her on their knees. But this Amazonian lady who rode out into the field in full armour was also profoundly religious. Which may explain why, in the struggle between her sovereign and the Pope, she stood squarely behind Gregory VII. Hence the high drama of the scene when in January 1077 the Emperor Henry IV, realising that he had met his match, came penitently to her ancestral castle of Canossa and waited three days barefoot outside in the snow before finally being admitted to make amends to the Pope.

This operatic humiliation was only an incident in the power struggle between Emperor and Papacy that was to continue throughout the Middle Ages, and reappear in the fierce rivalry between Guelphs and Ghibellines. Yet had they wet a finger and held it to the wind, these feudal figures might have realised that by the end of the eleventh century a whole new world was stirring.

Down on the coast, the Pisans had won a crucial victory by expelling the Saracen pirates from Sardinia in 1016, and were now trading actively along the whole Italian littoral. In Matilda's day, Pisa was already a thriving commercial community, and before long the other Tuscan towns, starting with Lucca, were beginning to experience an economic boom. When in 1095 Pope Urban II launched the first crusade, he not only set a cap on the religious revival, but also extended the trading horizons to the rich markets of the East. The next two centuries were a period of unparalleled economic growth, which set the urban communities on a collision course with the landed aristocracy that stood in their way. The port of Pisa, for example, increased in area from about 75 to 280 acres, and Florence expanded to three times its earlier size. Such prodigious growth needed the resources of the surrounding countryside to provide the community with food, raw materials and manpower.

While the old guard was divided against itself — the imperialist nobility against the allies of the reformers, feudal bishops and clergy against the supporters of the Papacy — the city burghers began to flex their muscles and demand not only free passage for their goods without the taxes levied along the highways, but also a say in the running of their own municipal affairs. From Lombard times there had been the old custom of 'gathering in front of the Church' to vent their grievances, and this was now adapted into associations known as 'popolo' and 'campagna', run by a committee of citizens called *boni homines;* gradually the idea of the free commune grew. It was a revolutionary challenge to the territorial governing class with its marches and counties, its royal palaces and castles with their attendant rights and jurisdiction. (In the *contado* of Florence, for instance, documentary evidence exists of no less than 130 castles. There must, in fact, have been a castle at just about every strategic point in the countryside.)

So whereas the nobles formed themselves into aristocratic clan societies known as *consorterie* or tower-societies to form a common front against fragmentation of their estates (and too often to pursue vendettas among themselves), the communes began to emerge in virtually every town and village in central and north Italy, with Tuscany, Umbria, Emilia and Lombardy as the pace-setters. (It is intriguing that these are now the 'red' centres of Italy.)

Not, let it be said, that these early communes were democratic in either the ancient or indeed the modern sense of the word. They were usually dominated by a small group of families, either merchants or lesser nobility, who carefully manipulated affairs in their own interests, the role of the rest of the population being limited to the simple act of acclamation. Yet the communes did represent a first experiment in self-government, and an attempt, as it were, to disentangle themselves from the feudal net.

The first surviving reference to a commune run by consuls in Siena appears in 1125, and in Florence in 1138 — though probably, like at Pisa and Lucca, they came into being some time earlier, perhaps around the time of the death of Matilda in 1115. The consuls, elected for a period of office, headed a council drawn from the merchant guilds that were likewise taking shape. And since trade meant prosperity, and many tradesmen were directly dependent for their business on the countryside, it is hardly surprising that almost the first concern of the young communes was to wrest control of their traditional *contado* from the hands of the great nobles. Which was the start of a new and bloody period for places like Chianti.

NOTE 1. GENEALOGICAL TREE OF THE NOBLES OF MONTE RINALDI AND GRIGNANO (KNOWN AS THE GOTTIZI FAMILY) FROM THE END OF THE TENTH CENTURY TO THE BEGINNING OF THE TWELFTH CENTURY

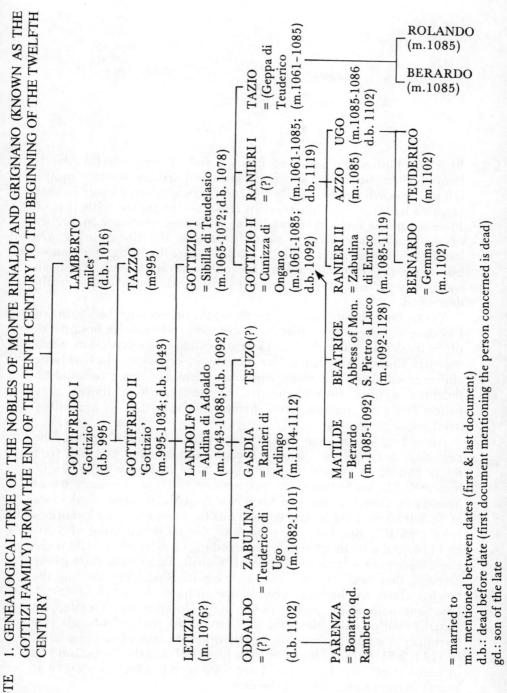

= married to
m.: mentioned between dates (first & last document)
d.b.: dead before date (first document mentioning the person concerned is dead)
gd.: son of the late

First the Florentines attacked Prato, a fief of the powerful Alberti family. Then their army of shopkeepers and artisans stormed up the hill to the north and besieged their ancient neighbour, Fiesole (whose *contado* had, for some unrecorded reason, been united with that of Florence in the ninth century). Three bites were necessary to dispose of this particular cherry — possibly because the citizen army was loath to leave its shops and its work-benches for long at a time — but when in 1125 they finally breached the massive old Etruscan walls, it was with such ferocity that the little town was virtually destroyed.

Next, their beady gaze turned south, where the bishopric of Florence ran deep into Chianti. As *contado* and diocesan boundaries often tended to coincide, the Florentines had no hesitation in claiming that Chianti was theirs. The Sienese, of course, could hardly be expected to share this view, and understandably began to build up defences against their aggressive neighbour whose limits, they believed, should remain safely behind the hills that so ominously overlooked Siena.

According to the Sienese historians Malavolti and Tommasi, the first clash between the two towns took place as early as 1082, after Siena had given provisions and other help to Henry IV when he besieged Florence (because, presumably on the instructions of Matilda, it closed its gates in his face). A battle, it seems, took place at S. Salvadore a Selva, known today as Lecceto, and the Florentines were repulsed. But they were back in the nieghbourhood of Siena in 1114, and a further battle is recorded on 18 November 1129 when the Florentines seized the castle of Vignale along with the Sienese garrison that was engaged in fortifying it. Since Vignale, on the heights above the highway near Fonterutoli, to the south of Castellina, was technically in the *contado* of Florence and Fiesole, but actually within the bishopric of Siena, this part of Chianti was obviously a ready-made bone of contention. In fact a few years later, in 1141, a Florentine incursion took them as far as the Porta Camollia of Siena itself, and four years later they scored a further victory at Monte Maggio to the west of the city.

But the Arno commune did not have things all its own way. In 1147, after capturing the Guidi family's stronghold of Monte Croce in the Val di Sieci, the Florentines struck next at the Castello of Monte Rinaldi, which by now had become the focal point of the Guidi possessions in central Chianti. On this occasion, however, they found themselves faced not only by the count's men but the Sienese army as well, and in the heat of a mid-August day (13 August 1147) they were well and truly trounced under the walls of the castle itself.

Admittedly these were only the opening rounds of a struggle that was to reach its climax over a hundred years later. For if the burgeoning young communes with which Chianti was surrounded — Pistoia and Arezzo, but above all Florence and Siena — had as prime objective the destruction of the feudal lords in their *contados*, they very soon found themselves in conflict with one another. Which led to some unexpected alliances: Sienna, for example, when threatened by Florence, had no hesitation in ganging up with the Guidi and the Alberti; while Florence, for its part, pragmatically gave help to the great feudal clans of the Sienese *contado*, such as the Cacciaconti and the Aldobrandeschi, and later made alliances with minor communes in the Sienese territory like Montepulciano and Montalcino.

While the cat was away, the mice could play, and the conflicts with which the Empire was involved elsewhere — notably in north Italy — gave Florence a free rein to its expansion. What is more, Emperors such as Lothair III and Conrad III showed less interest between 1125 and 1152 than their predecessors had done, or their successors would do. Even during the long years of Frederick Barbarossa's struggle on the plains of Lombardy, Tuscany was left largely to its own devices.

Thus in 1167 both Figline and Empoli were brought under the direct control of Florence, and nine years later (after the defeat of the Imperial forces at Legnano, when prospects for the nobility began to look far from rosy) the great feudal clans of the Guidi and the Alberti were drawn closer into the Florentine net. In 1180 Count Guido Guerra sought to mend his bridges with the commune by marrying Gualdrada, daughter of Bellincione Berti, a leading burgher. But the Alberti were rather less forthcoming, so in 1184 a citizen army stormed their great castle of Mangona, and took the head of the family prisoner.

Nor did the powerful Firidolfi-Ricasoli family escape the commune's aggressive attentions. According to the Brolio archives, the Firidolfi (figli di Ridolfo) owned some fifteen castles and churches in Chianti — including Radda, Castiglione, Vertine, Monte Luco, Lecchi, Panzano, Montegonzi, San Polo in Rosso and S. Giusto —

and had dominated eastern Chianti since the eighth century from their formidable castle on the summit of Monte Grossoli which over-looked both the Val d'Arno and the valley of Gaiole. So strategic was the site, indeed, that as ardent supporters of the Emperor, the Firidolfis had willingly offered Monte Grossoli as headquarters of the Imperial legate for eastern Tuscany. But by 1172 the fortunes of the Empire were at such a low ebb that the Florentines were emboldened to destroy the castle and seize the Imperial representa-tive. Moreover, once the Firidolfis had rebuilt the castle, they repea-ted the performance a decade later, and yet once again in 1198 after the death of Henry VI. But this time they installed their own representative in the place, a certain Ugolino Scolari. (Once the castle was firmly in the hands of the commune, the Firidolfis split up: one branch moved to Panzano; another, the Firidolfis of Rio Casole, near Montevarchi, becoming the forebears of the most ancient of existing Chianti families, the Ricasoli, who still own some of their ancestral estates and whose wine is the best known in Chianti Classico.)

The building of new encircling walls to include all its suburbs symbolised the triumphant commune's supremacy over the Arno basin and central Chianti, which incidentally was placed under the jurisdiction of San Piero Scheraggio. Symbolic, too, of the people's growing ascendancy over the nobility was the decision forbidding any towers in the city over a height of 50 ells (an ell being 45 inches). The tower of the Adimari, which had collapsed in one skirmish, had been more like 60 ells, and may not have been the highest any-way.

Equally successful were the Sienese efforts to subdue their own *contado*. In 1137 the Soarzi family surrendered a quarter of their lands at Montecastelli, and the following year Count Manenti ceded a sixth of his property around the castle of Radicofani. Eight years later the Abbot of San Salvatore in his turn gave up his rights on Radicofani, and shortly afterwards the Forteguerra family, headed by Count Paltonerius, surrendered San Giovanni d'Asso. When their castle on the Poggio d'Orcia was sacked and burned by the Sienese army, the Ardengheschi fmaily not only sold their property there, but were obliged to appear in person before the assembled populace of Siena and confirm their renunciation of Orcia with a solemn oath. And in 1168 Count Ildebrandino Cacciaguerra lost his lands near Asciano.

To set a seal on all this, the Imperial legate to Italy, Archbishop Christian of Mainz, was captured and imprisoned at Montefiascone. Since the extortionate ransom demanded was beyond the immediate resources of the Emperor (there was, after all, no foreign credit in those days!) the Sienese contributed heavily in return for a charter recognising their consuls and the city's rule over the annexed districts of the *contado*. Confirmed in 1186, this stated:

> In the name of the Holy and Invisible Trinity, we, Henry VI, by divine favour King of the Romans . . . make known to all the faithful of the Empire, present as well as future, that in view of the merits of our trusty subjects, the citizens of Siena, we grant them free election of their consuls . . . In addition we grant them full jurisdiction in the city of Siena, and outside the city in the comitatus, over the men belonging to the bishop of Siena or to any Sienese resident at the time this document is drawn up, saving the right of appeal in cases amounting to more than 20 lire . . . All nobles outside the city and all other men throughout the Sienese comitatus, except those noted above . . . we retain in our power. Also we concede to the Sienese the privilege of coining money in the city of Siena.

NOTES

1. As a matter of fact, whereas the *contadi* of Florence and Fiesole were unified in 854, the bishopric of Fiesole was never merged with that of Florence, though the Bishop of Fiesole was forced to reside in Florence after the destruction of his town (1123-5) until the eighteenth century. Chianti was claimed by the Florentines as part of the 'unified' *contado*.

SEVEN

And many a warrior-peopled citadel
Like rocks which fire lifts out of the flat deep
Arose in sacred Italy,
Frowning o'er the tempestuous sea
Of kings, and priests and slaves, in tower-crowned majesty.

Or so rhapsodised Shelley in his 'Ode to Liberty', although a less romantic commentator such as Maurice Hewlett compared the Tuscan communes to a pack of snarling dogs who, after snapping at each other furiously in the dust, make off for safety, yapping like mad. For if each fledgling commune was out to destroy the feudal lords that hemmed them in, and to hit out at each other in a free-for-all battle for commercial and territorial advantage, they all nevertheless had to keep a weather eye open on the super-powers, which in those days were the Emperor and the Pope. And indeed the ebb and flow of their struggle, like ever-moving clouds, was to throw its shadow over Chianti for more than a century and a half.

If it had started with the investiture dispute, the rivalry of the two heads of Christendom had been given, in this area at least, a new twist by the Countess Matilda. For only a few weeks after humiliating Henry IV at Canossa with Gregory VII, she made a will, re-confirmed in 1102, in which she left all her vast properties to the Church.

These possessions, some of them in Chianti, included not only allodial estates (which were hers to dispose of as she wished) but also the feudal lands that she held for the Empire. Henry V, the son of the man who had stood as a humble penitent at the gates of Canossa, would have no truck with such a thing, and immediately appropriated the whole inheritance for himself. Since the Pope had troubles of his own at the time, he took no immediate action. But later, at a favourable moment, the Papacy waded in with its claim, and the bickering over this particular issue continued for more than a century — at which point most of the land had been quietly taken over by the communes, anyway.

For the time being, however, Henry V, determined to keep Tuscany under his thumb, replaced the hereditary margraves by officials of his own choice. Their headquarters, moreover, were moved from Florence to San Miniato, still known as *del Tedesco*. But when Henry, the last of the Salian Emperors, died in 1125, and the Imperial crown itself was disputed among the German princes (Lothair III was little more than a puppet set up to demonstrate their right of free elections) the troubles behind the snow of the Alps left the Imperial nominees in Tuscany with only the local nobles to support them (who in any case were split by vendettas). As the Papacy was hardly in better shape, the resultant power vacuum gave the communes their chance. Whenever the Emperor himself appeared at the head of an army (to be crowned at Rome, or to deal with trouble in Sicily) the feudal order got a temporary shot in the arm, and the communes had to lie low for a while. But for several decades during the twelfth century they had the field to themselves, as we have seen. Not until the reign of Frederick I was the rising new movement checked.

Known to the Italians as Barbarossa because of his luxuriant russet-hued beard, this vigorous and authoritative new Emperor was outraged, when travelling to Rome for his coronation, to find that the cities of Lombardy and Tuscany had become to all intents and purposes self-governing under elected consuls. Having been brought up to the divine right of kings, nothing set his teeth more on edge than the idea of the middle classes usurping the royal authority. When Florence added insult to injury by refusing even to admit him into the city, it was more than he could stand.

With the help of a tough-minded chancellor, Rainald of Dassel, and the Imperial army, he began what sounds suspiciously like a reign of terror to put back the clock. True, Rainald was clever enough to camouflage his programme by basing it on the local nobility and towns, such as Siena, that were known to be friendly to the Empire. But while the communes were allowed to run their municipal affairs, a network of *podestàs* — mostly German — assisted by viscounts and local squires was nominated to bulwark the Imperial administration. In Tuscany, these *podestàs* resided at San Miniato, Montepulciano and Monte Grossoli. Both the Guidi and the Firidolfi-Ricasoli families backed them in Chianti, and were rewarded for their loyalty to the crown.[1]

Barbarossa's counter-measures were successful (even if in subduing the Lombard communes he found it necessary, in 1162, to raze Milan to the ground) until a new Pope appeared who was not prepared to let the Emperor become unchallenged master of the whole peninsula. Alexander III, a Tuscan from Siena, saw clearly that if only the various Lombard cities would stand firmly together with the Papacy behind them, they would eventually win through. Which is exactly what happened. Prompted by the Pope, a league of Lombard cities was finally formed, and in 1176, just when it seemed most invincible, Barbarossa's army was first struck by the plague, and then so decisively beaten at Legnano by the new league that the Emperor had to flee over the Alps disguised as a valet. The following year, exactly a century after Henry IV had been humbled at Canossa, a similar scene took place as Barbarossa knelt before the Pope in the atrium of St Mark's church at Venice.

For Florence and Siena, it was the signal for a new round of fighting. The issue was possession of Poggibonsi, and the boundaries through Chianti.

Already for some time the *via Francigena*, which passed through Siena and followed the valley of the Elsa until reaching the Arno at Fucecchio, where it turned sharply west to Lucca, had been the main commercial highway from north to south. Midway along, and controlling the whole valley, was the castle of Poggio Bonsi (Bonizio's hill) which once again was a Guidi fief. Needless to say this strategic stronghold, undoubtedly used for exacting tolls from travellers, had become a target for the Florentine burghers, who argued that it lay within their *contado* anyway. The Guidi, who had on previous occasions joined forces with Siena to prevent the Florentines from taking over their possessions, preferred that Poggibonsi should be in the hands of the Sienese. Their strategy had worked. A Florentine attack had been defeated, and in 1163 Pope Alexander III had used his influence as a good Sienese to stabilise the boundaries in Chianti along a line from the north of Poggibonsi running eastwards across the hills to the conjuncture of the Cerchiaio and the Pesa at Grignano, and then across to the Arbia at San Polo.

That was how things had stood since 1163. Now, intent on seizing Poggibonsi, the Arno commune played a similar sort of game. With the help of the Cacciaconti, the feudal lords of Asciano, and therefore at loggerheads with Siena, they gained a foothold in the east. When the Sienese struck out at the Cacciaconti stronghold, they were confronted with the Florentine army and decisively beaten. In the negotiations that followed, the Florentines not only acquired a part of Poggibonsi, but a large chunk of eastern Chianti as well, including the important castles of Brolio, Lecchi and Lucignano, as well as Tornano and Campi (which they nevertheless failed to wrest from the redoubtable Warnellottus).

Meanwhile, in the background to such local incidents, the superpower struggle continued. Barbarossa was in no mood to take his defeat lying down, and when in 1184 (his beard now white) he returned to Italy — ostensibly to marry his son Henry to the heiress

7. Ambrogio Lorenzetti's fresco of 'good government' in the Palazzo Pubblico at Siena (1338-1339) shows that vineyards were a prominent feature of Chianti in medieval times, though more in harmony with the landscape than the modern *vigneti*.

8. Modern industrialised vineyards below Volpaia.

9. A bill sent to Francesco di Marco Datini by Georgio di Monte da Uzzano for wine supplied to him. According to the late Professor F. Melis it can be dated 3 November 1398.

10. Trampling the grapes: a detail from Benozzo Gozzoli's fresco at the Camposanto of Pisa, painted in the latter part of the fifteenth century.

of the kingdom of Sicily, and thus straddle the peninsula — his attention focused on Tuscany. It was all very well for the northern cities to exercise the self-governing rights that had been granted to them at Venice. But no such charter had been given to their counterparts further south. To him it was the difference between legality and rebellion, and immediately he began to clamp down on their activities. Since the Tuscan communes, being so divided amongst themselves, were unable to present a common front as the Lombard cities had done, it was relatively easy for him to clip their wings.

When, four years later, the venerable Barbarossa set out on a crusade and was drowned in Turkey, the Imperial *podestà* was once again ruling with an iron hand from the pinnacle of San Miniato del Tedesco, and his deputy controlled Chianti from the heights of Monte Grossoli. And Henry VI, who had stayed behind as regent, proved to be every bit as formidable as his father — if anything, more so. The landed aristocracy had their old rights and possessions restored: by a decree dated 13 September 1187, for instance, Henry restituted to Ranieri di Berlinghiero of the Ricasoli family (who had commanded Barbarossa's troops in Tuscany against the papal forces) the concession to exact tolls from the castle of Ricasoli in the Val d'Arno. (The word 'pedagium', or pedaggio, was used, like on today's autostradas.) Likewise a diploma in 1197 confirmed the Guidi's tenure of Monte Rinaldi and Grignano. In contrast the communes, while allowed to continue their municipal self-government, had to be satisfied with jurisdiction of a *contado* of only five or six miles round the town. (Siena, of course, for the reasons that we have noted, did slightly better than this. And by a deed of 1193 the lords of Trebbio, who also held Castellina, allowed Florentine troops to be stationed in their stronghold, then known as Castellina de' Trebbiesi. So the situation was obviously not cut and dried.)

But on the whole, it was the mixture as before: the feudal fraternity were back in control under the Hohenstaufen banner. Which tempts one to reflect on the crucial role that an individual could play in medieval life — how quickly the whole situation could change with the arrival of a reforming Pope, or (as we shall see) with the death of a strong Emperor. For the peasant, or indeed the small-holder, in Chianti a great deal depended on the character of his lord; for the soldier, on the qualities of his leader. One discerns, as it were, both a permanent and impermanent level of being. On the one hand, you had the peasant family who had always been, and would continue to be, on the land, attached to its village or castle for generations; on the other the changing faces of its overlords as invasions and warring factions rose and faded away. If plague, fire, hailstorms and outside interference were the day-to-day problems that troubled the minds of medieval men, such dangers and threats to their well-being were bound to bring people together in a feeling of communal self-help. The notion of associations — be it of families, individuals or even animals — was deeply engrained in the shifting patterns of medieval life, and still has its echoes today. It was the catalyst for both communes and *consorterie*, and was later to become the secret strength of the Tuscan traders. What is more, in their reliance on the support of either Emperor or Pope, it was to be a motivating force for both Ghibellines and Guelphs.

NOTE

1. There is an intriguing document in the Brolio archives signed by Barbarossa on 23 January 1167. It seems that a member of the Mezzolombardi family, a certain Warnellottus, who owned the strategically placed castles of Tornano and Campi on each side of the River Massellone, had waylaid an Imperial messenger and seized the letters he was carrying from the Emperor to his nominee, the anti-Pope Pasquale. As punishment, Barbarossa stripped him of his lands and gave them to Ranieri de' Firidolfi. Yet, oddly enough, Warnellottus was still in possession of Tornano and Campi 36 years later when the same castles were contested by Florence and Siena.

EIGHT

At Easter in 1216, Mazzingo Tegrimi became a knight, which (although it largely depended on footing the cost of the appropriate ceremonies and games) was rather a grand thing to do. And so, to celebrate this increase in his *standing* he invited all the best people — 'tutta la buona gente' — of Florence to his country place at Campi, some six miles out of town. But hardly had they sat down to the banquet than an incident occurred. A clown snatched away the plate of food that had been handed to Uberto dell'Infangati, who happened to be paired with Buondelmonte de' Buondelmonti. (A single plate, it seems, had to suffice for two of the guests.) The chronicler reports:

> That angered Uberto greatly, and Messer Oddo Arrighi de' Fifanti, a man of valour, roughly reproved him on this account. In reply Messer Uberto told him he lied in his throat, at which Messer Oddo Arrighi tossed a plate full in his face. And the whole assembly was in an uproar. When the tables had been removed, Messer Buondelmonte struck at Messer Oddo Arrighi with a knife and wounded him severely.

Horseplay was normal among 'la buona gente', but this was too much. A vendetta might ensue. So to avoid trouble between the families, it was suggested that Buondelmonte should marry Oddo Arrighi's niece, who lived in a tower at the end of the Ponte Vecchio. Peace was re-established, a marriage contract drawn up, and the wedding was to take place the very next day.

But at this point, as our chronicler shows, the plot began to thicken:

> Thereupon Madonna Gualdrada, the wife of Messer Forese Donati, sent secretly for Messer Buondelmonte and when he came spoke to him as follows: Knight, you are forever disgraced by taking a wife out of fear of the Uberti and the Fifanti; leave her you have taken, and take this other (at which she brought forward her own daughter) and your honour as knight will be restored. As

soon as he had heard, he resolved to do as he was told without taking counsel with any of his kin. And when on the following day . . . the guests of both parties had assembled, Messer Buondelmonte passed through the gate of Santa Maria and went to pledge troth with the girl of the Donati family; and her of the Amidei he left waiting at the church door.

This insult enraged Messer Oddo Arrighi greatly and he held a meeting with all his friends and relatives in the church of Santa Maria sopra Porta. When all were assembled he complained in strong terms of the disgrace put upon him by Messer Buondelmonte. Some counselled that Buondelmonte be given a cudgelling, others that he be wounded in the face. At this spoke up Messer Mosca de' Lamberti; whoever beats or wounds him let him first see to it that his own grave has been dug; what this case requires is not half measures but clean work.[1] Thereupon they decided that the vendetta was to be carried out at the very place where the injury had been done, when the parties had gathered for the exchange of the marriage vows. And thus it came about that when on Easter morning, with his bride at his side, Messer Buondelmonte in a doublet of silk and mantle and with it a wreath about his brow came riding over the bridge, no sooner had he arrived at the statue of Mars than Messer Schiatta degli Uberti rushed upon him and, striking him on the crown with his mace, brought him to earth. At once Messer Oddo Arrighi was on top of him and opened his veins with a knife. And having killed him, they fled. The ambush had been in the houses of the Amidei.

Immediately there was a tremendous tumult. The body of the murdered man was placed on a bier and the bride took her seat on the bier, holding the head in her lap and weeping aloud. And in this manner the procession moved through all Florence.

While down the streets and from tower to tower, the vendetta began to rage. Not that there was anything very new about that; the pages of medieval Italian history are studded with such incidents. But what made this one different were the words with which the chronicler concluded his account: 'On this day,' he says, 'for the first time new names were heard: Guelph and Ghibelline.'

Sophisticated critics or paperback readers, everyone knows them. But before investigating their impact on Tuscany as a whole and Chianti in particular, we should glance back some nineteen years, to the autumn of 1197, when suddenly the whisper went round that Henry VI, the autocratic young Emperor, had died of fever at Messina at the age of 29, leaving an infant son of three as his heir.

For, as if by spontaneous combustion, the Tuscan communes

rose in revolt. What is more, they did something that had never happened before: they met at San Genesio, right beneath the lofty towers of San Miniato del Tedesco, and formed a league to withstand any further tyranny from the Empire. The Papacy itself, hitherto faced with territorial encirclement by the Hohenstaufen, readily gave its support to this Tuscan league, and even great feudal magnates such as the Guidi and the Alberti (less enthusiastically, to be sure, but realising that they must make the best of a bad job) appended their signatures, along with those of Florence, Siena, Lucca, Arezzo and the Bishop of Volterra, to the document of incorporation.

Once the deed was enacted, each commune immediately took advantage of the vacuum caused by the disputed succession to the Imperial crown to reconquer its *contado*. In practical terms, this meant that a series of minor civil wars swept through the countryside. Some feudal strongholds were meekly surrendered: the Guidi, for instance, withdrew to their possessions across the Apennines, and the Aldobrandeschi, who controlled so much territory south of the city, signed a treaty of friendship with Siena. Muratori quotes it:

> In the name of the Lord, Amen. We . . . swear on the Holy Gospels that henceforth and forever we shall be Sienese citizens, and shall preserve and protect every person of the city of Siena and its contrada and their goods . . . We promise to reside within the walls of Siena for three continuous months in time of peace as well as in time of war . . . and we swear we will give ear and attend to the commands of the Sienese consuls.

On top of which they promised to offer a candle each year in the cathedral to the patron saint of the city. One can imagine the satisfaction of the burghers as they watched these great magnates lining up every August, candles of submission in their hands.

Not all the territorial grandees did so well. The Alberti, recalcitrant as usual, got the worst end of the stick. To replace the loss of Prato earlier in the century, they had created an entirely new town which they intended should rival Florence as a commercial centre. Semifonte, as it was called, was built from scratch on a hill near Certaldo, and in the palmy days of Imperial control had already begun to siphon off a significant volume of business from Florence. Because of this, it became the object of quite special spite from the Arno traders. It took them five years of sieging to do the job, but when they finally breached the massive encircling walls, the town was destroyed so thoroughly that archaeologists have even had difficulty in establishing its site.

While the Florentine net stretched ever wider, the smaller communes were also at each other's throats. (The quarrelling between San Gimignano and Volterra, for example, was practically endemic.) But so far as the people of Chianti were concerned, the issue was again that of boundaries. For both Florence and Siena, indeed, the demarcation line across Chianti seemed to have taken on an almost mystical as well as a strategic significance.

When in the first flush of goodwill following the creation of the Tuscan league the Florentines again pressed their claim that it should follow the ancient diocesan boundary only a few miles from their rival's gates, the Sienese agreed to settle the matter by arbitration. The *podestà* of Poggibonsi was called in as an umpire, and (according to a treasured legend) stipulated that a horseman should set out at cock's crow from each respective city, and gallop down the highway: where they met would be the frontier. But the canny Florentines starved their bird so that it would crow earlier than usual, and thus were able to push the line forward from Grignano beyond Castellina to what is still known as the Croce Fiorentina. Whatever the truth of this tale may have been, the matter soon resorted to arms. In the subsequent skirmishing, mostly in the area of Tornano, Florence gained the upper hand and with the celebrated 'lodo' pronounced by the *podestà* of Poggibonsi in the church of San Miniato at Fonterutoli on 4 June 1203, most of Chianti passed definitively into her keeping. Yet even if this new boundary line between the two *contados* remained practically unaltered until the fall of the Sienese republic in 1555, it by no means ended the hostilities between them.

For, thwarted in the north, Siena turned in the opposite direction, and soon raised her banners over Montalcino. But when she attempted to do the same at the key town of Montepulciano, dominating communications as it did through the valley of the Chiana, the Florentines reacted sharply. A strong Siena, after all, was the last thing they wanted. The result was a succession of capricious wars, lasting through the greater part of the thirteenth century, and culminating in the major battles of Montaperti and Colle Val d'Elsa. Between the periodic assaults, sieges, and tip-and-run tactics with which their confrontation was marked, the Florentines periodically subverted such Sienese towns as Montalcino and Grosseto, while the Sienese carried out raids into Chianti.

In more rarified oxygen, meanwhile, the Empire was convulsed on the sudden death of Henry VI by the contest for the Imperial crown between the great German families of Hohenstaufen and Welf (or Guelph). The matter was only resolved by the murder of Henry VI's brother, Philip of Swabia, in 1208, and Pope Innocent III, who had no love for the Hohenstaufen, must have been happy to crown Otto the Guelph as Emperor the following year. But when

Otto, despite solemn vows to the contrary, followed the old policy of making himself master of all Italy by reconquering Sicily — and thereby straddling the Papacy — the Pope quickly changed his mind. Promptly excommunicating the Emperor, he decided to set up Henry VI's son, the 18-year-old Frederick (who, being his ward, had, he thought, been carefully indoctrinated) as anti-king. As part of this ploy, he instructed all Italian communes and principalities to repudiate Otto and acknowledge Frederick. In Florence, however, not everyone was inclined to obey the Papal order. Having only too vivid memories of how roughly they had been treated by his father and grandfather, many of them preferred to support Otto (who had recently done them some favours) rather than give their allegiance to the young Hohenstaufen.

Perceptibly, therefore, two parties formed. Those who supported Otto became the *parte del Guelfo*, whereas those who accepted the papal command took up the old Hohenstaufen battle-cry of 'Waiblingen' (after their castle in Swabia) which became italianised into *Ghibellino*. (Foreign names are often unpronounceable to Italians. When my good friends Philip and Frances Tyson-Woodcock took up residence at Panzano, they were surprised to find that the nearest the locals could get to their surname was Taxe-Boycock — though most of them settled for Filippo and Francesca.)

Anyway, Guelfo and Ghibellino it was. And what, looking backwards, may be mystifying is that at first the Guelphs were in opposition to the Pope, whereas the Ghibellines were simply following his instructions. Later (although the labelling is misleading) it was the other way round. As soon as Frederick II began to continue the policy of his ancestors, he and his supporters were denounced by the Papacy as enemies of the Church, while the Guelphs, who had always opposed the young king, found the Pope on their side.

Yet these groupings, which started in Florence and spread throughout Italy, were never absolutely organised as the party of the Emperor and the party of the Church. Originating from the factions that divided the ruling families, and later entangling the *popolo* as it grasped for political rights, they represented the efforts of each commune to enlarge its sphere of influence. As such they had a life of their own that was quite independent of Papal and Imperial leadership, and were, if you like, an attempt to use the conflict of the superpowers (in a way that we in the late twentieth century know only too well) for local and strategic advantage.

If on the whole the Ghibellines tended to be traditionalists with a stake in the land, the Guelphs attracted many of the minor nobility and the mercantile *popolani*. With 'civic liberty' as their slogan, they wanted to shake off the yoke of Empire, and looked to the Pope for support against the aristoctratic Ghibelline clans. Yet even so these lines of division were neither clear-cut nor permanent. It often happened that territorial rivalry between two neighbouring Guelph cities or even castles threw one of them into a temporary alliance with the nearby Ghibellines, or the other way round. Clashes between the parties within the city often led to a purge, and those who were expelled would join up with a rival town in the hope of eventually staging a come-back. In each centre, moreover, they formed a separate organisation within the state, much as the political parties still do in Italy today.

Soon, this polarising of interests resolved into a chequer-board pattern of alignments between the various communes. If Florence was Guelph, it followed that Siena must be Ghibelline: indeed as time wore on a steady balance grew up between Florence and her ally Lucca supporting the Guelph cause, while Siena, Arezzo and Pisa pinned their faith in the Emperor. These opposing leagues, moreover, were pledged to mutual support, with a precise *tallis* of forces to be supplied by each member. Significantly enough, after the two French Popes, Urban IV and Clement IV, had called on France for help· against the Hohenstaufen, Charles of Anjou, the brother of the King of France, became the nominal head of the Tuscan Guelphs, while on the other hand the Ghibelline communes, as clients of the Empire, relied chiefly on German troops.

All this had been gestating for some time, but the Buondelmonte murder brought it sharply to a head. The top clans in Florence aligned themselves with one side or the other. Since Schiatta degli Uberti, one of the grandest of them all (who had struck the fatal blow) had built up the Uberti family's influence thanks to Hohenstaufen support, it followed that the Buondelmonti threw their weight behind the cause of their rivals. And, like it or not, all the leading families began to emerge as either Ghibellines or Guelphs. Ranging from the trivial to the tragic, the hostility between the two factions spread into every aspect of day-to-day life. (Shakespearean sophistication apart, one has only to reflect on the elemental story of Romeo and Juliet.) A Guelph could be distinguished from a Ghibelline by the cut of his doublet, by the angle at which he wore the feather in his hat, by the shape of his battlements (square-topped, as opposed to the indented triangle of the Ghibellines) and even by the way he cut his bread.

Inevitably, too, the struggle spilt over into the *contado*. Whenever one side gained the upper hand in town, its opponents retreated to their castellos and carried on their vendettas, with the result that Chianti became the scene of bitter skirmishing between one strongpoint and another. 'It was impossible to plant vines or gather grapes or even to live in peace on a farm,' laments Malaspina, describing the effect on the countryside.

> Only close to the walls of the city, under military protection, was it possible to cultivate land . . . But elsewhere it was hopeless because of the highwaymen, thieves and robbers, who were attacking every day more openly, taking people prisoner in order to extort ransoms, and driving away their cattle to eat them or sell them. And when people would not pay, they would hang them up by their hands or feet, knock their teeth out and put toads in their mouths . . . everyone saw the devil everywhere . . . and the land was dying with no one to till it.

Understandably, a good many of the farming community fled for safety to the towns. And there, although still neither Guelph nor Ghibelline in spirit, they soon got drawn into the communal politics. Basically, as we have seen, this meant a hatred of any power that threatened the city's independence. If the Guelphs sought to achieve freedom from the Empire with the support of the Papacy, the Ghibellines leaned towards the Emperor in the hope that their loyalty would be rewarded with self-rule. The object was the same, even if the strategy differed. One way or the other, it meant involvement in the great power struggle between Emperor and Pope.

In which, as it happens, Chianti was to play a part.

NOTE

1. *Cosa fatta capo ha,* the famous phrase quoted by Dante that was to become proverbial.

NINE

Some (like the Pope who helped him get his crown) called him the Anti-Christ. Others thought he was 'stupor mundi', the wonder of the world. Perhaps it was his Mediterranean upbringing that made Frederick II, the blonde boy-king — without helmet, long curls blowing in the wind, smiling and waving his gauntleted hand — at once an imperious ruler and a poet, a philosopher and a bon viveur.

His court was the most cultured in Europe (the library fed continuously with new versions of Arabic texts by scholars such as Michael Scotus and Theodore of Antioch) and the glamour of his private harem was only matched by the splendour of the retinue with which he travelled. He is reputed, in fact, to have arrived at Ravenna in 1231 'with many animals unknown to Italy; elephants, dromedaries, camels, panthers, gerfalcons, lions, leopards, white falcons and bearded owls'. The monastery of S. Zeno at Verona had to find accommodation within its precincts for an elephant, five leopards and 24 camels, and when the elephant, which was kept at Cremona, died in 1249, the great debate was whether its bones would turn to ivory.

In many ways this greatest of medieval monarchs was also the first modern man of the Middle Ages. His zoological studies included the artificial incubation of poultry, and the hatching of ostrich eggs under the Apulian sun. He had barnacles brought from the north to prove that geese were not their produce, and he sealed the eyes of vultures to see whether they found their food by sight or by smell. Among the less tasteful of his experiments were those which led him to shut up a man in a wine cask to prove, as he affirmed, that the soul died with the body; and to disembowel two others to show the respective effects of sleep and exercise on digestion. Or when he had several children brought up in complete silence to answer the premise 'whether they would speak Hebrew, which was the first language, or Greek or Latin or Arabic, or at least the language of their parents'. A question, as it happens, that was never resolved, for the children all died.

As epitaph to this complex individual, who burst so many of the medieval limitations, Salimbene had this to say:

Of faith in God he had none; he was crafty, wily, avaricious, lustful, malicious, wrathful; and yet a gallant man at times, when he would show his kindness or courtesy; full of solace, jocund, delightful, fertile in devices. He knew how to read, write and sing, and to make songs and music. He was a comely man, and well formed, though of middle stature. Moreover, he knew how to speak with many and varied tongues, and, to be brief, if he had been rightly Catholic, and had loved God and His Church, he would have had few emperors his equals in the world.

God he may have loved, but certainly not the Church. He complained in a manifesto to the kings of Europe after he had been excommunicated by Pope Gregory IX:

The Roman Church is like a leech. She calls herself my mother and nurse, but she is a stepmother, and the root of all evils. Her legates go throughout all lands, binding, looting, punishing, not to sow the seed of the Word, but to subdue all men and wring from them their money.

The reason for his banning was that he had failed, as he had promised, to lead a crusade to the Holy Land. Whereupon he promptly set sail for Palestine and dumbfounded all critics by coming to terms with the Moslem ruler of Syria, and having himself crowned King of Jerusalem without fighting a single battle.

His battles, to be sure, were mostly with the Pope, and the quarrel between the two movers and shakers of society resounded in every Italian town. In 1248, encouraged by Frederick and his illegitimate son, Frederick of Antioch, who had been appointed *podestà* of Tuscany, the Ghibellines drove out the Guelphs and turned Florence into an Imperial headquarters. Frederick II himself never entered the Arno city after his court astrologer had predicted that he would die in Florence, though he was often enough in the countryside around it. Yet oddly enough the prophecy was fulfilled, for when he lay dying in an Apulian village he asked the name of the place and was told it was called Fiorentino. 'Ill did he understand the lying word of the demon, which bade him beware of dying in Fiorenza but not of dying in Fiorentino,' commented Villani sanctimoniously.

So great had been Frederick's power that his death, once again, left an unbridgeable vacuum. In the confusion that followed, the Florentines expelled the Ghibellines in their turn, who retreated through Chianti to the more amenable *ambiance* of Siena. Predictably, this sheltering of *fuorusciti* led to a fresh burst of hostilities between the two communes, in which, initially at least, Siena

— as so often in the past — came off worst and was obliged not only to withdraw its hospitality to the Florentine Ghibellines, but also to be bound in what was euphemistically termed 'an eternal league of love'.

Since the Guelphs had already been exiled, this spontaneous rising of the Florentine people against their Imperial overlords to the cry of 'Viva il Popolo' was, in fact, something of a revolution — if not proletarian, at least of the tradesmen and artisans: the commoners, shall we say, as opposed to the magnates. And yet, for all this, there are indications that the richer merchant class were in the game too — keeping a low profile, maybe, but nevertheless controlling the policy of the new government as they had done in the past. At any rate, *Il Primo Popolo,* as it became known, lost no time in showing its muscle. In a remarkable show of strength, the Florentines subdued Pistoia and forced free-port rights from Pisa — that is to say, the transit of goods without payment of customs dues. More significantly still, they calmly usurped Imperial privilege by minting the gold *fiorentino*, a beautiful coin with the lily on one side and St John the Baptist, the patron saint of the city, on the other. (Nothing, as it turned out, was to contribute more to their commercial success than this gold florin — worth 20 silver florins and 240 silver pennies — which soon became recognised, like the sterling pound in Victorian days and the Swiss franc now, as the yardstick for international monetary dealings.)

To symbolise their emancipation from the old feudal order, moreover, they reversed the colour scheme of the city's banner, which became (as it remains today) the red lily on a white background; while in 1255 they began building the impressive Palazzo del Popolo, or Bargello — as forbidding a fortress as any feudal castello — from which to rule all Tuscany in the name of democracy. And indeed for some years this is just what they did, dividing the territory into 72 *leghe*, or leagues, each in charge of a *podestà* (including the Lega del Chianti, which comprised the three most important towns in the region — Radda, Castellina and Gaiole — with a *podestà* at Radda).

The Primo Popolo was a brave period in Florence's history. But it was not to last. For whereas in 1255 the Pope, in an effort to dispossess the hated Hohenstaufen, offered the crown of Sicily to King Henry III of England (who promptly accepted it for his second son Edmund, and gratefully began filling the Papal coffers) it was actually Manfred, the illegitimate son of Frederick II who, on the death of Conrad IV, had himself crowned at Palermo in 1258, and by a series of successes against the Papal forces gave a fresh shot in the arm to the Imperial followers.

In the bewildering see-saw of Tuscan politics, it was now the turn of Siena and the Ghibellines to come up on the rebound. To which, naturally enough, Florence responded with arms.

TEN

The 'Libro di Montaperti' (so called because it was captured by the Sienese after the famous battle) was the official log-book of the Florentine commune. It recorded the day-to-day preparations for the campaign in 1260 against Siena. And as such it is one of the most absorbing of medieval documents.

Without Manfred's truimphs in the south it is unlikely that either the exiled Ghibellines or Siena itself would have challenged Florence's new-found supremacy. But when in 1259 they affirmed their allegiance to the young monarch, who responded by sending his cousin, Giordano of San Severino, as vicar-general of Tuscany with a contingent of German troops, it was clear to Florence's Primo Popolo that the challenge must be met.

In a sequence of officially minuted cameos, the scenario unfolds. First to be recorded is the *Capitani's* decision that Baldese di Bonaccorso of Antella should be put in charge of the parishes of San Leolino in Conio and Ligliano, while Uberto di Rovignoso remained in command at S. Giusto in Salcio and S. Polo in Rosso — all key points in Chianti strung along the boundary with Siena. A month later, on Thursday 1 April, Oddone Infrangipane of Altomena was appointed as chief bell-ringer of the army ('ad pulsandam campanam exercitus') and the following week instructions were sent to the *podestàs* of Poggibonsi, Colle and San Donato in Poggio to muster provisions for the army and check the defences of their communes. And on 14 April Biciccio, the tailor, was exempted from military duties for eight days to finish sewing the covers for the horses.

By 16 April the communal army (comprising the whole male population between the ages of 15 and 70, with the exception of the sick, the disabled, and certain groups needed for work at home) was in the field at Colle Val d'Elsa, where the contingent from Colognole (a castle above Greve) and Acone were left to guard Gagliano. On the 23rd the pay of the pigeon-keepers and the four grooms of the *caroccio* was fixed at 2 soldi each per day, and at Lucciano on the 28th (the day that the submission of nearby Casole was received) it was agreed that the *bifolchi* of the *caroccio* would be given 4 soldi a day for each pair of oxen.

The *caroccio* was the communal state-car that formed a sort of headquarters or rallying point for the army. Villani explains:

A platform on four wheels painted crimson all over, it carried two great crimson masts from which waved the great standard of the commune . . . and was drawn by a magnificent pair of oxen, covered with crimson hangings and reserved expressly for this service. . . and when an expedition was proclaimed the nobles and knights of the neighbourhood drew forth the car of state from the Opera, and brought it to the New Market. And the best and strongest and worthiest foot-soldiers were appointed as its special guard, and the whole people were wont to collect about it (*Cronica* Libro VI, Chapter 76).

On 3 May this colourful contrivance was at the villa di San Regolo on the Menzano estate, and six officials were ordered 'a far fare e condurre la macchina di guerra per espugnare il castello di Menzano'. The machine of war obviously did what was required of it, since 48 hours later it is recorded that the hostages from Menzano were handed over and shortly afterwards the little commune surrendered.

So far the expedition had been heading south towards Grosseto, where Giordano had the bulk of his army. But on 14 May it suddenly swerved left over to the Badia a Isola, and Ranieri Squarcialupi was ordered to guard the road, down which the supplies would come, from his tower. By 16 May the headquarters had reached the villa di S. Stefano, between Querciagrossa and Siena, on the extreme southern tip of what is now Chianti Classico. In doing so some damage must have occurred, because a payment was authorised to be made to Orlando Buonsignore 'pro incidenda' to the big house, and a further 40 soldi, also 'pro incidenda', to a tower by the villa.

The following day the Florentine army reached Poggio di Vico just outside Siena. But hopes of catching the city unprepared were dashed. The German guards made such a furious sortie that the Florentine vanguard was routed, and the *capitani* prudently ordered a retreat through Chianti, with little more than an Imperial banner to show for their trouble. Rewards were given to those who had taken prisoners (significantly referred to as 'teutonicus' in the record) and by 21 May the *caroccio* was back at San Donato, the commandant of which was instructed (with the threat of a personal fine of 200 lire and 1,000 lire from the vicario if he should fail to do so) to send 20 men the following day to reinforce the guard 'in Trebium et Castellinam', as Castellina in Chianti was then called.

Here the log breaks off for a while. But if this particular venture had proved a fiasco, it does not seem to have dampened the Florentine ardour, because almost immediately preparations for a new expedition were started. On 4 June the captains were nominated, and orders went out to all the parishes in the *contado* to supply grain for the army. From the assessments that are recorded we can get a glimpse of the agricultural resources of the various places in Chianti at that time.

Not surprisingly, the great Badia of Passignano heads the list with 36 *staria*. But it is revealing to note that Grignano and Vertine followed with 30 apiece, whereas Radda and S. Giusto were expected to provide 18 *staria* each; Monte Grossoli and Monte Luco 15; Lamole and Pietrafitta 12; Volpaia 8; Stinche and Collepetroso 6; Ricavo 3 and San Polo in Rosso only 2. All these little communities still exist, although some have grown and others diminished; but there is something rather agreeable in such a sense of continuity over so many centuries.

At any rate, once revictualled and reinforced by contingents from Prato, Lucca, Volterra, Arezzo, Colle, San Gimignano and even Bologna, the Florentine army was in the field again in August. Followed by an immense train of 20,000 pack animals, this determined cavalcade made its way towards Siena by the direct route through Chianti. On 25 August it camped overnight at San Donato in Poggio, on the 29th at Ricavo, on the 31st at Monsanese and on 2 September at Pieve Asciata, almost in sight of the towers of Siena, where it was joined by troops from Orvieto and Perugia. On the face of it, this great army with its multifarious banners should have made mincemeat of the Sienese who, after all, were outnumbered by at least three to one. But, as we know, it didn't.

Fortified by a copious meal of roast meat and 'perfectly matured wines', the Sienese Ghibellines under Farinata degli Uberti and Count Giordano's Germans hacked their way into the Florentine hosts at Montaperti with such fury that the waters of the Arbia, in Dante's words, ran red with blood. At a loss to explain the defeat, Florentine historians such as Villani attributed it to the treachery of Bocca degli Abbati, who is supposed to have cut off the hand of the Florentine standard-bearer at the height of the German attack. 'Seeing the banner on the ground and themselves betrayed at the very moment when they were powerfully assaulted by the Germans,' he declares, 'the knights and foot-soldiers were in brief order put to rout.' But more likely it was a left-flanking attack on the Florentine rear — an unexpected manoeuvre in those days of head-on encounters — that decided the issue.

At all events, it was now the turn of the Guelphs to flee, and as the raggle-taggle remains of the Florentine army made its way back through Chianti the exultant Sienese followed in its wake, destroying a number of castles that belonged to their foes — Monterinaldi, Meleto and Mugnana among them.[1] 'Before very long,' says the chronicler, 'there remained neither town nor castle, little or great . . . that was not subject to the Ghibellines.' Twelve days after the battle of Montaperti, Count Giordano and the Ghibelline exiles, headed by Guido Novello and Farinata degli Uberti, entered Florence and took over the government. To show their gratitude to Siena they signed a treaty renouncing most of the advanced positions that Florence had gained in Chianti over the past hundred years. On the whole, this was a fairly mild retribution: some of the more uncompromising Ghibellines, meeting at Empoli, were all for the wholesale destruction of the Arno commune. But in a famous scene, recorded by Dante in Canto X of the *Inferno*, Farinata, drawing his sword, swore that if they attempted to do so, he would lay down a thousand lives in defence of his native city. 'Ma fui io solo colà . . . (But when they made agreement, every one/ to wipe out Florence, and I stood to plead/ boldly for her — aye, there I was alone,' his shade told the poet.)

Be this as it may, Florence, although defeated, was spared and for a few heady years Siena — now taking the title of 'civitas virginis' — was paramount in an Imperial Tuscany. But the aristocratic factions continued: even as Guido Novello, the Ghibelline, became *podestà* of Florence, for instance, his cousin, Guido Guerra, was the acknowledged leader of the Florentine Guelphs. Moreover, just as Manfred scored this success in Tuscany, two French Popes (Urban IV and Clement IV) assumed the Papal mantle and called on King Louis IX (who was later to be canonised) for help against the hated Hohenstaufen. At the same time, the Papacy applied economic pressure.

This was not too difficult to do. For some time the lucrative job of collecting money for the crusades had been entrusted to the great trading companies of Siena and Florence, who through their agents in France, England and the Low Countries had built up a flourishing business in handling the Papal tithes. As the basis of their wealth, in fact, was largely built up on 'Peter's Pence', Urban IV quickly spotted that the way to their hearts was through their purses. Now that both Siena and Florence were officially Ghibelline, therefore, he put them under interdict. What is more, he excommunicated the merchants and ordered their debts to be withheld. And so, faced with bankruptcy, the great business houses had no alternative but to switch sides. Especially as behind the stick was a carrot.

In another wily move, the French Pope secured the assistance of his compatriot in France. Tempted by the offer of the Sicilian crown, together with money to finance a 'crusade' against Manfred, Louis IX agreed to send his brother Charles of Anjou on an expedition to Italy.

And to raise the money, Urban turned to the compliant Tuscan bankers who were able to advance funds at interest rates of anything between 20 and 60 per cent. Not surprisingly, most of the influential bankers and merchants, although outwardly Ghibelline, quickly became either openly or secretly Guelphs and put their money at the Pope's disposal. It was a matter of 'interesse', as they say in these parts.

Charles sailed from Marseilles to Rome, where he was invested with his new crown by the Pope, while the bulk of the French army marched down the east coast of the peninsula. Inexplicably, as it turned out, Manfred took no action to counter this threat before they joined up. (The Pisan fleet could surely have disposed of Charles's small flotilla, had it not been for a quarrel with Manfred's representative. And the main French forces took several months to get down south.) But whatever tactics Manfred had in mind to safeguard Sicily, the result was disaster. On 26 February 1266 his army was crushingly defeated at Beneventum, and he himself was hacked to pieces. (This was the year, incidentally, that Dante Alighieri was born in Florence under the sign of Gemini.)

If it was Montaperti in reverse, the Ghibellines nevertheless took some comfort in the news that the 15-year-old Conradin (the son of Conrad) was setting out from Germany, against the advice of his mother, to recapture the Sicilian throne. Siena and Pisa, for their part, refused to recognise Charles as overlord, and even little Poggibonsi resisted his attack for a full five months before finally surrendering.

In the meantime the fair-haired young prince, with his German knights, strengthened by Ghibelline partisans, passed through Chianti on his way south via Pisa and Siena. From the battlements of Viterbo, where he had taken sanctuary, the Pope spotted the Imperial army as it moved along in a luminous haze of dust. 'He will vanish like that golden dust,' he remarked to his attendant cardinals, 'They are leading him like a lamb to the slaughter.'

At Togliazzi, Charles turned this prophecy into fact, and a few days later Conradin's blonde head was sliced from his body in the market place of Naples. By his death, this last of the Hohenstaufen (that 'viper's brood', as so many Popes had called them) left the field open to Charles of Anjou and his Papal patron. But it was under the walls of Colle Val d'Elsa on 17 June 1269 that Florence and its new French allies finally had their revenge over the Sienese and the Ghibellines. Here on the borders of Chianti, Siena's fighting force was destroyed as effectively as that of Florence at Montaperti, and Tuscany was welded into a Guelph franchise obedient to the Pope and the French. The dominion of the German Emperors was replaced by that of the hawk-nosed Frenchman. Instead of the Hohenstaufen, there was the House of Anjou.

Yet just as the fortunes of the Holy See had depended on the outcome of Charles's expedition, so also had those of the Tuscan bankers who had financed it. And, manifestly, they had backed the right horse. As creditors to the new order, they were able to establish a dominant position in the trade and banking affairs of the peninsula. On the wave of an economic boom underpinned by the Pope, the King of France, and their new Angevin master, the great banking houses stretched their tentacles into most of the Western world. This alliance between Christianity and capitalism ('In the name of God and of profit' as Marco Datini always prefaced his letters) produced a bull market that lasted well into the fourteenth century, enabling Florence to lay the foundations of her greatness and to look forward from the Middle Ages to what would be known as the Renaissance.

NOTE

1. The damage to palaces and houses within Florence, and to castelli and farmhouses throughout the *contado* caused by the Ghibellines to the Guelph leaders who had fled from Florence and taken refuge at Lucca in 1260-6 were recorded in detail ('Estimo dei danni') by the Guelph party. This 'Estimo', which has survived (in the Florence state archives), is a very important source of topographical information, together with the *Libro di Montaperti.*

PART THREE: THE LATER MIDDLE AGES AND
THE RENAISSANCE

ONE

Violent it was. Yet thirteenth-century Tuscany saw the flowering of a distinctive culture — *La Vita Civile*.

By this term the Italians meant a new way of life that followed in the wake of their expanding trade and the great transfer of knowledge brought back from the Near East by the Crusaders. It was both pious and mercantile. Interwoven with the values of hard-headed commerce, like strands in a tapestry, were the notions of chivalry and the ideals of a free society. It was a culture that overlapped the boundaries of city and countryside, for the landed aristocracy had their town houses and the rich townsmen their castles. In fact Villani, writing in the early fourteenth century, took it for granted that most wealthy citizens spent the summer in the country, which for many meant Chianti.

Not all of them, of course, spent their days in the same elegant ease as the members of the Spendthrifts' Club — a group of young Sienese nobles who pooled their resources to lead a superbly luxurious existence, and were consigned into an appropriate circle of the *Inferno*. In this exclusive fraternity, grumbles Dante, 'Caccia d'Asciano lost woods and vineyards, and the ingenious/ Abbagliato, like a man of fashion/ displayed his wit', while Niccolò dei Salimbeni 'first found out/ how to make cloves a costly cult and passion/ in the garden where such seeds take root and sprout.'

It may have been to this same Niccolò, who specialised in the concoction of dishes prepared with exotic spices, that Folgòre da San Gimignano (who was also, it seems, a member of the club) dedicated a sonnet describing the pleasures to be enjoyed each month of the year. And very beguiling they sound too: in January to sit round a blazing fire or lie with silk sheets in bed; in February to hunt hind and wild boar; in March to fish eels and trout. (Lent, laughed Folgòre, was simply for 'crazy priests who pray and tell lies'.) While in April the green countryside was 'tutta fiorita di bell'erba fresca', June was the time for romance and July for feasting indoors, sheltered from the heat. But in August one should be back in the hills, far from enervating sea breezes, to 'feel as fit and bright as the stars' and ride from one castle to another enjoying the country delicacies of Tuscany.

And this was followed by the October vintage when one drank and danced through the night (after which it was necessary, in November, to go to the baths of Petriolo for a cure).

Dante would not have approved, and didn't. 'Was there ever a race so frivolous of heart as the Sienese?' he exclaimed with some petulance. And yet, against this, the establishments of many local tyrants were centres of learning and culture. Ezzelino da Romano, who was as cruel as they come, employed savants such as Guido Bonatti (one of the most distinguished medieval astrologers), Master Salio (a canon of Padua), and Riprandino of Verona. There was also at his court, a chronicler assures us, 'a long-bearded Saracen named Paul, who came from Baldach or the confines of the Far East, and by his origin and appearance and actions, deserved the name of a second Baalem'. Bonatti was also, for a time, in the employ of Guido da Montefeltro, and is said to have directed his master's military expeditions from his *campanile* with the precision of a fire alarm: the first bell ordered his soldiers to arms, the second to horse, and the third to battle.

Indeed, in a still relatively clockless world, bells ruled the everyday life of a medieval citizen. Bells pealed for masses and the monastic offices, and for any unusual or special occasion. They rang the daily timetable, much like a school bell, though rather more pervasively: thus the Angelus bell signalled the closing of the gates at sunset; the *campana bibitorum*, or toper's bell, called for 'time' in the taverns; the *coprifuoco* signalled the moment at which fires and lamps must be extinguished, and at dawn seven bells heralded the opening of the gates and the resumption of the daily routine.

Campaniles were a crucial part of town and village life. The 'Storm Bell' (no doubt easily distinguishable from the rest) was rung only for sudden danger, and the 'War Bell' announced the start of a military campaign. (In Florence, this was the celebrated *Martinella* or donkey-bell, which pealed continuously night and day, while messengers were sent out into the countryside to recall citizens to their duty; and as the time for the action approached, all the other bells in the city took up the refrain.) Not surprisingly, therefore, the job of bell-ringer was one of the most responsible in the commune. At Siena, for example, the records lay down that he was not to leave the immediate vicinity, and must sleep by his bell — though one doubts, with all this clanging, whether the poor wretch had much chance to shut his eyes.

Preserved in the Palazzo Piccolomini at the corner of the Campo, these state records — which run intact from 1248 onwards — show that from the early days of communal government the affairs of Siena were decided by meetings of counsellors, who when summoned by the bell would foregather in the Church of San Cristoforo. Certain officials, such as the heads of the trading guilds and the rector of the hospital della Scala, were counsellors by right. Otherwise they were elected from among citizens with at least ten years' residence, and in 1262 numbered three hundred persons (100 from each Terzo) along with two notaries who recorded the proceedings. Before every meeting the agenda was pinned up on the church door, and the delegates solemnly deliberated each question before it was put to the vote; if carried by a majority vote a committee was then nominated to put it into execution. (To eliminate cheating, counsellors were required to vote with their hands open and fingers outstretched.)

From weighty matters — whether for instance the constitution should be entrusted to the local consuls or to a professional *podestà* (who would supposedly be impartial) and whether to go to war (which required a two-thirds majority vote at three successive meetings) — to such mundane questions as the action to be taken against a recalcitrant castello, everything was debated. Sometimes the discussions have a medieval tinge. On 30 August 1255, for example, they centred around the punishment of the small feudal stronghold of Torniella in the Val di Merse that was suspected of treachery with Florence. While everyone agreed that the castle should be levelled and its inhabitants jailed, some counsellors urged that they should be blinded, have their hands and feet cut off, and then be sent to the gallows. That, they declared, was what the population wanted. Well, perhaps one eye and one hand? suggested a delegate. Or would it not be simpler just to hang them? thought another. Fortunately, when it was put to the vote, the moderates won, and the prisoners of Torniella were subjected to a relatively humane treatment.

Inevitably, though, finance and defence were the prime considerations. In these turbulent times — *tempi strani*, as they were called — the army ate up most of the communal funds, which had to provide for the pay of the German Imperial troops, the fortifications of the city, the cost of provisions and armaments, the maintenance of strategic castelli, to say nothing of repairing the ravages of war. And there is no doubt that the army was well looked after. It was equipped with special blacksmiths, farriers, engineers, doctors and even musicians. In 1259 extra rations of corn were imported for its use from Sicily and Puglia, and the feast provided before the battle of Montaperti shows the importance that was given to good victualling.

But there were also public works in the city itself, which was fast outgrowing the encircling walls of the original *Saena Vetus*. Siena must be almost the last remaining medieval city in Europe, and the earliest attempt at town planning — when the suburbs were first brought within a new defensive circle — dates back to 1218. It was then that a network of roads was thrust through the tangle of old buildings that had grown hugger-mugger in the constricted space. The main highways that connected the gates of the city had to be 10 to 12 *braccia* wide, that is, 20 to 24 feet, and were paved in stone by the commune, whereas the upkeep of the narrower lateral *vie* (which had to be 6 *braccia* or 12 feet in width) was the responsibility of the local householders. Naturally enough, a good deal of expropriation was involved, which, so far as one can gather, was paid cash on the nail.

The fountains, too, which served for washing and drinking as well as watering places for cattle, were carefully regulated by decree, each with its appointed function; and likewise the various market places. In those days the market was held on Saturdays in the Piazza del Mercato, which still stands below the Campo, where space was rented out by the *braccia* to bakers, hosiers, coopers, saddle merchants and other stall-owners who set up their tents and their booths much as they do at the Lizza on Wednesdays now. (A regulation of 1262 allowed wine-barrels to be sold only from mid-August to mid-October, against a tax of 100 soldi.) Prominent also was the *bisca pubblica*, or gambling den, which occupied three tents and, human nature being what it is, brought in a substantial revenue to the communal coffers, though the fishmongering concession produced even more. (It was rented out for 435 gold lire a year, as opposed to the street-cleaning concession — mainly carried out with pigs — that rated only 36 lire.) Concessions, in fact, formed an important part of the fiscal scene. Even the prisons were run by a contractor, who charged from 2 to 5 soldi a day for each unfortunate inmate, and a fixed tariff of 2 per cent on the amount involved for those who were imprisoned for debt. But the main source of revenue was the *gabella*, a direct tax on houses and property as a whole, as well as on wine, oil, flour and salt, all of which were purveyed at the public weighbridge. In addition there was the *lira*, a sort of yearly capital levy on each family resident in the city, calculated on its estimated worth; and in the countryside the *massaritie*, a fixed tax on each farm dwelling, and of course the notorious *dogana* or *dazio* which was levied on all goods that entered the city. (This archaic practice lingered on right up to the introduction of IVA (or VAT) a few years ago: so that if you did your housekeeping in the next-door commune, you would be charged an additional *dazio* if the *daziere* happened to spot it.) The *dazio* was collected at the gates of the commune, and needless to say was circumvented whenever possible. Like the village priest who slyly dressed a porker in clerical robes and stretched it out in a coffin. When stopped by the customs official he threw up his arms and said sadly, 'Praise be to God. The pig is dead.'

'Good job too,' replied the *daziere*, and waved him through.

What we would now call the media had a place in their lives also. News had to spread, and since (notarial documents apart) there was a marked aversion to quill and parchment, it was largely done by proclamation. While in Siena sixty red-hatted messengers carried ordinary messages at two soldi a time, three grandly arrayed individuals known as *banditori* rode round the city on horseback and to the sound of a trumpet announced the decisions of the government, as well as their sentences. (A daily sight in the Piazza was that of a forger being burnt at the stake, or a bugger suspended by his genitals.) And at various times of the day the town-crier went his rounds broadcasting more mundane matters — such things as births, marriages and deaths; bankruptcies and sales; lost property and coming events — a sort of ambulating gazetteer who conveyed all the titbits of news that now feature in the back pages of the local newspaper, and who at the same time acted as a sounder of public opinion. The local postman still fulfils the same useful function, bringing local gossip along with the mail, and transporting a chicken or two on the back of his Vespa.

TWO

Since space within the walls was restricted, the buildings spread upwards, and visually speaking architecture was at its most spectacular. The thin fortified towers of the *grandi*, says a chronicler, looked like a thicket of canes. There were over a hundred of them in Siena, mostly built around tiny courtyards, and a seventeenth-century print of the siege of 1555 shows at least two dozen of these thirteenth-century skyscrapers still erect above the city at that time. On a smaller scale one can still see how they looked at San Gimignano, just as Monteriggioni with its 'diadem of towers' in the encircling defence wall gives the feel of Chianti's fortified little towns. And Ambrogio Lorenzetti's fresco of good and bad government, painted between 1337 and 1343, shows how cheek to jowl were even the agreeable dwellings of the richer citizens.

Understandably the great families preferred their spacious castles in the country where they could indulge in a taste for wine, women and revelry (and of course hunting and banqueting) without getting tangled up with the plebs or confronted by former retainers now strutting around as *boni homines*. From time to time, it is true, a blood feud between the Tolomei and the Salimbeni, the Piccolomini and the Malavolti or the Saracini would erupt in the narrow streets, which would resound with accusations and knife-blades, but on the whole their appearances were limited to glittering cavalcades that moved occasionally through the pullulating stone caverns. After the collapse of the Empire, the grandees were excluded from political power by the merchants and *popolo*, although they still wielded considerable influence behind the scenes. From 1277 onwards, the highest political posts were in the hands of a new merchant class, grown prosperous on trade. A bloodless revolution brought a shift from banking to wool, so that shopkeepers and artisans, known derisively as the *popolo grasso* and the *popolo magro* — the fat cats and the lean ones — then filled the crowded stage.

Living and toiling higgledy-piggledy in close-packed huddles of houses and workshops, many of these people spent their whole existence within the walls of the city. For nearly all of them the first common experience was that of baptism, which took place at midday on Easter Saturday or on Whitsunday eve. Crowds of children were congregated at the cathedral where, after being touched on the breast by the bishop and anointed with holy oil, they were plunged three times into the font (with who knows what sobbing and yelling) before being given their names. By old established custom the eldest boy of the family had to be *Giovanni*, and the eldest girl *Maria*, the second boy *Martino*, though subsequent comers were named according to the whims of the parents, which sometimes ran to such excesses as Vigoroso, Bencivenne or Diotisalvi. (Out in the country, it must be admitted, priests were rather less convinced about the merits of water, and an *ordo officiorum* from the church authorities in 1213 stipulated that children should not be baptised in wine or olive oil.)

On the other hand, when it came to getting married, the Lombard convention of *morgincap* continued to be applied, until gradually the old Roman idea of the dowry returned to favour. *Morgincap*, which we encountered in the marriage settlement between Landolfo and Aldina, was nothing more than a literal translation of the German *Morgengabe*, the gift that the bridegroom made to his bride the morning after the wedding night to compensate for her lost virginity. Although Liutprand had decreed that the gift should not exceed a quarter of the husband's total possessions, this particular proportion seems to have been adopted as a general rule, and included even such items as clothing and arms. Basically it gave the woman security against the claims of her in-laws should she suddenly find herself widowed (which was only too likely), remembering that the head of the house retained the legal right to administer the family property. During the eleventh and twelfth centuries the Roman concept of the dowry came back into fashion (along with the wife's right to restrain her husband from dissipating her fortune) and in 1300 it was laid down that the husband's 'gift' should not exceed 50 *libbrae*, however great the dowry might be (or 25 *libbrae* if the dowry was less than 100 *libbrae*).

All this was usually drawn up in a legal deed by a *notaio*, or in the case of poorer people testified in front of witnesses, after which the father or guardian took the bride by her right hand and presented her to the husband-to-be as his 'legitimate bride', and he accepted her by placing a ring on her finger. Harking back to the old times when the bride was purchased, the groom also made a symbolic gift to the bride's father of a fur coat — usually a wolf-skin of carefully predetermined value. And then off they all went to the marriage banquet amid the same sort of ribald jokes that are still bandied about today.

Burials, likewise, were very much of a family affair, and it was not until the Black Death in 1348 that the last rites were entrusted to professional undertakers. Until that time relations, friends and priests gathered around the dying man's bed, and if he had not already made a will, became witnesses to his orally expressed legacies, which were legally binding. Then came the extreme unction and, if the death throes were protracted, some devout persons (in particular priests) had themselves lain in the ashes of the fire, hoping no doubt by this final act of expiation on earth to hasten their entry into paradise (Rub. eccl. Flor. Cod. Riccard.3138).

At any rate, the last breath had hardly been drawn than the corpse, after being quickly washed in hot water and scented with hyssop ('Purge me with hyssop and I shall be clean,' as the psalmist sang) was bundled off to its last resting place. The law required that it should be buried on the same day, and Boncompagni tells us that a person still living in the afternoon might already be in his grave by nightfall. In fact, in the haste, it was not unknown for people to be buried alive.

If this sounds a bit primitive it is probably because neither culture nor intellectual life had yet spread to the bulk of the population. And yet education was more widespread than might be expected. While all Italian youth did not sweat in the schools (as the German historian Wipo has suggested) most small boys seem to have been taught to read, write and do sums. Indeed quite often one of them would be brought by the *consiglio* to read an ordinance in public or a lesson in church — a tradition, incidentally, that is quite widespread today. And there were also teachers of grammar and rhetoric, whose disciplinary methods, judging from Benozzo Gozzoli's portraits of the life of Sant' Agostino at San Gimignano, strike a familiar note: on his first day at school the chubby little saint is already seen squirming under the master's switch. Yet the relationship between tutor and pupil was often cordial enough. One schoolboy who sent his teacher a basket of pears received in return a gracious little sonnet wishing him a hundred years of purgatorial indulgence for each juicy piece of fruit.

Certainly most school children began wage-earning as soon as they could. But others persevered with their studies, and if the records of the law school are anything to go by, examinations were every bit as hard as today. Siena's university, *Lo Studio*, was founded by scholars from Bologna in 1246, and a learned Portuguese, Pietro Hispano, taught philosophy and medicine there before becoming Pope John XXI. This does not mean to say that the undergraduates were always as intent on their studies as the relief on the tomb of a medieval professor in the university might suggest. They were only too liable to rush out into the Piazza and stage boxing matches or mock fights, watched anxiously by the city fathers lest this should develop into minor civil wars.

For within the narrow streets, life was carried on almost entirely in public. The shops and *botteghe* opened directly on to them, so that passers-by could chat with the cobbler, the saddler, the tailor and the barber as they plied their trade; while pack-mules jostled with the butcher cutting a sheep's throat amid housewives bargaining for a roll of *pancetta*. Outside one door wood would be stacked alongside leather being cured, and outside another carpets would be shaken in the faces of the itinerant vendors selling cooked meats and cheeses. What is more, the pedestrian had more to put up with than just elbows and oaths. A sharp eye had to be kept open for rubbish tipped out from the windows, and to avoid tumbling over people as they performed their natural functions (though by a 1250 decree this was forbidden in public by anyone over 14 years old).

Mercurial, noisy, voluble and proud, it was raw rather than romantic. But at least the green and red clothes must have been colourful against the solid stone and brick walls, and the bustle and hubbub of the street was probably more cheerful than the dank interiors of the houses.[1]

Every now and then in *dugento* buildings that have survived unchanged you come across deep-windowed chambers with a marvellously satisfying feel about them, especially when vaulted in rose-tinted brick. But for the most part these were the well-to-do dwellings of the aristocracy or the Church. The ordinary citizen does not seem to have had much more than a kitchen, a store, and a bedroom with an enormous curtained bed into which the whole family crowded, usually quite naked. (A fresco in the Church of San Niccolò di Bari shows three girls asleep in the same bed, while the saint hovers round. His miracle, it seems, was to have prevented anyone from jumping in with them.) Even in comparatively rich establishments the furniture rarely consisted of more than a footboard, a painted chest, and a three-legged table; and if the kitchen at least was well supplied with earthenware pans, the general level of comfort can hardly have been greater, as a Sienese archivist remarked, than a hillside farmhouse in Chianti, in which smoke filtered out of the window while water seeped in through the door.

There was, after all, still no glass in the windows, which were usually covered with pigskin rendered as transparent as possible with olive oil; nor were there any chimneys. People just lit a blaze in any convenient corner, and since so many of the houses were built of wood they easily burnt down. Fire was such a constant hazard, in fact, that the communal authorities themselves underwrote the risk and compensated householders when a conflagration occurred.

It is rather surprising, too, to find that neither music nor flowers enlivened the general drabness. (Though even today plastic plants feature more prominently in *contadini* houses than the genuine article, and, unlike elsewhere in Italy, it is rare to hear a Tuscan singing at work.) The most that our medieval friends ran to was a fig tree in front of the house, and even this caused trouble if it happened to spread over a neighbour's walls. Dante's great-grandfather, Caccia-guida, for one, was forced by the rector of San Martino in Florence to cut down a plant that was too near the church.

The thirteenth-century home must have been a dispiriting place in which to spend one's whole life, as so many of the womenfolk were obliged to do, only occasionally putting on a long-sleeved *gamurra* with a train of Sienese wool to venture out to church — an act of piety which probably came as a welcome break in the monotonous routine of cleaning and cooking.

On such occasions they adorned their faces with cosmetics made of white lead, alum, plaster of Paris or cotton waste, though the jewellery they could wear and even the number of pearl buttons they could have on their dresses was regulated by decree. But rings were worn on each finger, and if horsehair wigs were popular among the bald, some women also emphasised their charms with tresses and pigtails that had been snipped off corpses. Nor were they alone in making themselves up. Boncompagni tells us that young men used cosmetics as much as women, and were 'constantly combing their hair in front of the mirror'. In 1250 the authorities ordered that youths should not let their locks grow below shoulder length, and since this was not just a pious but also a permissive age, it is hardly surprising to find constant references to illegitimate children, some of whom quite happily took the name of 'Bastardinus'. In one of our Passignano documents, dated March 1110, a certain Umbertus made over some land in Chianti to his 'concubine Hermingarda', and the constantly repeated laws forbidding priests to marry show that Boccaccio's tales of monkish indiscretions must have been founded on fact.

But there were other diversions too. Chess, we are told, was the favourite pastime of a Florentine bishop as early as the eleventh century, and even then it aroused the gambling instincts of the medieval Tuscans, who were only too ready, says Boncompagni, 'a rendere omaggio a Bacco e Scacco'. Throwing the dice was also a popular sport, especially among garrison troops who had time on their hands in some hilltop fortress, though real gamblers preferred to congregate around the *tavola reale* — a mixture of baccarat and deck quoits in which the object was to throw on to a predetermined square.

11. The layout of Uzzano in the Val di Greve shows how this sixteenth century villa incorporated the previous castle structure, with outbuildings clinging against the defence walls.

12. No longer daunting to passers-by, the tower of the old Lombard castle of Grignano now symbolises the peace and well-being of modern Chianti.

13. Leonardo da Vinci's drawing of the Capella of the Madonna delle Neve, done in August 1473 and now in the Uffizi. The original engraving seems to have been executed in negative form, but, by holding it to a mirror the scene appears much as it is today, with Vignamaggio and the Val di Greve in the background.

In the countryside, of course, the daily routine was enlivened by riding and hunting, and also from time to time by travelling bands of minstrels who moved from castle to castle. For the most part they played the harp, the viola and the lyre (as Boncompagni tells us, the term *sinfonia* already meant instrumental music), and some of these *trovatori di canti* were renowned for tear-jerking songs — often improvised around people in the audience who would duly shower largesse if their vanity was tickled. As likely as not there would be entertainers too, whose acts included acrobatic somersaults and dancing on a cord, or ventriloquists whose imitations of birds or donkeys braying could usually raise a laugh. And along with them would be dancing girls to provide medieval go-go. Altogether it cannot have been so dissimilar from a modern cabaret, though if the evening turned out to be a flop they risked more than a few groans or a ripe tomato. Boncompagni tells the story of two clowns calling themselves 'Malanotte' and 'Mal di Corpo', whose performance fell so flat that Count Guido Guerra (at that moment the owner of Grignano) sent the one up on to the roof to spend an 'uncomfortable night' in the snow, and the other to suffer more 'bodily pain' than he had bargained for by being roasted between two fires.

On a more humdrum level, life in Chianti continued to centre around agriculture which, despite all the feuding between Florence and Siena, continued to pick up as the boom in the urban centres gained momentum, if only because mouths have to be fed and the townsmen had more money to spend. Increasingly the trend was for long-lease contracts (usually 29 years, with the rent payable either in cash or with products from the soil) to be replaced by *mezzadria* agreements. Boiled down to its essentials, this meant that the land-owner provided the land and the working capital, and the farmer the labour; the profit being divided between them in predetermined shares. In the early days, when much of the land was still uncultivated, the landowner sometimes received as little as a third of the produce: in fact a Passignano document of 1076 refers to such a share-out as normal practice. But in 1092 the contracts show that in the richer low-lying lands the proprietor was already getting a half share (though in the sparser hill-farms two-thirds still went to the farmer) and by the thirteenth century a fifty-fifty agreement was the general rule. What is more, it was not just landless *contadini* who contracted to do the working side of such agreements. Even great religious foundations like Passignano were not above using their available manpower to cultivate other people's land on a *mezzadria* basis. As early as 1132 the Abbey made an arrangement with a wealthy shoemaker to farm his land and give him half the wine and oil crop, as against only a third of the produce from some other high-lying fields that had to be reclaimed.

Farmland, moreover, could also be used as security for loans. In 1203 Abbot Alberico of Candeli (near Bagno a Ripoli) made a loan against which he took some land as a lien. This he had cultivated, pocketing half of the revenue and placing the remainder in the repayment account. But while practices certainly varied from district to district, and even from village to village, they tend to confirm that agriculture was flourishing and that labour was more than abundant. The warm, dry atmosphere of the Chianti hills gave a specially tasty flavour to fruit, such as figs, pears and sweet green apples, and also to nuts, particularly almonds and chestnuts; but above all to olives and grapes. These scant resources supported an extraordinary number of people – in fact by the end of the thirteenth century the rural population had so saturated the countryside that many were being forced to emigrate to the cities. And yet, surprisingly, there was still no great emphasis on the making of wine. Since agricultural sales figures show that at the end of the century the production in the area of Impruneta and Greve was 65 per cent wheat against 18½ per cent oil and only 16½ per cent wine, it is clear that food was considered more important than the wine – which although certainly drunk with relish was still called 'Rutilante' rather than by the name that later was to become so renowned. All the same, a shift of emphasis was already on the way. Fifty years later, during the serious economic recession that was aggravated by the Black Death, wine already accounted for 22 per cent of the production, whereas wheat had fallen to 54 per cent.

While heavy ox-drawn carts conveyed the cereals to market, wine and oil were transported by mules in long narrow containers. The great regional centre, of course, was the *Mercato Vecchio* in Florence, but there were local ones as well, and as early as 1073 one comes across references to the market at Barbischio near Gaiole; while place names such as Mercatale clearly indicate their origins. For rural dwellers market day was the big event of the week and seems to have been well organised; from 1192 onwards regular price lists were issued, which was important when one considers that prior to the thirteenth century there were no shops of any sort in Chianti, or for that matter in the whole of the Florentine *contrada* (though we do have record of a pork-butcher at Passignano in 1188). On the other hand, plenty of ambulating salesmen peddled their wares from place to place, as they still do even now, and until quite recently this was the only regular way of shopping for housewives with no means of transport. Most of them were quite young, for it was a dangerous job; at any moment they ran the risk of being waylaid on the road and having their whole stock in trade forcibly removed. Not surprisingly, therefore, they tended to journey round in groups and if possible to trail in the wake of some well-guarded personage — a trick that was known in Tuscany as travelling 'in the shadow of a signore'. In fact one smart sixteen-year-old managed to make his way from Chianti to Rome behind the bishops of Florence, Lucca and Siena in quick succession.

In such rural surroundings one would hardly have expected to find much in the way of industry. Yet the records show that from the thirteenth century onwards there were a number of fulling mills along the rivers of Chianti. Indeed, until the textile industry got under way in Florence a century or so later, the fulling of cloth was more widespread in the country than in the city. Moreover, pottery was already being made in the furnaces around Impruneta and Ferrone. All the same, such marginal activities were few, and one is left in no doubt that the role of this area was the production of food.

NOTE

1. Young men and artisans tended to dress in a doublet and hose, and working men often wore a *camicia* split at the sides and belted at the waist. They also had breeches, called *panni di gamba*, and long soft leather jack-boots. But people of standing appeared in a *gonella*, a sort of gown — cut short for the young and full length for older men — and also a cloak that was fastened at the neck and reached down to the feet. Women, for their part, wore scanty underclothes but fine gowns of velvet, brocade or damask, and on top a long-sleeved gown known as a *gamurra* that came down to the ground. On top they would put a mantella or cloak, and as headdress a hood.

THREE

Tuscan cooking is not just the application of raw material to naked flame so fast that it scorches (as an American once unkindly remarked). Nor is their food quite as dull as the monotonous fare in local trattorias might suggest. All the same, many Tuscans would agree that they are conservative feeders who prefer fried-in-olive-oil cooking to cordon bleu cookery. 'How we suffered,' sighed one of my neighbours, describing a meal in a celebrated French restaurant. 'Everything was so messed about with sauces, you couldn't see what you were eating.' When it comes to the table, the Tuscans prefer plain straightforward food.

This being so, it is rather a surprise to find the first medieval gourmets in Siena. For even if Dante sent the local spendthrifts packing off to Hell because of their extravagance (just as he consigned Pope Martin IV to purgatory for being overfond of Bolsena eels washed down with *vernaccia*) at least Niccolò dei Salimbeni's chef left posterity with the earliest surviving cookery book from the Middle Ages.

Until then, culinary secrets had been handed down by word of mouth, and may not have been rich in curiosities, anyway. The Lombards had been content with freshly slaughtered and roasted cattle along with their mead, and if the Franks were a shade more discriminate, with some knowledge of the old Roman cuisine, they were still no great adepts with the pan and the pestle. True, Gregory of Tours is said to have been particularly fond of 'a hot baking-pan full of the food made from beaten eggs quickly mixed with chopped dates and round olives' which suggests something like an omelette, but Charlemagne, his biographer tells us, 'enjoyed the roast meat which his hunters used to bring in on spits more than any other food'.

So when Niccolò dei Salimbeni upset Dante's frugal spirit by having pheasants and chickens roasted over a fire made of cloves, he was breaking fresh ground, though whether, as a commentator suggests, he 'had gold florins cooked in sauce, which he would suck and throw away' is another matter. Francesco Buti, writing a century later, simply states:

This Niccolò de' Salimbeni was one of the Spendthrift Brigade, and because they all tried to discover sumptuous and gluttonous dishes, it is said that blancmanges and Ubaldine fritters were invented then, and other similar things, about which their cook wrote a book.

On the face of it, *Crispetti Ubaldini* (a sort of pancake made of flour and eggs, with saffron and honey) sounds neither sumptuous nor gluttonous. But at least it has a connection with Chianti, since Landolfo of Monte Rinaldi, it will be recalled, had married Aldina degli Ubaldini a few generations previously. Yet most of the recipes given in this thirteenth-century cookery book can be traced to Arab sources, and may have been brought back to Siena by the Crusaders.

Limonia, for example, was roast chicken stuffed with dates and ginger, along with egg whites, crushed pine kernels and the cloves to which Dante referred. It was served with a sauce made of pounded pine kernels, ginger, white wine and verjuice (the juice of sour grapes) together with lemon juice, sugar and egg yolks, with a dash of cinnamon and mace. *Brodo Sarta Cerrito* also featured roast chicken, though in this case simmered in a casserole with its liver, breadcrumbs, grapes prunes, almonds and dates, white wine and verjuice. And then there was an intriguing concoction of steak and onions fried in olive oil with cream cheese, cinnamon, ginger and a pinch of saffron, to which scrambled eggs were added when the mixture was cooked.

Yet these elaborate dishes were probably not exceptional: well-to-do people were addicted to rich sauces, and a fourteenth-century manuscript in the Riccardiana at Florence explains how to make *sanguine* sauce — a mixture of shredded meat, raisins, cinnamon, sandal, sumach and wine. Other favourites were *peverata*, or pepper sauce, made of meat, fish, peppers, cinnamon, ginger, and given a brilliant yellow colour by the addition of saffron; and a white one called *camellina* featuring sugar, cinnamon, cloves, bread and vinegar.

Sweet-sour effects were obviously popular, and although Fiumi's study, 'On the alimentary conditions in Prato in the Communal Age', showed that the most favoured dishes consisted of mutton, pork, chicken and game, along with fish from the Bisenzio river, there seems to have been no hesitation in mixing them all up together. Moreover, the richer the dish looked, the better. At some banquets the sauces contained precious stones, pearls and gold pieces (which may explain the remarks about Niccolò), and Iris Origo, quoting a codex from the University of Bologna, reminds us that the *plat de résistance* was sometimes a peacock, stuffed with pounded pork, capon and nutmeg, all beaten up in the white of an egg. After the bird had been cooked, its skin and feathers were put on again, and a skewer held it up 'so that he seems alive'. To add to the illusion, some cotton wool was put in its mouth and lighted 'so that he casts fire out of his mouth'. And for even greater magnificence, says our source, 'you may adorn him with leaves of beaten gold'. Yet, alas, I daresay the eye appeal was better than the taste, like the *torta* that followed, in which live song-birds filled a pie with little windows that was then suspended on a tree made of pastry.

The quantities of food that appeared on such occasions were enormous. The wedding celebrations in 1368 of the Duke of Clarence (second son of Edward III) and Yolanda, the daughter of Giangaleazzo Visconti, ran to eighteen courses, each accompanied by a sumptuous gift. And the Datini papers show that the shopping list for the Merchant of Prato's wedding breakfast included 56 chickens, 60 large game birds, three sheep, about half a bullock, two pig's heads weighing 53½ lbs, 250 eggs and 406 loaves of bread.

In contrast, the diet of the majority of the population in Chianti was based chiefly on bread, which even in those days was rough and unsalted. ('Thou shalt by sharp experience be aware / how salt the bread of strangers is,' lamented Dante in exile (*Paradiso*, XVII, 58-9), though foreigners in these parts, breaking their teeth on the hard, tasteless stuff, are inclined to reverse the charge.) But large quantities of chestnuts were also eaten, both roasted or boiled or ground into a flour from which *Castagnaccio* was made with raisins and nuts. Moreover every *contadino* had his kitchen garden full of broad white Tuscan beans, chick-peas, spinach and onions, which together with rosemary, sage, thyme and of course garlic, flavoured almost every dish. Meat only appeared on the table on special occasions, and was substituted by cuts off the smoked hams that hung in the store-room, along with the fat Tuscan sausages which were grilled on the fire or boiled with lentils. Fish, on the whole, was not particularly popular, apart from the trout and eels that could be caught in the river, though occasionally salted tunny and herrings would be sent up in barrels from Pisa. And then there were *pecorino* and *ricotta*, the hard and soft sheep's milk cheeses made in the neighbourhood, as well as mushrooms in the autumn and the odd pheasant or partridge that could be trapped as a welcome change from the farmyard chicken and ducks.[1]

This spare but healthy diet made up the two meals of the day. *Desinare*, eaten around nine or ten in the morning, was not so much breakfast as luncheon, and *cena*, at sundown, was a sort of pre-bedtime supper. Since work began at dawn or even earlier, half of it was done on an empty stomach — a habit that still persists today. Alvaro, my factotum, who always rises with the lark, has already completed half his daily rounds before eating his first meal, which he now takes at midday; but only because the work break is between twelve and one. In the past, when most farmers operated on a *mezzadria* basis and could fix their own timetable, they preferred to down tools for a snack around the time usually associated with breakfast, though they had already been in the fields for three or four hours. Many government officials still do their stint from eight to two on nothing more than a cup of black coffee, but since neither tea nor coffee existed in the middle ages their predecessors made do with a glass of wine and a hunk of bread — by no means an indication of poverty, since it was what the doctors prescribed as the healthiest thing to do. In fact although undoubtedly there was poverty in other parts of Italy (particularly in the south) one does not get the impression of any actual hunger in Chianti during the Middle Ages, except when war, pestilence or bad weather caused the crops to be destroyed.

Cecco Angiolieri, the earthy Sienese poet who was the thirteenth-century's equivalent of an angry young man, wrote that when he woke up feeling that his body 'was full of salt' (in other words, with a hangover) his first thought was for a draught of wine 'che tutto il dì mi fa stare in bonaccia'. In celebrating the tonic effects of Chianti vintages, he was only anticipating Galileo's remark that 'wine is composed of wit and light', or even the words that Dante put into the mouth of Statius in canto XXV of the *Purgatorio*: 'Think how the sun's warmth mingles with the vine / with its moist sap, and turns to wine in it.'

Wine was also distilled into a sort of *grappa* or aqua vitae known as *l'aqua ardens*, apparently much prized for its medicinal qualities: in fact Taddeo di Alderotto (who founded the Bologna school of medicine and gained a niche in Dante's *Paradiso*) wrote a therapeutic treatise on *de virtute aquae vitae quae etiam dicitur aqua ardens*'. There are references to *vinadri*, or wine retailers, in Florence as early as 1079. But once the guild system got under way they were grouped, from 1282 onwards, into l'Arte dei *Vinattieri* — whose crest, a red octagonal drinking bowl on a white background, can still be seen engraved on a stone outside their headquarters in the via Lambertesca.

From the statutes of this guild, which cover 86 pages of a big leather-bound book and are as solemnly tabulated as the articles of association of an Edwardian golf club, one gets an insight into how the wine trade was organised.

A good half of them dealt with the admission of members and the responsibilities and privileges of the elected officers. But the standards that had to be maintained are also exhaustively laid down. Each retailer had to be provided with correct measures, and to maintain the approved standard of cleanlinesss in his shop, which could not be less than a hundred yards away from any church; he was forbidden to sell cooked foods or to allow children under fifteen years old in the premises, and he was liable to severe penalties if he sheltered thieves, prostitutes or 'young ruffians'.

By this time wine was already being sold in the familiar chubby straw-covered *fiaschi,* manufactured by *becchieri* in places like Empoli, Montelupo and Certaldo. (The production of glass was so far advanced in Tuscany that a Florentine called Salvino d'Armato, who died in 1315, is credited with having been the inventor of spectacles.) But even so it was still not called Chianti. Although the area with which we are concerned was probably known as *Clante* by both the Etruscans and the Romans, and certainly appears in the *Libro di Montaperti* under its present name, the red wine of Chianti was termed *vermiglio* and the white *vernaccia* until the latter part of the fourteenth century. Only in the Datini papers do we first find it referred to as Chianti.

But it was drunk in vast quantities. In fact by 1298 the import tax on wine was second only to that on salt. According to Villani an average of 55,000 *cogni* entered the gates of Florence each year, and since a *cogno* was 100 gallons this made an annual total of 5.5 million gallons. No wonder that the city fathers, to finance the building of the Palazzo della Signoria, thought of imposing a further tax on retail sales. In January 1298 it was ordered that the money thus raised 'would be spent to buy the land and houses and buildings on the spot where the Palazzo della Signoria will rise'. Thanks therefore to the tax on the wine of Chianti, the authorities were able to complete Arnolfo di Cambio's great project (which incidentally incorporated in its structure a number of aristocratic *torres* — one of them, called *La Vacca,* that belonged to the Foraboschi family became the tower of the Palazzo itself).

Even before it became known as Chianti, the wine from this region already had the robust flavour that has always been so characteristic. To a large extent this is achieved by the practice known as *governo,* which is still a unique feature of Chianti vintages. Under this process, carefully selected grapes are put aside and left to dry: they are then added to the wine to create a second fermentation. The point about this is to purify the liquid of any organic material that might spoil its fluidity and sparkle. Above all, it does away with the sediment.

A goldsmith called Ruberto Bernardi seems to have first laid down the principles of *governo.* In a paper published in 1364 he recommended that 'black' grapes (including the dark Trebbiano which no longer exists) should be dried in the cellar and then mixed with the wine — in contrast to which his friend Giovanni di Duranti believed that the same process should be achieved with white grapes left out in the sun and then crushed and boiled in a pan. Among his other tips was that wine barrels should never be 'contaminated' by being washed out with water, and that some of the previous year's wine should be left in them to act 'as a guard'.

Everyone had his own methods, to be sure. But the practice of scenting the wine with iris flowers seems to have been very widespread. The iris, in fact, is so much a feature of Chianti and the surroundings of Florence that in all probability the celebrated red *giglio* that the city adopted as its crest was derived not from the lily but from a stylised iris. The City of the Iris: it is a pleasant suggestion, which does justice to the *contado*.

Again, the sweet dessert wine that all Chianti farms produce for festive occasions is not really *vin de messe* as its name, Vin Santo, might suggest. Until 1349, indeed, it was known as *vin pretto*, or 'special wine'. But in that particular year the great council of the Roman and the Greek Orthodox Churches was held in Florence, and on sipping the 'pretto' that concluded the banquet, Bessarion, the head of the Greek Church, is said to have exclaimed with pleasure: 'But this is Xantos!' imagining, of course, that the Greek wine had been served as a subtle compliment. His Florentine hosts, for their part, thought he implied that it was *'Santo'*, or holy wine, and as a result of this misappropriated benediction it has been known as *vin Santo* ever since.

Half a century later, in the correspondence between Francesco di Marco Datini (the merchant of Prato) and Amideo Gherardini (the ancestor of Leonardo's Monna Lisa) we come across the earliest use of the term Chianti applied to wines of Vignamaggio in the Val di Greve. On 26 October 1404 Gherardini wrote that he was sending half a barrel of his own personal stock from Vignamaggio, one of the choicest wines of *Chianti* (which it still is); and one can visualise the hard-headed old merchant sitting over a bottle of it with his faithful crony, the notary Ser Lapo Mazzei (himself the ancestor of Lapo Mazzei, who now heads the Chianti Classico consortium). 'In tasting these good wines,' recalled Ser Lapo, 'We did nothing but laugh ... for my part ... I would spend money like dust to obtain them.' Though Datini, one suspects, may have preferred to send the best of his Chianti wine to people like Francesco Federighi, the treasurer of the Florentine Commune. For even in medieval days, such thoughtful little *bustarelle* were not unwelcome.

NOTE

1. Pigeons also represented a basic source of fresh meat for peasants, together with swallow nestlings – which explains the 'piccionaia' turrets that are to be found on many farmhouses (together with the small round holes for the swallows' nests).

FOUR

One day many citizens came together in the Piazza de'Frescobaldi to assist at the funeral of a woman, it being the custom of the country on such occasions for the men of title to sit on wooden benches, while the simple citizens sat on the ground on straw mats . . . With the Cerchi partisans on one side and the Donati partisans on the other, someone stood up to smooth out his garment or for some other reason. At once, from suspicion, those of the opposite stood up and laid hand on their swords. Their opponents did the same and blows fell. The neutrals who were present interposed and stopped the fight. Notwithstanding, many people rushed to the houses of the Cerchi, demanding to be led against the Donati; but the Cerchi refused.

Dino Compagni, *Cronica.*

The astonishing boom that Florence experienced during the last quarter of the thirteenth century was above all due to its Guelph connection with the Pope and the kings of both Sicily and France. As a result of the special privileges that they enjoyed within the dominions of these monarchs, the Florentine bankers were able to turn their city into one of the richest and most important trading centres of Europe. Moreover, working quietly behind the scenes, these money men took over the reins of government by the simple dodge of electing an executive of six priors chosen from the *Arti maggiori* or 'Greater guilds'. Compared with the Guelph and Ghibelline governments of the past, it was democracy of a sort — though in fact a middle-class oligarchy instead of an aristocratic one — and it was supported by an efficient police force. Indeed, by the famous *Ordinamenti* of 1295, the *Grandi* (amounting to something like 1,000 persons) were specifically excluded from power, and subjected to various restraints and penalties.

Needless to say, this was hardly to their taste. Corso Donati, a feudal figure who had led the cavalry attack that had smashed the Ghibellines at Campaldino in 1289 (the battle in which Dante Alighieri had also taken part) was all for seizing power and abolishing the *ordinamenti*. But other magnates — especially those involved in the business life of the city — believed that, though excluded from the Priorate, it would be better for them to exert their influence through the guilds to which they belonged. They therefore grouped themselves behind Vieri de' Cerchi, the head of the richest trading company, whereas the more militantly inclined (who viewed such conciliatory action as something like treason) rallied to Donati. No longer was it now a split between the Guelphs and the Ghibellines, but between the two Guelph factions. The hawks, reflecting the aristocratic feelings of the official *Parte Guelfa*, became known as the Blacks. The doves, secretly supported by the ruling priors because they had accepted the *ordinamenti*, were called the Whites.

Soon the city was divided into two armed camps and history was plagiarising itself in the streets of Florence. The Blacks angled with Pope Boniface VIII to have Charles de Valois, the French king's brother, brought in to re-establish order. The Whites, who were dead against any French interference, sent a mission to the Pope in the hope of preventing such a visitation. (One of their envoys was Dante, and it may be that the Pontiff and the Poet who immortalised him so terribly then met face to face.) But their mission was in vain, for in the meantime Charles de Valois had arrived in Florence and taken the side of the Blacks. Corso Donati and his followers held a five-day bonfire of their adversaries' houses, and fifteen prominent Whites — of whom Dante was one — were condemned to 'be burned with fire till they are dead'. It is said that Dante, hearing the news in Rome, rode hotfoot back, only to learn at Siena that his worst fears had been realised.

But that was not all. In the vicious purges of 1302 no less than 599 other Whites were sentenced to death and only saved themselves by escaping into the countryside. Among them were Ser Petracco, a government secretary and the father of Petrarch, the other great Florentine poet, who was thus linked to Dante by a common death sentence.

Many of the exiles barricaded themselves in their strongly fortified castles in Chianti: the Tosinghi and the Cavalcanti at Gaville and Le Stinche; the Gherardini at Montagliari. And, as outlaws with a price on their heads, they set about harrying their enemies in Florence. Muratori tells us that the Gherardini frequently sallied out from Montagliari, their banners waving, and scoured the valleys of the Greve and the Pesa, from Colle Petroso to San Casciano, pouncing on anyone they found carrying crops to Florence. 'They likewise captured and ransomed any members of the opposition they could lay hands on, and set fire to the country houses of their foes.' When, during August, they destroyed a large convoy of Florentine merchandise not far from Grignano, after a pitched battle that lasted the better part of a day, the Priors decided that enough was enough. On 10 September 1302 the Florentine army besieged Montagliari, though inconclusively: in the end it was agreed that the Gherardini should be free to move across the valley to their villa at Vignamaggio, while the Florentines 'furiously destroyed the castle'. So furiously, in fact, that no trace of it remained. A similar fate befell the Cavalcanti in the Fortezza delle Stinche on its high wooded spur between Montagliari and Monte Rinaldi. But in this case there was a curious transference of the castle's name to one of the most notorious of Florentine institutions. Villani says:

> And when the castle had been destroyed, the prisoners were brought to Florence and incarcerated in the new prison erected by the Commune on ground formerly owned by the Uberti next to the Church of San Simone. And because the prisoners were the first to be lodged in the new jail, it received the name of Le Stinche.

Significantly, too, a good many White Guelphs joined forces with the Ghibelline expatriates, who still hoped, with the help of the Emperor, to force their way back into Florence. In 1310 they might well have succeeded had Henry VII (who had been egged on by the Pope to cross the Alps, and then subsequently betrayed) not run into a formidable Guelph axis dominated by the royal house of France. The Blacks not unnaturally saw Henry as a threat to their liberties, and Dino Compagni tells us that when the Imperial emissaries arrived in Florence to seek the customary oath of fealty, Bruno de'Brunelleschi retorted that 'his countrymen had never yet bowed their sharp horns to any master'. But their sense of vendetta was so strong that, rather than allow the exiles back and present a solid Tuscan front, they preferred to call on Robert of Naples, the French king's relative, for help against the mutual enemy.

When, in September, Henry VII arrived outside the eastern gate of Florence, he found a stronger army than his own entrenched behind the walls, to say nothing of torrential rain and the Arno in flood, with the result that he had to call off the siege. He himself died some months later, in the little village of Buonconvento to the south of Siena of the fever that did more damage to his army than the Guelph arms had achieved. But although Florence was saved, the Neapolitan connection was to have disastrous effects on Chianti in the century to come.

For most of the Middle Ages these hills and valleys had been the back area — and sometimes the centre — of a battlefield: a small part of a larger story that often outstripped the boundaries of time and place. From now onwards, as the Lega del Chianti, they would increasingly be involved in the fortunes of the great city whose silhouette loomed to the north, and within whose jurisdiction they fell.

The great boom of the thirteenth century reached its peak around 1295, and by the early days of the fourteenth century it was fading. In 1308 the banks of the Mozzi and the Franzesi failed, followed two years later by the even more important establishment of the Cerchi (which, despite its connection with the banished Whites, had continued to operate). As these — and other firms that had contributed to put Florence at the forefront of international banking — were financed not only by their owners but also by the savings of innumerable small tradesmen, each crash meant loss and misery to a large number of little shareholders. And, with the approach of the Emperor, the expense of keeping up the army increased sharply.

At first, it had been a democratic army — which meant all the male population. The infantry had been drawn from the poorer classes and the cavalry from the nobility and better-off citizens: it had been the pride and duty of any man of standing to maintain a horse for the *comune* and to go into action when required. But whereas the old aristocracy had such spirit in its blood, the newly rich merchants who had chased them out had very little desire, or indeed ability, to go to war. Taken up with making money, they preferred to pay somebody else to do the job (an arrangement which, with a shrug, they called *la cavallata morta*). It is true that the municipal authorities could still call on the Legas of their *contado* for a fair number of troops. For the battle of Altopascio in 1325 the territory of Castellina in Chianti provided 664 infantrymen and 37 mounted cavalry, of which 200 persons from the little town itself — a large proportion of the total population which then, as today, numbered about 3,500 inhabitants. But more and more they began to rely on mercenaries.

In this the *comune* was following the Emperor. Since feudal levies tended to head for home as soon as their required term of service expired, the German kings had built up professional armies manned by well-armed troops who stuck by their units as long as they were paid and who, commanded by noblemen brought up to the ideas of chivalry, acquired a sort of regimental pride. (The first mercenaries to reach Tuscany were, in fact, Germans; though soon they were recruited from every country in Europe.) But once war became simply a business, such team spirit disappeared and they became profit-seeking adventurers who fought for whoever paid most. A commune like Florence would hire a troop of mercenaries for a particular campaign, and then sign them off as soon as it was over — only to find the same troops employed against them by their enemies a few months later.

Not surprisingly, some of the *condottieri* who headed these private armies were able to seize political power and become despots or tyrants. 'For every town in Italy is a den / swarming with tyrants; any churl's Marcellus / who comes along to play the partisan,' lamented Dante, implying that any demagogue supported by sufficient manpower to defy the local constitution would be hailed by the population as a hero. In this way Uguccione, an exiled Ghibelline nobleman, finding himself at the head of 800 German knights (who had lost their paymaster when they buried Henry VII) became lord of Pisa. His lieutenant, the even more celebrated Castruccio Castracani degli Antelminelli became ruler of Lucca, and earned his nickname, castrator of dogs, by fighting the Florentines tooth and nail.

As part of his harrying tactics, this legendary figure managed, with the help of the Frescobaldi family who then had control over Castellina in Chianti, to subvert the strongholds of Capraia and Montelupo as well as the Castellina itself. In April 1325, recalls a contemporary Florentine poet, Castruccio 'acquired for gold / the castle of Castellina which one of the Frescobaldi had sold'. However he does not seem to have held his strategic position in Chianti for long, since the Castellina contingent fought against him at Altopascio on 23 September of that same year, and at least 17 Castellinesi were numbered among the prisoners that were taken, along with the Florentine *carroccio*.

Castruccio did, however, make a pleasant little gesture to their fellows from the Val di Greve. As a penniless youth (relates Giovanni Cavalcanti) he had been wandering in that part of Chianti and found himself at a place called Nozzole. It was a hot day, and he asked for a glass of water. 'You seem a well bred lad,' replied the farmer, 'and it seems a shame that you should drink water when I have wine to spare.' Castruccio replied that he had no money to pay for it, so he had better have water.

'Wine and bread are what you need, and I would feel ashamed if I didn't offer them to you,' insisted the farmer. After he had eaten and quenched his thirst, Castruccio suggested that he should leave his lance behind in payment, but his host would not hear of it. Years later, though, the same farmer found himself among the prisoners led before Castruccio after the battle of Altopascio, who, when he recognised him, repaid the hospitality he had received at Nozzole by freeing on the spot all the men from the Val di Greve.

Certainly, tough soldier though he was, Castruccio comes down to

us as one of the more *simpatiche* figures of that time. He liked to
enjoy himself, his biographer says. For instance, one night he went
to a friend's house in Lucca where a number of women were
provided for dancing and other amusements. When his advisers
suggested that such carryings-on were bad for his image, Castruccio
would have none of it. 'He who is considered wise by day will never
be considered foolish by night,' he replied with a smile.

On another occasion he bumped into a young friend coming out
of a brothel. The youth was obviously embarrassed at having been
seen, but Castruccio only shrugged. 'Don't be ashamed when you
come out,' he gibed, 'only when you come in.' Of another friend
he remarked that he was altogether too destructive. When asked
why, he answered: 'Because as a beautiful youth he took husbands
from their wives, and now, as a handsome man, he takes wives from
their husbands.' Shades of Julius Caesar, to be sure, though
Castruccio's wit could also be caustic. Asked by a dinner party bore
when one should eat if one wished to remain healthy, he snapped
back: 'If one is rich, when he is hungry; if one is poor, when he can.'

If some *condottieri* were regularly employed, like the famous
Sir John Hawkwood, others were little more than brigand gangs
that terrorised the countryside. Muratori tells us of a German
company under Werner von Urslingen (whose motto 'Enemy of God,
of Pity and of Mercy' was inscribed on his breastplate) that played
havoc with the Sienese contrada until bought off with a payment of
25,000 florins, and after repeating the performance throughout
Tuscany, finally returned home across the Alps with a huge booty.
We hear likewise of the Great Company commanded by a Count
Lando, as well as the White Company, the Company of the Star,
the Company of the Hat under Niccolo di Montefeltro, and the
Company of St George with which Hawkwood, from his headquarters in the Abbey of San Galgano, devastated the Sienese part of
Chianti and captured Castelnuovo Berardengo, until persuaded to
depart with a bribe of over 50,000 *fiorini d'oro*.

Most of these companies must have spread through Chianti like
clouds of locusts. We know that the White Company, manned by
English mercenaries under a German *condottiere* named Albert
Sterz, crossed through from the Val d'Elsa to the Val d'Arno in
September 1363 via San Donato, Panzano and Greve on their
way to take the castles of Figline and Incisa, after which, says
Ammirato, they returned by the same route and robbed whatever
was left.

There were local troubles too, such as in 1351 when the sons of
Arrigo Ricasoli and members of their *consorteria* besieged their
uncle Ranieri, the *pievano* of San Polo in Rosso, who was reputed

to be immensely rich. The Florentines sent a task force under Luca di Totta da Panzano, which in its turn besieged the Ricasolis for over a year in the nearby castle of Vertine. (Both of these castles still stand and were only recently sold by the Ricasoli family.)

In Panzano, a street is named after Luca di Totto. This notable member of the Firidolfi clan was described by a contemporary as 'a liar, robber, assassin, traitor, gambler, highwayman, arsonist, who associates with outlaws and men of evil condition, and who lives by extortion and from the sweat and labour of others'. About par for the course in those days. But Luca was also four times a Prior and *podestà* of Florence, and hero of the woollen workers during the *Ciompi* uprising in 1378. What is more, since he wrote his memoirs, he can qualify as Chainti's first resident author.

In these *Ricordanze*, Luca admits to taking part in a vendetta — a typical Black versus White affair, by the sound of it. For in 1346, his cousin Antonio da Panzano was killed by two Gherardini brothers from across the valley. One of them then fled to Naples, where he died; the other, Carlo, took refuge in Prato. Since Luca was Florentine ambassador to Siena at the time, a good two years elapsed before he could get around to the business of avenging his cousin.

By then Carlo was hiding with a 14-year-old nephew in the church of S. Margherita a Montici, a Gherardini fief. There Luca and his retainers tracked him down, and after a fierce hand-to-hand battle (watched breathlessly, we are told, by a crowd of 5,000 spectators) the nephew was captured and Carlo clambered up to the top of the *campanile* — a rather short-sighted move, as it turned out, for Luca promptly set the church tower on fire. And then, as his adversary attempted to jump clear of the flames on the bell-rope, smartly sliced the cord. Carlo fell helplessly to the ground and the game was won. This piece of medieval drama is often re-enacted outside the castello at Panzano (in period costume and with much play on the gory bits, such as the final decapitation of Carlo), where it never fails to beguile the modern inhabitants.

By all accounts, Luca seems to have followed his star regardless of family and class (among other things, he seduced his daughter-in-law). For in the famous but short-lived workers' insurrection of 1378, known as the revolution of the Ciompi, he featured as a demagogue, encouraging the mob to burst into the Palazzo Pubblico and acclaim a young wool-comber called Michele di Lando as Gonfalonier of the city. Barelegged and dressed in a ragged shirt, Michele became master of Florence for six weeks until economic pressures brought the brave, brief proletarian rule to an end.[1] Michele di Lando came from Chianti — he was born at Lucolena — and among other things he made propaganda for the wines of his valley during the

brief time he was in office. And Luca di Totto, the aristocrat (who
may, of course, have been soured by the sanctions taken against him
for his part in the sensational murder of Sandro da Quarrata in 1370)
sounds very much like a forerunner of the modern left-leaning intellectual.

Yet if, as Professor Caggese says in the *Cambridge Medieval
History,* there were no events of 'universal import' but only a multiplicity of 'local dramas' in fourteenth-century Tuscany, the worst
scourge was undoubtedly the Black Death which hit both Florence
and its *contado* more than most places. Moreover, this followed
a whole chain of disasters. From July 1345 six months of almost
continuous rain made sowing impossible, and the following year
the corn crop was less than a quarter of what it should have been.
All the farmyard stocks had to be slaughtered for food. 'In 1346 and
1347 there was a severe shortage of basic foodstuffs,' says Muratori,
' . . . to the point where many people died of hunger and people
ate grass and weeds as if they had been wheat.' Prices rose and even
bread cost more than many of the poor could afford.

A financial crisis in both Florence and Siena aggravated the agricultural problem. Overextended credit to Edward III of England and
Robert of Naples caused the three most powerful Florentine banking
houses — the Bardi, the Feruzzi and the Acciaiuoli — to be declared
bankrupt between 1343 and 1345. By the following year the Florentine banks had lost 1,700,000 florins, which meant that money to
stimulate agriculture and even import grain was woefully lacking.

Then in the spring of 1348 came the Black Death. If it is associated more with Florence than with any other place, it is surely
because Boccaccio's sombre description in the introduction to the
Decameron has never been bettered. One particular passage has a
relevance to Chianti.

I spare to rehearse with minute particularity each of the woes that
came upon our city, and say in brief that, harsh as was the tenor
of her fortunes, the surrounding countryside knew no mitigation;
for there — not to speak of the castles, each, as it were, a little
city in itself — in sequestered villages, or in the open champaign,
by the wayside, on the farm, in the homestead; the poor hapless
husbandmen and their families, forlorn of physician's care or servants' tendance, perished day and night alike, not as men but
rather as beasts. Wherefore they too, like the citizens, abandoned
all rule of life, all habit of industry, all counsel of prudence;
nay, one and all, as if expecting each day to be their last, not
merely ceased to aid Nature to yield her fruit in due season of
their beasts and their lands and their past labours, but left no

means unused, which ingenuity could devise, to waste their accumulated store; denying shelter to their oxen, asses, sheep, goats, pigs, fowls, nay even to their dogs, man's most faithful companions, and driving them out into the fields to roam at large amid the unsheaved, unreaped corn.

Other chroniclers confirm the grim story of abandoned houses, hasty burials, cattle wandering over the countryside and crops left to waste. At San Gimignano, about 58 per cent of the population perished, in Siena slightly less. We have no definite data about Chianti, but since the plague was exceptionally severe throughout Tuscany (as opposed to Lombardy and Emilia, which escaped more lightly) it seems more than likely that in six months or less, half the population must have perished.

A grim and horrifying holocaust: an expiation, men believed, for their sins — for lechery, avarice, the decadence of the Church, the arrogance of the *Grandi* and the drunkenness of the peasants. There was plenty to choose from.

NOTE

1. The incident serves to remind one that six hundred years ago the same 'leftish' pressures lay bubbling beneath the surface as they do today. In scanning the voting lists of the 1976 elections, when two-thirds of the population of Castellina-in-Chianti voted Communist, it is worth reflecting that there is nothing very new about this radical tendency.

FIVE

> When Adam delved and Eve span
> Who was then the gentleman?

Well, obviously it wasn't Eve. And when Lord Montagu of Beaulieu (who descends, I believe, from five dukes, six earls and four kings — one on the wrong side of the blanket) murmurs that 'we were all nouveaux riches once', he means that wealth had to have a beginning, either by seizing someone else's land or by lending money at exorbitant rates to those who had done just that. Or, of course, by marrying or bedding down with a well-endowed heiress — a procedure known (perhaps tactlessly) as 'an injection of new blood'.

In the early Middle Ages wealth had meant land, which was concentrated in the hands of the feudal lords and the great prelates. But while rich in terms of real estate, they were usually strapped for cash. Their land and their serfs provided supplies and service, but little ready money. So when funds were needed for a tournament, a campaign or a visit to the Emperor (which involved dressing with the utmost luxury, keeping strings of richly caparisoned horses, and spending improvidently on gold and silver plate and rich hangings brought from the Orient) they simply contracted a loan from the *mercatores* — the new class of traders who had sprung up with the urban movement. Schevill says:

> A great nobleman would ride into the nearest town, tap at the door of a trader with his spear, and putting his cross, in lieu of his name which he could not write, to a mysterious Latin document, would vanish as soon as a few pounds of pennies had been delivered into his hands. Likely enough he did not actually handle the cash, for the moneylender was also a merchant and cunningly supplied the goods the money was intended to buy from his own stock. When after a few months the debt had to be repaid, the improvident borrower, incapable of making restitution, grasped eagerly at an extension offered him at a higher rate of interest and registered no objection against throwing in an extra field or vineyard as a security for his loan. The process, begun in the

eleventh century, was accelerated in the twelfth and carried to a climax in the thirteenth.

In this fashion the Cerchi family stripped the Abbot of the Florentine Badia of his possessions and the Cavalcanti did the same to the nuns of the Santa Felicita, while the Guidi, the Ubertini and other feudal figures in Chianti suffered the gradual transfer of their land to the Frescobaldi, the Peruzzi, the Bardi and the Acciaiuoli, who had risen from pawnbrokers to great bankers. If the typical Chianti noblemen of the high Middle Ages had been little more than rogue barons, hardly literate and probably bloodthirsty, who clung to rocky fortresses like the Ricasoli at Monte Grossoli, the Firidolfi at Panzano (and I suppose Landolfo at Grignano), they were rivalled from the thirteenth century onwards by the new commercial magnates from Florence. But although these 'knights of the age of gold' may (as a Veronese lawyer sniffed) 'have stood in the squares and at their counters exercising some base profession . . . and not know how to put their arms on', at least they were politically active, spent their money with style, and by their patronage of learning and art paved the way for the Renaissance.

For purists, of course, there may be a debatable distinction between nobles and aristocrats, since the word noble comes from the latin *nobilis*, and originally meant a known or distinguished person (almost, as Sir Iain Moncrieff once remarked, what our TV friends would call a celebrity); whereas aristocracy originates from the greek *aristos* and *kratia*, meaning government by the best people. But by the late thirteenth century blue and new blood had intermingled to form a patrician class that qualified for the title of *Grandi*. Living together in the cities they acquired similar tastes and combined both aristocratic and bourgeois attitudes to such an astonishing degree that, jobbing backwards, it is hard for a twentieth-century observer to distinguish between them — although I have no doubt that they themselves could, and did. Francesco Datini's wife, for example, was not slow to remind her husband of the differences in their social origins. 'I have a little of the Gherardini blood, though I prize it not overmuch,' she told him, 'But what your blood is, I know not.' Neri Capponi once told me, with a hint of glee, that only two or three of the great Chianti families could trace their pedigrees back to the *noblesse feodale* (or rather, *uradel*, since their earliest tenures were probably allodial). The Ricasoli, for sure; the Guidi, and perhaps the Ginori (though one was permitted to have doubts). All the others, such as the Capponi themselves, had mercantile rather than territorial pedigrees. (The original Capponi, which means capon, came from Pisa; and as Neri points out, must have been misnamed, or he wouldn't be here.)[1]

If this makes for pleasant dinner-table chat, the remarkable thing is that they are still around at all. Seven hundred years is quite a long time, to be sure, and one is bound to reflect that when Enoch Powell gave a party at Westminster to celebrate his book on the House of Lords, and invited all those peers whose ancestors had sat in Henry VII's first Parliament, it was a very small gathering. The Antinori, the Castelbarcho of Uzzano, the Buoninsegni, the Pucci, the Della Robbia, the Capponi and the Mazzei are to be congratulated, therefore, on their staying power.

In some ways they have proved more durable than their buildings which, massive though they were, have been worn down to stumps by time and conflict. I am thinking of Monte Grossoli, perched like an ancient molar on its hill now abscessed by quarries; or Barbischio, where only two angles remain of the tower from which the young count Guido di Ugo di Battifolle was chased out for raping his tenants a few times too often; or Montenano, now invaded by vegetation. Chianti is exceptionally rich in medieval bastions: the chain of Florentine castles to the south — Rencine, San Polo in Rosso, Lecchi, Tornano, Cacchiano, Lucignano, Rentennano, Brolio, Montemarchi, Montecastelli and Castagnoli — were 'marked', like football players, by their Sienese opposites, Monteriggioni, Querciagrossa, Aiola, Selvole, Pievasciata, Cerreto, Sesta, Cetamura Berardenga and San Gusmé. A bit to the rear stand fortified villages such as San Casciano, San Donato in Poggio, Panzano, Montefioralle, Lamole, Radda, Volpaia, Vertine and Castellina, which for the most part had grown from Roman and Lombard *curtes*. With its fragmented plots of land, the *curtis* was a necessary centre from which the agricultural workers radiated out to the *mansi*, that were often scattered over a wide area, and its layout was almost always the same. Within an oblong or elliptical circuit of thick walls, punctuated by watch-towers, were the stores, the stables and the dwelling places clustered around a massive tower called the *cassero* (from the Arabic Q'asr, or castle) which was both the owner's quarters and the ultimate point of defence if the walls were breached. (A secret escape passage usually led from it to safety outside if all else failed.) But few of them have remained intact.

Vertine, one of the few strongholds that was not destroyed during the Aragonese invasions in the fifteenth century, is an authentic example. Walk through the horseshoe-arched gateway by the silver-grey *cassero* and the whole thing assembles itself before your eyes like a picture thrown on to a cinema screen — better in fact, for the atmosphere is curiously unchanged, and the absence of medieval costumery only heightens one's perception that life in those days was basically agrarian. The haphazard jumble of buildings nearly all dates from the end of the twelfth and early thirteenth centuries, and even an extravagant restoration of the *cassero* hardly detracts from an otherwise unvarnished glimpse of things as they were. True, the watch-towers have gone, and the southern gateway has got lost, so that to see what the outside of a medieval Chianti stronghold looked like one must go to Monteriggioni, whose 'circling rampart crowned with towers' (*Inferno*, XXXI, 41) still gazes out over the countryside from the massive walls, though little of interest remains inside.

In Volpaia, too, you get the same mesmeric feel of the Middle Ages, while Montefioralle, when seen in the distance in the evening light, seems to condense all the verities of history in one singing chord, like an organ arpeggio as one enters a cathedral. But if at Panzano or Radda or San Donato you can trace the original configuration (so long as you know what you are looking for and have a cadastral map), I have found it easier to do so on the spot here at Grignano, which was only partly rebuilt after its final destruction by the Aragonese army in August 1452.

Rather more than half the defence walls still stand, enclosing an area on the crown of the hill about 250 feet long by 100 feet in width — just under three-quarters of an acre — and almost exactly the same size as the original nucleus of Volpaia. But whereas the *cassero* at Volpaia forms part of the walls, at Grignano it stands at the head of a small piazza, flanked by a tiny monastic building on one side and a high store (which may have been a second tower) on the other. These must have been hurriedly patched up by the Florentine authorities after that disastrous August day when the whole place was put to the flames, though the nature of the other constructions, whose foundations can still be picked out in the garden and on the southern slopes of the hill beneath the walls, can only be conjectured after pottering around the alleys of Vertine or Volpaia.

It is surprising how much masonry can be crammed into quite a small space. Tradition has it that no less than fifty families lived at Grignano in its medieval heyday, and certainly the Florentine records state that the inhabitants were exempted from all taxes for ten years to compensate for the damage they had suffered. But I doubt if they rebuilt much. A sixteenth-century map from the *Capitani di Parte* shows the torre and the two other buildings much as they are today, with the old mill astride the river Cerchiaio where it runs into the Pesa, and the church of S. Lorenzo half-way up the hill. Both the church and the mill have now been replaced by newer buildings in different locations, and the records of S. Lorenzo, dating back to 1635, which start off with a reference to the *antichissima torre decapitata*, only register two families and the priest as living in the place at that time. For by then, I presume, the rest of the community had moved from their cramped quarters within and beneath the walls to more spacious and convenient farmhouses that were erected on the spots they were working, once the danger of war had receded and peace had returned under the autocratic hand of the Medici grand dukes.

It is fascinating, indeed, to find exactly the same farmhouses recorded in the 1635 *stato dell'anime* of San Lorenzo a Grignano as still figure in the parish books today: the fifteen households are just as they were, neither more nor less, with the sole exception of the *molino vecchio* which has been replaced by the *molino nuovo*, and a house called Navicuzzo that was built in 1945. There's continuity for you! 'Navicone', for instance, was the church farm then as it remained until 1967, when it passed into the hands of my good Dutch friends, Kitty and Tyo van Marle. And there, lo and behold, is Galileo Galilei recorded as the owner of Grignanello just up the hill.

These old church books are full of pleasant surprises. About a mile away, in what used to be called Grignano di Sotto but is now known as La Piazza, the *stato dell'anime* in the church ran back to 1705, and on the very first page is the entry: 'La villa dell' Illmo. Sig. Abata Buonarroti, luogo detto alla Torre' along with a *casa da lavoratore*, which is none other than the farm which Michelangelo bought in 1545 and which was held by his descendants until a hundred years ago.

What with one thing and another, the little bit of countryside that I can see from my windows is exceptionally well documented, and one can tick off on one's fingers the stages it has passed through for nearly three thousand years. From the shards that have been found, we know that the site of Grignano has been inhabited since the early Iron Age. In 400 BC it was probably an Etruscan outpost, controlled from Volterra, against the Celtic tribes under Brennus which swept over the Apennines from the Adriatic coast. The Romans built a 'fundus' here above the old Cassia highway, and the Lombards a castle that was damaged after the battle of Montaperti in 1260. It was owned by the Counts of Monterinaldi and was confirmed as a fief of Guido Guerra by the Emperor Frederick II in 1220. Subsequently it passed into the hands of the Bernardi family (possibly his descendants) and became one of the fortified strong-points of the Lega del Chianti — smaller in built-up area than places like Castellina, Radda or Vertine, yet a shade larger than others such as Panzano, Cacchiano or Meleto, and strategic enough to figure on the maps at the Vatican and the Uffizi (whereas many other Chianti villages didn't). But it never recovered from its destruction in 1452, since a century later only a dozen or more of the 174 inhabitants of the parish of S. Lorenzo a Grignano actually inhabited the old site; and once the usefulness of the place as a Florentine defence point disappeared, it gradually devolved into an ordinary *mezzadria* farm — though at least, in the hands of the seventeenth-century agriculturist Biffi-Tolomei, a model one. By 1850 even the parish priest had moved to the adjacent church at S. Maria, and the proud old *torre* had become just a picturesque 'old Chianti watch-tower', as an American tourist described it some 75 years ago. By lucky chance (at least for me) it remained a single cadastral unit, neither incorporated into a Renaissance villa, as so many discarded *torri* were, nor fragmented into a dozen or more jumbled up bits of real estate, which was the fate of so many others. (Sir Osbert Sitwell tells us, for instance, that when his father bought Montegufoni in 1904, some 80 people were living higgledy-piggledy in one half of the house, once the palace of the Acciaiuoli, and it took over twenty years to sort the property deeds out.)

So in a way, surrounded by its vines and its woods, Grignano encapsulates all that has happened in Chianti. Other places do the same, though not many medieval buildings have come down so clean. Most of those that have survived were, by necessity, within walled centres and have all but disappeared in a hodge-podge of masonry, so that you will find the remains of a twelfth-century wall *a filaretto* incorporated into a barn or hidden in an ironmonger's shop. As the eye becomes attuned, one can quickly pick out what is of medieval vintage. Regularly squared off stonework with finely cut pointed arches are the prize exhibits: dating from the high period of the twelfth and thirteenth centuries when if people built, they did so to last, and even a battered vestige still has a singing patina that is instantly recognisable.[2] By the fourteenth century, you get a more rustic feel. The masonry is still fairly regular, but the stones tend to be longer and flatter — excavated, maybe, from buildings that had been destroyed, and juggled into place with the help of their flags. Or at least, that is the impression they give. But then from the fifteenth century onwards, the texture changes completely. By that time plaster was becoming fashionable and a regular pattern was no longer necessary; builders simply piled on whatever was to hand in the same haphazard fashion as they do today. Basically, therefore, the older the period, the better the masonry, especially as, in the early days, they used lime rather than cement — which was so rock-strong that anyone now faced with the task of hacking away channels for pipes must sympathise with those victorious troops who were required to dismantle a castle. No wonder they took it out on their unfortunate prisoners.

A few isolated constructions dating back to the thirteenth century are still to be seen here and there in the countryside, such as Vercenni, a fine fortified farmhouse near Radda; Monteraponi and Galenda, where inhabited towers have been incorporated into much later farmsteads; and San Polo di Tiene, the delightful 'bijou residence' of some minor feudal character. But on the whole it was chiefly religious buildings that were spared the attentions of the demolition squads. It is surprising, in fact, how many Romanesque churches have survived, often in quite remote spots, and now long deconsecrated, such as Mello, Lusignano, S. Stefano a Cerreto, Cignano and S. Leonardo a Catignano, which serve to remind one how well populated Chianti must have been in the high Middle Ages. Within the boundaries of what became the Lega del Chianti (the present communes of Radda, Castellina and Gaiole) there were eleven *pivieri* controlling some 70 parish churches.[3] All were constructed of locally quarried *alberese* limestone, and followed the same simple design. That is, a basilical layout with three naves separated by pillars and arches; a semi-circular apse and a tower which if necessary could be used for defensive purposes. With the exception of S. Maria Novella in Chianti — which had delightfully sculptured capitals — they were devoid of almost any decorative motives. Their attraction lies in perfect proportions and the glowing texture of the regularly cut cinder-grey stone. And also that they were erected not to satisfy someone's grandiose ambitions, but for country folk to worship in without any fuss. They are homely buildings of human dimensions, and the fact that there are so many shows how admirably they corresponded to the spiritual needs of the time.

NOTES

1. The Ricasoli had not only been the largest landowners in Chianti since Lombard days, but also one of the leading families in Florence, and they made no concessions to the mercantile way of life, preferring to supplement the revenues from their estates by taking up positions as military captains, *podestàs* and governors in Florence and elsewhere. The Guidi too, had impeccable references, if that is the right word: one recalls that in the *Inferno*, Dante allows a certain Master Adam of Brescia to say, 'But might I here see Guido or Alexander / Damned, or their brother, I would not miss that sight / For all the water in the fount of Branda.' And well he might, for Master Adam had been employed by the Counts Guidi of Romena to counterfeit the gold coins of Florence, and as a consequence was burnt at the stake in 1281.

Not that such an aberration was anything out of the ordinary. It constituted, if anything, a sort of patent of nobility. For in a survey of 72 urban magnate families that was carried out in the 1330s, it transpired that no less than 46 of them had been convicted for offences against the common law. (The Gherardini headed the list with 13 convictions for serious offences; next came the Aleis and the Frescobaldi with 10 apiece.) As serious offences included arson, murder, devastation of Church property, attacks on communal fortifications, highway robbery and treason, we need not cherish too many illusions about the general behaviour of the old Chianti *nobili.*

2. 'Have you ever wondered', said Rose Macaulay to Lawrence Durrell, 'how it is that the utilitarian objects of one period become objects of aesthetic value to succeeding ones?'

3. *Piviere* is the district of the *pieve* which was at the time the only church having a baptistry and a cemetery. *Popolo* was the congregation, but also meant one of the parishes that were grouped under a *pieve.*

SIX

Two periods in the Middle Ages were the most critical for Chianti. From the middle of the twelfth century until 1268 it had been a battlefield between Florence and Siena; now, in the last decade of the fourteenth century and for most of the fifteenth, it was destined to become a victim of the power struggles that convulsed the peninsula.

As the fourteenth century drew to its close — with the Empire crumbling and the Papacy paralysed by the Great Schism — Milan, Venice, Naples and the states of the Church (which the political skill of Cardinal Albornes had fused into a unified structure) had all risen to big-league status by gobbling up their weaker neighbours, and the oligarchic government of Florence was intent on doing the same in Tuscany. This was the age of the tyrants: top in the catalogue of which rogues was Gian Galeazzo Visconti of Milan who, in a bid to make himself king of all Italy, burst through the Apennines into Umbria and Tuscany. And once having established a firm foothold in Perugia and then Pisa and Siena, he began a concerted attack on Florence.

Under the leadership of Giovanni d'Azzo degli Ubaldini and Giantedesco dei Tarlati, the joint Milanese and Sienese armies struck into Chianti. Their initial target was the Florentine outpost at S. Giusto alle Monache, which they besieged with cannon — the first time, note our sources, that this new technique of bombardment had been used in Tuscany — and when some 300 lb of ball had breached the walls, the garrison was forced to surrender and the castle was levelled to the ground. This was in June 1390. Not long afterwards, some Florentine mercenaries under the Count d'Armagnac managed to bribe their way into the Sienese stronghold of Monteriggioni. But they were expelled the same day by the Sienese, whose counterattack took them deep into the neighbouring territory, from which they returned laden with prisoners and booty, leaving smoking ruins in their wake.

At this point Niccolaccio Ricasoli led a general uprising in Chianti against the Florentine republic. Fairly general, that is, because his brother Arrigo opposed him — whereupon Niccolaccio seized his castle of Montecastelli and set about burning the recalcitrant family's possessions with such unfraternal zeal that a stiff price was put on his head by the authorities in Florence.

This dog-eats-dog situation went on with only short interruptions for a full twelve years, during which Gian Galeazzo's troops ranged through Chianti more than once on a safari of destruction. In 1397, for instance, under Alberigo da Barbiano, they routed a Florentine army at San Donato in Poggio and destroyed the old Castellina in Chianti. But although still thwarted of his prize, the indefatigable Milanese tyrant had no intention of giving up. By 1402 he had captured Bologna and drawn, as it were, a ring of iron around Florence. A massive army, still under Barbiano, moved over from Arezzo and, after joining up with reinforcements at Siena, headed for its target through Chianti via Castellina, Panzano and the Val di Greve, all of which were thoroughly sacked and burned in the process. Since both Ammirato and Malavolti speak of 10,000 cavalry and 'a great number' of infantry, one can guess that not much was left standing in their wake. But just as almost certain disaster threatened Florence, there was a sudden *coup de théâtre*. On 3 September 1402 Gian Galeazzo died of the plague, and almost overnight his vast dominion, which was held together solely by force, fell abruptly apart. By the time the dust had settled, his two young sons were left with very little else but the possession of Milan.

Saved in this providential fashion, Florence was able to resume the forging of its own Tuscan empire at the expense of its immediate neighbours. Florentine foreign policy, it must be said, never ceased to be mercenary: its rivalry with Pisa had to do with overseas trading; its support of the Guelphs was to make sure of the papal banking business; and its desire for territory was to control as many land routes as possible. Trade, in its view, followed the Red Lily (just as in later times it was to follow the Union Jack).

And so once Arezzo had fallen again into the Florentine net and Pisa had been successfully besieged in 1406, it was understandable that cities like Siena and Lucca felt increasingly nervous, and were only too anxious for the security of an outside ally. The next one to turn up was King Ladislaus of Naples — a capable soldier and a subtle diplomat who, like Gian Galeazzo, had set his heart on dominating Italy.

Ladislaus occupied Rome, and gradually got a grip on the states of the Church. But although he never attacked Tuscany before his death in 1414, the tension of war first from the north and then the south led the Florentine state to beef up its defences. In Chianti the outlying castles like Rencine were strengthened, and following the destruction of old Castellina by Barbiano's troops, the Signoria decided on 1 April 1400 to consolidate their southern fortifications by building an impregnable new fortress on the strategic heights hardly more than ten miles from Siena. Sited a short distance from the ruins of the old medieval town, and incorporating some existing farm buildings, this was Castellina in Chianti as we know it today.

At the same time they revamped the statutes of the Lega del Chianti. Since the thirteenth-century statutes have been lost, those of 1384 with their subsequent amendments give us our earliest glimpse of the rules and regulations that circumscribed the lives of the people in these parts.

Given that there was, at that time, no clear distinction between civil and criminal or even commerical law, everything was dealt with by statute. So as you turn over the old parchment pages, like some dusty manual of military law, you come across a curious juxtaposition of items: goats, you find, were not allowed in Radda or Gaiole; a light had to be kept burning continuously in the church of San Cristofano; no one was allowed to start his *vendemmia* before 29 September 'because prior to that date the wine would not be good'; all the inhabitants of Radda were expected to grind their corn in the communal mill (one of the main sources of revenue); playing cards had to be destroyed; and parents would be punished for the misdeeds of their children under twelve years of age. Penalties were listed for those caught gambling or stealing fruit or grazing cattle on someone else's land: the list is a long one, and discussing it with the local farmers I was surprised to find how many of the old prohibitions have lingered on. You can still be fined for swearing or blaspheming, I am told (though only if the *carabinieri* happen to hear you). Moreover the principle still holds that one's taxes are paid to the commune in which one resides.

Radda was the headquarters of the Lega del Chianti, which covered the relatively small region now known as Chianti *storico* — Radda, Castellina and Gaiole — and came administratively under the control of Certaldo. (The other parts of Chianti Classico formed part of the Lega della Val di Greve, the Lega di Cintoia, and the Lega di S. Donato.[1] It was the seat of the Florentine *podestà*, who was paid 625 lire for his six months' term of office, and, assisted by three public notaries, held court in the church of S. Niccolò. These notaries served as his deputies in the other town of the Lega and each had at his disposition a troop of fifteen foot soldiers and twelve 'secret police' who were posted in the various *castelli* to report on any transgressions, a function that is still in theory carried out today by a uniformed official called *la guardia comunale*.

The lists of the *podestàs* continue in an unbroken sequence from December 1384 until March 1772, when the Lega del Chianti was abolished under the administrative reforms of the Grand-Duke Peter Leopold. They include members of such well-known families as the Acciaiuoli, Albizzi, Bardi, Buondelmonti, Canigiani, Capponi, Carducci, Cavalcanti, Corsini, Davanzati, Firidolfi, Frescobaldi, Galilei, Ginori, Gondi, Guicciardini, Machiavelli, de' Medici, Pazzi, Pitti, Rucellai, Serragli, Strozzi, Torrigiani and da Verrazzano, all of whom at one time or another made their mark in the history of Florence, and in many cases had their estates in Chianti. But the star of the list, so far as the locals are concerned, will always be Francesco Ferrucci, who served as *podestà* in Radda for three terms, from 14 February 1526 until 14 August 1527, before achieving fame as the hero of Florence's resistance against the Prince of Orange in 1530.

It is intriguing to look down the lists to spot who was at Radda during Chianti's most critical moments. Bonaccursus Capponi, an ancestor of Neri, took office on 1 June 1390, just a week before S. Giusto alle Monache surrendered to Gian Galeazzo. The records simply state that he died, without elucidating further, so one cannot know whether some long-forgotten drama occurred. A Frescobaldi was concerned with Niccolaccio Ricasoli's revolt, and secured compensation for Arrigo and the other members of his family for the damage they had sustained. Johannes Orlandi — quite possibly a forebear of my good friend Orlando Orlandi who, when running the modern commune of Castellina in Chianti, helped so many of us to get established here — was confronted with the destruction of the old Castellina, though a certain Talentus Rinaldi would have received the instructions to build the great new fortress. And a Corsini would have seen Castellina sacked again in 1402. But the worst task of all must have fallen on Joannes Stasii Barducci Attavanti, who, having taken up his duties as *podestà* on 20 July 1452, was just in time to witness the first of the two Aragonese invasions, which brought about the virtual destruction of medieval Chianti.

The causes of this new war were as follows. In 1434 the oligarchic junta in Florence, headed by the Albizzi, had been forced to give way to a signory led by Cosimo de'Medici. Around the same time Francesco Sforza, who I suppose could claim to have been the greatest of all the freebooters in this age of mercenary soldiers, had seized a large chunk of the Papal territories. Already he had his eye on the Duchy of Milan, then in the possession of Filippo Maria Visconti, by whom he was frequently employed, and whose daughter he married in 1441.

Six months after this event, the long contest between King Alfonso of Aragon and the French Duke of Anjou for the kingdom of Naples ended in victory for the Spaniard. And on the death of Filippo Maria,

Sforza was acclaimed Duke of Milan in 1450 after a three-year struggle with Venice for the prize.

For years Cosimo de'Medici had backed Sforza, on the grounds that if Venice got hold of Milan, the Serenissima would have dominated the peninsula. And there is no doubt that Florence's financial support was a big factor in his success. But it did mean that Venice, because of the help given to its opponent, was moved to abandon its long-standing friendship with Florence and make common cause with Alfonso instead.

In reaction to this, Florence proclaimed an alliance with the King of France and the new Duke of Milan on 9 April 1452. The die was now cast. In May Venice declared war on Sforza, and in June King Alfonso did likewise on Florence. Milan and Florence were thus confronted with an attack by Venice and Naples.

On 12 July the Aragonese army, commanded by Alfonso's son, Prince Ferdinand of Calabria and Federigo of Montefeltro (whose hook-nosed profile adorns the splendid palace he built at Urbino), attacked the Florentine outpost of Foiano, beneath Cortona, and then moved over to Siena, where needless to say they were welcomed with open arms. In fact some Sienese contingents joined the young prince as he thrust a pincer movement into Chianti.

Brolio and Cacchiano held firm in the east. But to the west the invaders besieged and sacked the castles of Rencine, Grignano, le Stinche and Pietrafitta one after the other before assembling around Castellina on 20 September. And here, as local historians proudly recall, they met with a notable setback. The new fortress resisted escalade after escalade for 44 days before the Neapolitans finally gave up the siege on 4 November, and retired to winter quarters in the abbey of San Galgano.

The conflict would have continued but for the news of the capture of Constantinople by the Turks. For, faced with this problem, Venice began negotiations with Milan, and both Naples and Florence eventually gave their adherence to the Peace of Lodi which was concluded in April 1454.

In Chianti, life slowly began to pick up again. Rencine was refortified, the *cassero* of Grignano repaired, but the ruins of le Stinche and Pietrafitta were left to gather moss. The inhabitants of the devastated areas were exempted of all taxes for a period of ten years to enable them to rebuild their shattered villages. A quarter of a century passed, and to the new generation it must all have sounded like old folk's tales. Until July 1478, that is, when the Aragonese invaded Chianti again.

To see why they did one must look at the Pazzi conspiracy, that extraordinary Renaissance melodrama in which the Pope himself

a

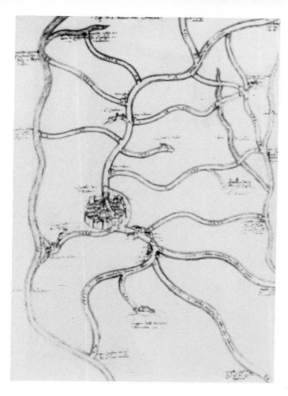

14a and b. The maps of the Capitano di Parte were compiled in the latter half of the sixteenth century. There were over 100 for Chianti alone, showing roads, rivers, villages and even individual houses, though not properly to scale. In these two examples, Radda appears with its walls still intact (a); whereas Gaiole is depicted as an unfortified village with a long market place (b) both very much as they still are today.

b

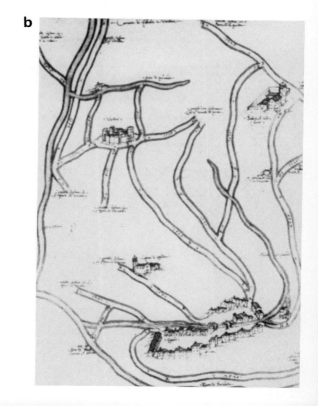

15. The tower of the Castello di Mugnana: a fine piece of medieval masonry.

16. Characteristic of medieval architecture in Chianti is the Abbazia di Monte Scalari.

plotted the murder of Lorenzo de'Medici in the cathedral of Florence. But after the victim escaped, following a chase round the principal altar of this great temple of Christendom, there was an *anna livia plurabella* of reprisals. The Archbishop of Pisa was hanged in his full vestments from a window of the Palazzo Pubblico; the other conspirators were hacked to pieces by the crowd, and the Pope's young grand-nephew was imprisoned by the signoria.

If Sixtus IV had been anxious to get rid of the Medici before this, he was doubly determined from now on, and letters in the Siena state archives show how the Papacy gave its support for an alliance between Ferdinand of Aragon and the Sienese republic to launch an offensive against Florence (Capitoli, 199-200).

Commanded once again by Ferdinand, the joint armies split up into two forces. The one attacked Colle, San Gimignano and Poggibonsi, driving the Florentine defenders back to San Casciano. The other, under Federigo of Urbino, who was back in the fray, seized Rencine and then headed for Castellina.

This time the fortress was no match for their artillery. The walls were breached, fierce hand-to-hand combats took place, and in the end the garrison was obliged to surrender. Five days later Iacopo Piccolomini, the Sienese commissioner in Chianti, reported that Radda and Volpaia had fallen too, and on 24 August Federigo sent a dispatch to Siena to say that the Florentine troops were being engaged at Brolio (Concistoro, Carteggio, Vol. 185, 58-9).

The archives at Florence are full of a flurry of orders rushed hastily out to the local commanders. Pier Giovanni Ricasoli was instructed (rather tardily, it would seem) to move provisions to Radda along with four squadrons of cavalry, 230 foot soldiers, 2 swivel guns, 2 barrels of powder, 20 bombards and 100 lb of lead. He was also told to send munitions to Barbischio, Monteluco a Lecchi and Volpaia, as well as saltpetre, mess-tins, explosives and sappers to Panzano — which was presumably being used as a supply base, although Antonio di Lucca was at the same time instructed to move the food provisions there to a safer location. Whatever happened, warned the Dieci di Balia, no supplies must be allowed to fall into the enemy's hands. Sappers must be despatched to put the mills out of action, and to destroy all the ripe crops around Castellina. From all this one gathers that the signoria in Florence were in a considerable flap.

As indeed they had very good cause to be. For on 13 September came news that the castle of Brolio, which controlled eastern Chianti, had been taken and razed to the ground; after which, moving northwards through Coltibuono, Lamole and Gaville, the invaders proceeded to take possession of all the rest of Chianti. And once again they practised their scorched earth tactics, burning crops and villages and deviating water supplies. Disconcerting tales filtered through of cruelty performed by the Sienese: Ricasoli reported that one of his captains, Giorgio Schiave, was being tortured on the rack in the dungeon at Grignano, and asked for permission to retaliate on some prisoners that he held. 'We are all part of their booty,' lamented a literate survivor in his diary.

Lorenzo de'Medici's own situation was almost as desperate. The widespread destruction of crops meant famine in the city, and this in its turn would bring plague, which was already raging in Chianti as a result of the total lack of hygiene. And then there was the Pope, who was after his blood, and had already placed Florence under interdict. Had Ferdinand, when almost at the gates of the city, not proposed the customary winter truce on 24 November, the Medici would probably have been doomed.

As it was Lorenzo, gambling on his luck and his powers of persuasion, left Florence secretly early in December, and took a ship from a small Maremma port to Naples. For three months the Magnificent argued with eloquence and charm to achieve a settlement. It cost the Florentines some territory and a great deal of money. But at least Lorenzo returned home with peace and without loss of honour.

In another Renaissance scene, this time before the middle door of St Peter's, Pope Sixtus, wearing the triple crown and seated on a purple chair of state, received a delegation from Florence. After granting them his pardon for having attacked them, he then performed a solemn mass of thanksgiving. Thus re-admitted to the Christian flock, the citizens of Florence were able to settle back and enjoy the high period of the Renaissance.

As part of the reconciliation, Chianti was returned to them. But no one can doubt that it was in a very sorry state.

NOTE

1. The full list of the *Leghe di Contado* is given in the *Statuto del Popolo del Comune di Firenze*, made out by Paola di Castro in 1415, which remained in manuscript form until 1778.

SEVEN

Where was the painter's art till Giotto tardily restored it? ...
Sculpture and architecture for long years sunk to the merest trav-
esty of art, are only today in the process of rescue from obscurity
... Now indeed may every thoughtful spirit thank God that it has
been permitted to him to be born in this new age, so full of hope
and promise, which already rejoices in a greater army of nobly
gifted souls than the world has seen in the thousand years that
have preceded it.

Matteo Palmieri (1406-75).

Normally, the Renaissance is taken to mean a period of European
history from some time in the fourteenth century to some time in
the seventeenth — even if the flowering of medieval humanism began
much earlier: in the twelfth century, perhaps. I think it was Vasari,
writing around 1550, who first used the term; and it still remains a
convenient (if overworked) expression to describe the quickening of
thought and liveliness of art that radiated through Tuscany during
the fifteenth century. Though it should not be forgotten that Vasari
was far from being alone in his self-conscious appreciation of his
times. Petrarch, Boccaccio, Salutati, Bruni, Ghiberti, Alberti and
others had done so before him.

No matter, though. What counts is that, by destiny or chance, a
group of artists in the tumultuous, money-grabbing atmosphere of
Florence was able to channel its individual talents into a great
torrent that enriched humanity. The same phenomenon had occurred
in Egypt and Hellas so many centuries before; it would happen again
later in the Paris of Louis XIV and the Impressionists. (Even in our
own day car stylists of Turin and the architects of Scandinavia have
achieved just such a link between man and his temporal preoccupa-
tions.) But the plant that spread its grace and beauty over Europe
during the Renaissance was an extreme expression of mortal genius.
And its roots were in the soil of Tuscany.

Strictly speaking, Chianti was peripheral to the Florentine Renaissance. Its inhabitants were less interested in mythological paintings

than in the thickness of the walls of their castles, and what the Aragonese were doing over the neighbouring ridge. All the same, these hills
and valleys were the rural backdrop to the city: a capillary source, if
you like, of its inspiration. Painters and sculptors rediscovered the
purity of its lights and its forms, and translated them into sublime
works of art. This beguiling, manicured landscape set the scene for
so many of their masterpieces.

It was part of the Florentine heritage — not only for the artist
but for everyone who lived in that marvellous, murky city where the
tiled roofs came so close to one another that what was left of the sky
was a mere narrow slit. Can one blame those who could for escaping,
if only for a while, from the damp exhalations of a March day or the
unbearable sultriness of summer, for the pure oxygen of the countryside? Just the knowledge that they were in fresh air — 'l'aria buona'
as they called it — filled them with intoxication. To which was added
the pleasure of tending their own little *orto*, their vines and their
olives.

This move towards country life has been explained by Lorenzo
Gori Montanelli in his book on Tuscan rural architecture:

> When the growing strength of the commune overwhelmed the
> feudal landowners and forced them to live in the city, a new rela-
> tionship was established between the citizens and the countryside.
> For the old feudal magnates never gave up the links with their
> land. On the contrary, they were able to improve their estates with
> the money they made in the city, and this interest in rural pursuits
> spread to other town-dwellers, who began to buy land, taking
> advantage of their wealth and the crisis in agriculture which was
> wiping out the small peasant proprietor.

So it happened that the old feudal castrum became *la casa da
signore*: part villa, part farm, part estate centre. And within this villa
landscape the tributary farms were grouped into new managerial
units, entrusted to salaried officials known (after mercantile usage)
as *fattori*. Gradually, as Florentine commercial prosperity declined —
for the period of the high Renaissance was also a time of recession —
agriculture came to be regarded as an attractive investment. True, the
rate of return was lower than in business or even on state loans. But
at least it had a security that business now lacked. Land gave power,
status and a modest profit, but above all it meant security: over the
years this influenced investment and the social composition of the
landed class. As Guicciardini pointed out, 'To buy land is one of the
objects for which merchants are accustomed to labour.' He might
have added that they brought a new commercial approach to exploit-

ing the soil, and the way costs and profits were shared out. For landowners who were obliged to spend most of their time in the city, the *mezzadria* system was an ideal arrangement: so enthusiastically was it extended that by 1430 there were nearly 15,000 such contracts in the Florentine territory, and something like 70 per cent of the land in Chianti itself was farmed in this fashion. Admittedly, behind the dry, formal language of the *mezzadria* contracts was the tantalising knowledge that both *contadini* and *padroni* would cheat each other whenever they could. One recalls Franco Sacchetti's pithy little tale about the wife of one of these urban landlords, a goldsmith from the Ponte Vecchio, who took her husband's farmer as a lover. When called upon to explain by her irate spouse, she indignantly replied: 'I did it for the good of the household . . . in order that he would make us an accurate measure and give us an honest staia.' A drastic (if effective) way of ensuring that the farm showed a profit.

Cosimo de'Medici had his villa at Careggi, where he relaxed from the affairs of state, chatting in the fields with the workers as they pruned the vines and grafted fruit trees. Lorenzo hunted with his falcons and his dogs around Cafaggiolo, discussing philosophy with Pico della Mirandola and writing quite tolerable verses. And where the first citizens set the fashion, the others followed suit. To modern Chianti residents there must be a hint of *déjà vu* about the instructions given to an architect to transform an old farmhouse into

an airy villa with a loggia so that we can have meals outside, with just a few big rooms where we can receive our friends, and only a few bedrooms because we are a small family. And I want all the steeply sloping land to be levelled. Take care, also, with the cellars and store-rooms, because the produce of this land is so plentiful.

Benozzo Gozzoli, Pinturicchio, Utens and others have left pictures of the country houses, and many of them can still be seen in Chianti today. Some, like Uzzano and Vignamaggio, were very grand indeed. But others differed from ordinary farmhouses only in the quality of their finish: the one was built for work, the other for pleasure. The *casa signorile* had wide overhanging eaves, sculpted cornerstones, and massive grey *pietra serena* surrounds to the doors and windows (which usually had grilles, on the ground floor at least). Often it was built — like Uzzano or Monterinaldi — on the foundations of a castello or around an old *torre*. Normally the layout included a *loggia* and a courtyard flanked with outbuildings, and probably a pleasure garden as well as an *orto*. But, these apart, it shared the same architectural features as its farmhouses: a tiled roof, dark red brick floors, and beamed ceilings with intervening terracotta coloured tiles. Sometimes there might be coffered or vaulted ceilings, and almost always a massive *pietra serena* fireplace with the crest of the owner. Otherwise proprietor and peasant lived in similar surroundings, which — unlike, alas, their twentieth-century counterparts — fitted into the landscape with natural and functional grace.[1]

For even those brought up in the city seemed to have an inborn feel for the countryside. There is almost a tenderness (along with a sharp eye for pros and cons) in Machiavèlli's letter to Francesco Guicciardini describing a couple of farms he was helping his friend to buy. In the midst of the farms was the house, with an inside courtyard, a *loggia*, and living rooms on the upper floor in which, says Machiavelli, 'You could live not dishonourably.' Moreover, he adds, by spending a further 100 ducats,

> You can lay down a lawn and surround the hill around the house with vines, and then make eight or ten ditches in the fields between your house and the first farm, in which if I were you I would plant winter fruit trees and figs; I would make a fountain with the clear water from the spring in the middle of those fields in front of a seat, which is as beautiful as anything there is.

Indeed, many of the great names of the Renaissance had their roots in Chianti, or eventually found their way there. The little town of Greve claims to be the birthplace of both Amerigo Vespucci and Giovanni da Verrazzano. (The one gave his name, rather inaccurately, to the New World; the other is credited with having discovered the island of Manhattan where he was warmly welcomed by the inhabitants, and a bridge named after Verrazzano now spans the Hudson River.) Vespucci's little house can still be seen at Montefioralle, just above Greve, where Verrazzano's statue adorns the operatic marketplace; the Castello da Verrazzano is perched on a hill just about two miles across the valley from Vignamaggio, where Leonardo da Vinci is said to have begun his portrait of Monna Lisa Gherardini.

There is a tradition that he painted her against the view as you look from the terrace up the Val di Greve, though I doubt if he did. The background is clearly allegorical and if anything more like the curiously indented landscape in the Val d'Arno near Castelfranco. In any case, the dates don't quite fit. As Professor Carlo Pedretti told me recently: 'It's better to steer clear of the Monna Lisa.'[2] (Though at least Vasari has left a description of how Leonardo kept La Gioconda amused. 'He employed singers and musicians or jesters to keep her full of merriment and so chase away the melancholy that painters usually give to portraits.') But we do know that Leonardo's first drawing — done on 5 August 1473 when he was 21 years old — had as its subject the Chapel of the Madonna della Neve, with Vignamaggio in the background.

Leonardo went in for solitary walks through the Chianti hills, just as Dante had done two centuries before. The story has it that the exiled poet was trudging south up the Cassia when a little way past Castellina he stopped and asked a peasant woman how far it was to Siena. Without hesitation she replied: 'Scendi la valle, sali sul monte, e vedrai Siena che apparirà di fronte.' A piece of spontaneous verse which so enchanted Dante that he fell to wondering whether there was any point in going to teach language to the Sienese when their vernacular speech was already so graceful.

Domenico Ghirlandaio had a plaque in his studio which proclaimed: 'The most perfect guide is nature' and he, too, must have known Chianti well, though not perhaps as intimately as his erstwhile pupil, Michelangelo Buonarroti. Michelangelo's letters to his nephew Lionardo about the purchase of his property up the hill from here have fortunately survived. On 19 April 1549 he wrote from Rome: 'Concerning the Chianti farm, I say that I prefer to make the purchase rather than keep the money around.' And a few weeks later the deal had been concluded, since on 25 May he wrote again to Lionardo: 'I learn from your last letter that you got the Chianti property. I think you say for 2300 florins of seven lire each. If, as you say, it is a good property, you did well not to worry about the cost.' By 1 June the payment had been made.

This morning, I took one thousand gold scudi to the Altoviti, and five hundred to Bartolomeo Bettini, in order that they be paid to you in Florence for payment of the Chianti farm. Let me know how much is lacking, so that we may expedite matters for the sake of the harvest.

And almost immediately afterwards, on 12 July, he agreed to buy the neighbouring *podere*. 'I am of the opinion that, if the security is good, for 250 scudi you should take by all means the Chianti property which is near the one you purchased.' On the maps of the Capitani di Parte published a few years later, the two properties are clearly marked. The *torre*, flanked by a villa, and the nearby farm called Casavecchia are both shown as 'Luoghi Lionardo Buonarroti'.

From these letters it sounds as though Michelangelo bought them sight unseen. But I wouldn't be surprised if he hadn't already set eyes on the *torre*, at least. At the time of the purchase he was already 74 years old Twenty years previously, in 1529, he had been elected to the board of works and given overall authority as governor of the fortifications of Florence, to elaborate the defences of the city and *contado*. It was he who had insisted that the most vulnerable section of the encircling walls was that on the southern, Chianti side of the Arno, and who had insisted on fortifying the hill of San Miniato. And, as part of his duties, he would certainly have inspected the advance posts in Chianti. At that time Castellina was the key point. But a little way behind, as a second line of defence, lay a network of towers centred on Grignano and Panzano, all within signalling distance of each other. Some can still be identified, and the *torre* that he bought was one of them. It seems more than likely, therefore, that he had already been on the spot, and that the villa was built during the last years of his life. From the evidence of the masonry and the maps, the argument holds.

We do not know how much time Michelangelo was able to spend here, though his letters show how fond he was of Chianti wine. 'I'd rather have two flagons of Trebbiano than eight shirts,' he wrote on one occasion to Lionardo, adding that much of it went as a present to the Pope. In another letter he complained that the wine was not up to standard: perhaps it had been spoilt in transit. He had certainly been mortified at the poor figure he had cut when he offered it to friends.

On the other hand Machiavelli (whose plans for the fortification of Florence Michelangelo had incidentally taken over) left a vivid description of his life in Chianti.

When, following the return of the Medici after eighteen years of exile, Machiavelli was summarily dismissed from his job as chancellor and secretary of the Florentine republic, he retired, a disillusioned man, to his home at S. Andrea in Percussina. He had every reason to be bitter. Politics were his life and no one had been more loyal to the state. But by unlucky chance a foolish young Florentine, who was plotting the murder of Giuliano de'Medici and Cardinal Giovanni de'Medici (who later became Pope Leo X) had written the names of possible supporters on a piece of paper and then dropped it in the street. Machiavelli's name was on the list and he was given six screws on the rack before his innocence became clear. But, although pardoned, he remained under a cloud of suspicion. In March 1513 he decided to leave Florence and settle down in the country.

He was by no means a rich man. All he had inherited were two houses in Florence near S. Felicita, and four small farms along with some houses at Percussina. Of the houses, one was used as an inn, and the other he turned into a villa as best he could. The inn had a *loggia*, a barn and an *orto*; the villa a small tower and a vegetable garden too.

Here, in the quiet of the long winter nights, he wrote *The Prince*, which was completed on 10 December 1513. 'Filippo da Casavecchia has seen it,' he wrote on that day to Francesco Vettori, 'and will be able to inform you about it, and the discussions I have had with him, though I must still expand it and polish it up.'[3]

At Percussina he also wrote the *Istorie fiorentine*, probably between 1520 and 1524, since in a letter to Guicciardini dated 30 August 1524 he says, 'I've been waiting and staying at the villa writing the Histories.' But from our point of view the letters to his friends are of more immediate interest. For in them, along with remarks on contemporary politics, some gossip and some jokes, he gives a picture of his daily life. That of 10 December 1513 to Vettori has become a part of Italian literature:

I get up in the morning with the sun, and go into a wood of mine I am having cut down. I spend an hour or two there looking over the work done on the previous day and passing time with the wood-cutters, who always have some quarrel on their hands, either among themselves or with their neighbours . . . When I leave the wood I go to a spring and from there with a book under my arm (Dante or Petrarch, or one of the minor poets like Tibullus, Ovid, or someone similar) to an *uccellare* which I have. I read of their amorous passions and their loves; I remember my own — and for a while these reflections make me happy. Then I move on down the road to the inn, talk with passers-by, ask news of the places they come from, hear this and that, and note the various tastes and fancies of mankind. This brings me to lunch-time, when I and my family eat such food this poor house and my slender patrimony affords. When I have eaten, I go back to the inn, where I usually find the landlord, a butcher, a miller, and a couple of brick-makers. With these I act the rustic for the rest of the day, playing at *cricca* and *trich-trach* which lead to a thousand squabbles and countless slanging matches — our fights are usually over a farthing, but we can be heard shouting nonetheless from San Casciano . . .

When evening comes, I return home and go into my study. On the threshold I strip off the muddy, sweaty clothes of everyday, and put on the robes of court and palace, and in this graver dress I enter the antique courts of the ancients where, being welcomed by them, I taste the food that alone is mine, for which I was born. And there I make bold and speak to them and ask the motives of their actions. And they, in their humanity, reply to me. And for the space of four hours I forget the world, remember no vexation, fear poverty no more, tremble no more at death: I am wholly absorbed in them.

A fresh insight on Old Nick, whose name has been twisted into such a universal symbol of duplicity and intrigue (Am I a Machiuel? — thus Shakespeare already). Yet the political tenets that he argued in Chianti — the pragmatic thoughts of a born and bred Tuscan — have remained alive and valid for four and a half centuries.

Machiavelli may have taken pleasure in rural occupations, such as snaring small birds and supervising the chopping of his woods. But his mind was never far from the affairs of state. Galileo Galilei was considerably more interested in agricultural matters, especially wine.

'Such was the delight that he took in the quality of his wine and the tending of the grapes,' observes his pupil Viviani, 'that he used to prune and bind them himself with more than usual care.' Galileo lived in his villa, *Il Gioiello*, near Arcetri. But he also inherited a farm in Chianti only a short distance from Grignano, which figures in the sixteenth-century map as 'Luogo di Francesco Galilei'. It must have been the produce of this farm that he had in mind when he wrote that before drinking wine one should consider what was inside the bottle: so excellent was red Chianti, he enthused, that it put all the other vintages to shame. 'Don't forget to bring a fiasco of your wine,' his daughter used to remind him, and when he visited her in the convent he never failed to take the sisters some fiaschi of Chianti and other delicacies (including even caviar, it seems).[4]

Nor must we overlook Francesco Ferrucci, who was *podestà* of Radda from February to August 1527 before becoming the hero of all Florence in the last desperate days of her independence, when the city was besieged by the joint armies of Pope Clement VII and the Emperor Charles V. From his command posts at Empoli and Volterra — and also within Chianti itself — he staged non-stop guerrilla attacks on the invaders wherever he could find them in the countryside, and kept the vital supply routes open. Finally his contingent of 3,000 infantry and 300 cavalry met the bulk of the Imperial army, led by the Prince of Orange, at Gavinana, in the mountains above Pistoia. Ferrucci's initial onslaught nearly won the day: the Prince of Orange himself was killed. But then reinforcements arrived, and the Florentines were annihilated by sheer weight of numbers. Wounded and exhausted, Ferrucci was taken before the Imperial leader, who himself finished him off on the spot. But at least Ferrucci's efforts enabled Florence to go down with her flags flying. And the mayor of Radda will show you with undisguised pride the documents he wrote during his period of office in Chianti (though only a specialist could make head or tail of his spindly script, I admit).

These, then, were some of the great figures who brought the tang of the Renaissance to Chianti, where the ancient rhythms of agrarian life went immutably on, unconcerned with the expanding horizons of the world outside. Each farm was a self-sufficient entity that pursued its own well-established routine. Corn was threshed with sticks tied together with a length of cord and then carried off to the local mill: every farmhouse had an oven to bake the flour into bread. Each farm had an olive press with a great wooden screw (now much prized as antiques). And then there were the white oxen that ploughed the soil and hauled the vat into the vineyards when the grapes were being harvested; the pigs that were slaughtered in late autumn and turned into smoked ham and sausages; the chickens and geese and seasonal offerings such as mushrooms and nuts. These were the important things in life. 'The thrushes are far from plump this year,' sighs Amedio Gherardini, all that he can send to his friends is a handful of figs; another time he complains that the corn could not be harvested because his workmen were on strike. Renaissance or not, the farmer's lot was the same.

But this did not mean that a touch of Renaissance elegance did not creep into Chianti. From the Gherardis' villa, a certain Valerio wrote to his friend Alessandro Strozzi that he was missing out on the delights of a house-party:

> Guess what, [he enthused] I'm a rustic. And shall I tell you where it is that I'm living so happily? It's called after the vines and the best month of the year: Vignamaggio. And it is surrounded, in fact, with vines on all sides ... My companions are Carlo and Giulio Gherardi, you know them well, they are the pride of florentine society ... The head of the family is here too, Andrea, a man of the old school of thought, I promise you: serious but unassuming, cultured, witty and highly religious. And there are others in the party too ...
>
> You will find the villa in the Val di Greve, just where Chianti begins, at the fifteenth mile. It is reached by a stony road that climbs continuously, sometimes steeply, sometimes on the level. The house itself is on the top of a hill and commands, like an imperious dowager, such a marvellous view that the Gherardi can say, as did Pliny, that 'wherever the eyes rest, they are refreshed.' The villa, in fact, owns over 20 farms. The western facade, which you see first when you approach from the city, is very grand, with a high roof that you can spot from far away. It has regular square windows with stone surrounds; the lower ones have grilles, and there is a wide door at the top of some steps. The proportions are admirable and it's all most luxurious.
>
> From the main door you enter into the hall, and then to the dining-room, and so to a courtyard. Another hall, with a door at the end of it. The rear facade of the house is just as beautiful,

with a magnificent triangular terrace in front of it. There are enough rooms for twenty guests to have a bed of their own, and all this downstairs. It seems like a labyrinth. Often I have to ask to find the way to my own.

Everything that has to do with the running of the estate and the house is well organised: stores, canteens, hen-coops, pigeon-lofts, stables for the oxen and mules, reservoirs, wine and olive presses. But the most splendid thing of all is the vaulted temple of *il Padre Libero* which has 25 altars . . .

And now you'd like to know something about the land itself. There are plenty of shady woods, but also vineyards, olives and orchards. Here fauns and dryads cross arms, there *Pomona* and *Cerere*. The woods are mixed up with the fields and the furrows run into the undergrowth. A lot of work is necessary to keep this luxuriant earth under control and make it yield harvests . . .

A little while ago we celebrated the feast at the chapel of the Virgin of the Snows, which belongs to the Gherardi . . . We scrambled down a steep narrow path to the river Greve — still hardly more than a stream with clear water running around pebbles and rocks and disappearing over waterfalls. On the other side is a steep hill shaded by huge chestnut trees, which were delightful in the hot summer weather. When we arrived panting at the top of it, we found the chapel snuggled among the trees, a worthy spot in which to worship . . .

Many people were there of all ages and conditions. Some had come from quite far away, especially the merchants and salesmen who turn up for such fairs. There were monks and pilgrims too, and folk from the ploughmen's association, who were all entertained to a large open-air luncheon. There were more than twenty priests. After the religious celebrations, the ploughmen and their friends each holding a green branch with ribbons tied to it, joined in a procession inside and outside the church, which ended with the Donation: a large quantity of corn brought up on pack-horses. After that we all ate, sitting on the shady grass or on tree-trunks, and lay down drinking. And then there were games and dances and fooling around with the girls, which led to some scuffles once heads had been turned by the wine. After vespers, a group of eight children all dressed in white took part in a race up the steep slope. Their clothes were less white when they finished, but the winner received a red piece of cloth as a prize.[5]

This letter was dated 6 June 1656. But I have no doubt that the scene would have been very much the same a century previously, just as the description of Vignamaggio might have been written today.

NOTES

1. In the seventeenth century Prince Fahr el Din, the Druse Emir who carved out a principality within the Ottoman Empire that later became the Lebanon (many Lebanese, in fact, consider him to have been the founder of their country) spent a period of exile in the Grand Duchy of Tuscany. On his return, he took a number of Tuscan architects and artisans back home with him. As a result, many of the old houses at Deir el Kamar (Camille Chamoun's village in the Chouf, some 25 miles from Beirut) are almost replicas of Chianti farmhouses. These buildings, now the pride of Lebanon, are classified by the 'Association pour la Protection des Sites et Anciennes Demeures' as *Vieux Libanais*.

2. A branch of the Gherardini family emigrated to Ireland in the early Middle Ages and took the name of Fitzgerald (son of Gherard): in fact a Gherardini was created Earl of Kildare in 1316. (Cf. *Unpublished Gherardini Documents*, by Reverend Samuel Hayman, Dublin, 1870.)

Monna Lisa, the daughter of Anton Maria di Noldo Gherardini, was born in 1479 and married Francesco di Bartolommeo di Zanoli del Giocondo in 1495. It seems likely that Leonardo painted the portrait in the summer of 1503, when she was 24 years old, but by then the Gherardinis no longer owned Vignamaggio.

The Fitzgerald connection suggests the possibility of a tenuous (though fascinating) link between Monna Lisa Gherardini and the 35th President of the United States.

3. *Complete Works*, Vol.2, p. 746.

4. Baron Bettino Ricasoli has reminded me that Galilei also spent the better part of a year at the villa called La Torricella, just south of Brolio, as a guest of the Ricasoli at the time of his indictment.

5. In Siena, the Palio dei Ragazzi is still staged today. After dark on the patron saint's day of each *contrada*, the local children run a race around the block, and the winner is awarded a red piece of cloth – after the original *palio*, which was red.

PART FOUR: THE MEDICI, THE RISORGIMENTO AND THE MODERN WORLD

THE MEDICI DYNASTY

Cosimo I	1537 — 1574
Francis I	1574 — 1587
Ferdinand I	1587 — 1609
Cosimo II	1609 — 1621
Ferdinand II	1621 — 1670
Cosimo III	1670 — 1723
Giovanni Gastone	1723 — 1737

THE HABSBURG — LORRAINE DYNASTY

Francis II	1737 — 1765
Peter-Leopold I	1765 — 1790
Ferdinand III	1790 — 1824
Leopold II	1824 — 1859

ONE

History, as any Sienese will tell you, ended in 1557 — that is, when the Emperor handed Siena and its territory over to the House of Medici. On that fatal July morning, the clock simply stopped. And why should one not sympathise with this partisan view? For, after four centuries of stalwart resistance, the proud old commonwealth was finally thrust under the thumb of its hated rivals. Though it would be more correct to say that both Siena and Florence had fallen victims to the Medici machinations . . .

Gavinana made it clear that Florence had been broken by the combined might of the two greatest powers in Europe. By making a formal submission to the Emperor, the Signory had hoped to avoid falling into the vengeful hands of the Medici Pope. If so, they were quickly disillusioned. The city was given over to Clement VII who (disregarding the terms of the capitulation) immediately had the last two *gonfalieri* hanged, and established Alessandro de'Medici — the illegitimate son of Lorenzo, Duke of Urbino — as head of the republic on 5 July 1531. Furthermore, the Signory was abolished, and by imperial patent the Medici became hereditary rulers, thus paving the way for the Grand Duchy of Tuscany. But for the Emperor's support from the moment they were banished from Florence, it is unlikely that they would have achieved this objective — a fact that was tacitly acknowledged in the decorations at Cosimo I's wedding in 1539: six red eggs (the Medici balls) in a nest being sat on by an (Imperial) eagle.

And indeed from this point onwards, things began to change. Traditionally, Florentine policy had been for friendship with France. But now, faced with the enormous power of Charles V's Spanish-Austrian Empire, this had to be modified, though not of course without a good deal of careful diplomacy; for the Medici's main problem (as for all the Grand Dukes of Tuscany in the 300 years before its annexation to Piedmont) was how to preserve their independence in the treacherous world of great nation states. Neither the German emperor nor the French king were easy patrons: each tended to believe that whoever was not his friend was necessarily his enemy. So, looking back, one is bound to agree that the Medici steered

171

through the chicanes with superlative skill (Cosimo's son Francis was married to the daughter of the Emperor Maximilian II; Fernando's daughter Maria to Henry IV of France; then Cosimo II made a *rapprochement* with Spain by marrying an Austrian princess, and Cosimo III was paired off with a cousin of Louis XIV). All the same, independence from both sides meant protection from neither — and when, from time to time, some outside support became necessary, it turned out to be expensive. Loans were exacted without compunction and repayment was seldom expected. For example, the death of Henry IV of France in 1610 caused the Medici a severe financial loss, and it cost Cosimo III 150,000 crowns to stave off an Imperial threat to consider Tuscany as merely a fief of the Empire. For, ironically, it was precisely the myth of the Medici's fabulous wealth that led to the depletion of their fortunes. On this their prestige depended: but it had to be backed up by cash. In the final analysis, diplomacy for the Medici boiled down to an expensive game of hand-outs. Unable to back up their diplomatic efforts with a convincing show of force, they had to rely on money instead.

On top of this, their extravagance and collecting mania played havoc with both state and family finances. 'We have no money in Florence,' complained Gian Gastone to his sister the Electress, 'though not a German has been to Florence but maintains there are millions in the fortress of Belvedere. The proof is our family is riddled with debt, and each member of it in particular.'

Inevitably, therefore, they resorted to grasping fiscal measures. From prostitutes to wigs, the Medici taxed everything they could. As Edward Wright commented in the reign of Cosimo III, 'The people of Florence are very highly taxed; there is an imposition laid on everything they either wear or eat.' (Peasants were even forbidden to extract salt from the brine of pilchards and anchovies, on the grounds that this contravened the salt monopoly.) So oppressive indeed did the régime become that Schillman considered Cosimo I to be 'Le fondateur de l'état-police' — a little unfairly, perhaps, since the use of police espionage was standard practice. Yet there is no doubt that the Medici were now presiding over a form of government that was quite different from the old Florentine republic. They had predominated in that, to be sure. But in the past they had always been careful to keep on good terms with the other powerful families who could possibly take their place. After 1539, there were no such pretences. Uncompromisingly and often brutally (one has only to think of the persecution of his rivals, the Strozzi) Cosimo I set out to ensure the continuity of his family. Like so many despots, he bulwarked his position by weakening the privileged classes and increasing the number of officials who were dependent on himself. The old city magistrates and professional corporations were stripped of their power, which now passed into the hands of the 'pratica segreta' — a small team of civil servants heading a bureaucracy in which provincials gradually came to outnumber the Florentines, and which was directly under the control of the Grand Duke.

No longer just Florence, but Tuscany as a whole was the stage for the Medici dictatorship. And inevitably this had its effect on the cultural and intellectual life, which now depended on the prince's whims. How they were expressed is shown by a letter sent from Cosimo III's secretary to Pisa University: 'His Highness will allow no professor . . . to read or teach the philosophy of Democritus or of atoms, or any save that of Aristotle.' Education, moreover, was strictly placed under the *aegis Jesuit*. Sir Harold Acton recalls how the famous librarian Magliabechi pointed out the Riccardi palace to a visitor and remarked: 'Here letters were born again,' and then, turning to the College of Jesuits across the way, added 'There they returned to their grave.'

It was during this period — which Schevill calls 'the great lethargy' — that Florentinism began. That is, a concern merely with the valuation (and sometimes over valuation) of the city's heritage: Lenzoni and Salviati, for example, praising the Florentine language, and Vasari eulogising the unchallenged position of Florentine art just when it was beginning to wane. Because of course it was better to play safe: Galileo was but one example of the dangers that independent and unorthodox thinking continually ran. And whereas experiments lacked, an elegant dilettantism began to creep in. Business — for so many centuries the life-blood of the city — went intellectually out of fashion. As Davanzati himself said, his treatise 'On Money' was written 'for entertainment, not instruction', and 'On the cultivation of Vines and Trees' to show his ability to imitate Tacitus' prose. Soderini expounded on the preservation of vines, as he put it, 'That our language not be wanting in georgic compositions'. While agriculture might be a favourite subject of discussion in the literary academies, nobody had any intention of dirtying his hands.

For all this, there was a significant switch in investment from business into land, even if only for the sake of security, since agriculture was regarded as a hedge against loss rather than a source of profit, especially in a period of recession. Though to be fair, the economic crisis of the seventeenth century (which Procacci considered to be 'one of the key points of Italian history, since it put Italy behind in the empire-building exploits of powers such as Britain, France and Holland') involved the whole peninsula, and not just Tuscany. True, Tuscany suffered like the rest. Whereas Florence had been producing 20,000 bales of woollen cloth a year between

1560 and 1580, and 14,000 pieces of wool in 1602, this figure had shrunk to a mere 5,600 by 1644. The insecurity of traditional forms of investment was shown by the enormous losses that were suffered when the Capponi bank crashed in 1640. Small wonder, therefore, that people preferred to put their money into land. For whatever else the Medici did, at least they kept Tuscany from becoming embroiled in the destructive wars that swept the other parts of Europe. When one considers the devastation that Chianti underwent during the Florentine wars up until 1539, this was no mean achievement.

Paronetto, in fact, has called the seventeenth century 'The century of Chianti'. For now at last, through its wine, Chianti really came into its own. As we know, large quantities were already being produced well before this time. When turning in a claim to the Florentine commissioners for war damages in 1530, for instance, Andrea Ricasoli had stated: 'When the battle neared Florence . . . about 50 Sienese . . . came to a place of mine in Chianti called La Leccia and destroyed 200 barrels of wine' (that is, 10,000 litres.) But quantity apart, the robust and harmonious flavour of the Chianti vintages was more and more appreciated. Michelangelo found it an acceptable gift to present to the Pope. Vasari thought it worth a frame, entitled *Ager Clantius*, on the ceiling of the Sala dei Cinquecento in the Palazzo Vecchio (see photo). And a whole host of poets were beginning to sing its praises. Redi in particular (who as Cosimo III's doctor carried out intriguing experiments with vipers and poison) advertised his delight in Chianti wine, not only in his well known 'Bacco in Toscana', but also by a backhand compliment in the *Arianna Inferma*:

> E quel che importa, il medico l'approva
> E in centomila casi stravaganti.
> Ha fatto ancor di sue virtù la prova
> Celebrandola più del vino di Chianti.

From around the middle of the sixteenth century Chianti began to be exported to England, and in many ways the English market and English shippers became as important to the production of Chianti as they did for other famous European wines such as sherry, port and claret. A certain Mr Longland built up a thriving business shipping it from Livorno, though the creation of a wine that could travel well was, from all accounts, a continual technical problem. Moreover the Medici princes frequently used Chianti as diplomatic gifts. Ferdinand I sent several consignments to Queen Elizabeth of England, and Cosimo III did likewise to Queen Anne. In fact he made a habit of presenting Chianti vintages to the friends he made in England — such as Charles Calvert (Lord Baltimore), Lord Stafford, and Charles II's favourite Duchesses (Cleveland, Lennox and Portland). But quite apart from these personal presents, Cosimo III anticipated Ricasoli's later ambition to place Chianti wines firmly on the English table, and commissioned Magalotti to study the ways and means of capturing the British market. Ricasoli's ancestors, of course, were already busy exporting Chianti to England, as numerous letters from Brolio to their agent in London confirm. But although the international reputation of Chianti can clearly be said to date from the seventeenth century, its distinctive make-up was not finally decided upon until Ricasoli's day, and even after. Three centuries of development in the wake of technical innovations and changes in taste were still to come, for wine itself has a history: it is the product of slow evolution in which so many factors play their part. And who knows, the wine we drink today may still not be the ultimate in what Chianti has to offer.

TWO

Somewhere in Denis Rixson's notebooks I came across an entry suggesting that without going into what he called 'a value-laden discussion about the past in terms of degeneracy and decadence', one would do well to question the habit of judging societies according to their pathology or health. 'How does one determine decadence?' he asks.

> Nowadays we do not expect monarchs in procession to vomit out of carriage windows at their subjects as Gian Gastone did. Nor do we allow them 370 'ruspanti' to pander to their every desire — if only to save the exchequer. But perhaps we have too much of value judgement in our approach. The Medici were more like old cars — obsolete, out of date and destined to be cast aside — but no less attractive or worthy for that.

Which, come to think of it, is not a bad description.

When, however, the last of the Medici died in 1739 — tragic, dissolute old Gian Gastone — the arrival of the Habsburg-Lorraine dynasty tied Tuscany firmly to Austria. True, the Lorraine princes made some desultory attempts to steer clear of their predatory relatives in Vienna. Francis-Stephen, for instance, took the title of Francis II to emphasise his continuity with the Medici. But during his 28-year reign he spent barely three months in Tuscany: for the rest of the time he was commanding the imperial armies or acting as co-regent with his wife, the Empress Maria-Theresa. Pressure from the great powers, what is more, made it difficult to combine both the imperial throne and the Grand Duchy of Tuscany, so on Francis' death the less grand of the two was hived off to his younger son Peter-Leopold. Yet whereas when held by one person, the interests of the two states were obviously identical, when held by two it was quite another matter. The passing of Tuscany to the cadet branch brought a continual tension between Austrian and Tuscan interests — and if Leopold II eventually lost his throne, it was because he placed loyalty to his family above loyalty to Tuscany.

A clear case in point was the question of taxes. Expensive Spanish

176

garrisons were maintained from 1731 onwards, when Gian Gastone became bedridden, and the powers had to decide about the Tuscan succession. On top of this Francis II had to fund a seemingly bottom-less Austrian war debt, and extracted the money by that most rep-ressive of institutions, a tax-farm. Tuscany exported 12 million scudi in 1756 and another 4 million lire in 1766 to the Imperial treasury. But this was not all. Francis also introduced compulsory military service (which was always unpopular in Italy) and in 1758 three thousand young Tuscans departed to join the Austrian army. At the second levy they deserted *en masse*. Such measures rankled, yet there was not much that could be done: small states are always at the mercy of the larger ones, and there was no real alternative to the Austrian domination. (During the French invasions Napoleon had no qualms about Tuscan feelings and just shipped off ten thou-sand men to join the ranks of the Grande Armée.)

All the same, Tuscany suffered less than the rest of Europe during the Seven Years' War and under Peter-Leopold the Grand Duchy even began to project the image of a model state under a philosopher-king. For a brief spell its light shone encouragingly until eclipsed by the flame of the French Revolution, after which it petered out in universal reaction.

In Chianti what counted most were Peter-Leopold's agricultural measures. For his policy of freedom for both land and produce coincided with a general increase in European demand for agri-cultural products. Predictably, therefore, there was again a return to the land. Agricultural academies were formed — of which the most famous was the Georgofili. There was a revolution in the economics of agriculture, and (to quote Cochrane) 'The big aristocratic families finally consummated the withdrawal from commercial and indus-trial activities that had begun two centuries earlier.' In the 1720s they still held 59 per cent of the capital behind Florentine business, often playing an active part in the management of wool, silk and banking enterprises. By the 1750s their stake had been reduced to 28 per cent. A lot of money was obviously being invested in land, and a good many of today's big Chianti estates date from that time.

With good reason, too. Between 1766 and 1773 the export trade in corn was freed, and numerous internal restrictions and tolls were abolished. Now that surpluses could be exported, there was an incentive to increase production. Over the next 25 years grain prices almost doubled, and production increased by at least a quarter. Oil prices rose and new olive groves appeared — thanks to a tree-planting contest organised by the Georgofili. Wine pro-duction also increased significantly, and once the Grand Duke had cancelled the state monopoly, much of it was turned into spirits.

By any token, these were the indices of increased prosperity, and not surprisingly, free trade became an article of faith in Chianti — though not everyone shared equally from its benefits. The *mezzadri* paid rent in kind, not in cash: hence if their profits were higher, so were their rents.

Yet on the face of it, the results were impressive. Businessmen, landowners and farmers collaborated to increase production. The Georgofili had a model farm near Bagno a Ripoli (where the Chiantigiana road begins) and gave monetary prizes for specific innovations. More resistant grains like 'Siberian oats' and 'gran nero' were introduced, and there were attempts at crop diversification. Wheat fields were interspersed with vines, olives, potatoes, fruit and mulberry trees: indeed one is inclined to wonder whether the intercultivation that we know in Chianti today (that magic classical tapestry of garlanded vines and olives in the corn, which is so like the Roman system) was not really a re-creation of the eighteenth century.

And there were new crops as well. With the planting of tobacco the famous Tuscan cigar appeared; the Grand Duke removed all legal restrictions on its sale, and the Georgofili issued a free pamphlet on its cultivation. Such helpful actions aided new ventures and spurred on forward-looking agriculturists like Gianni's cousin Biffi Tolomei ('the educated farmer'), whose possessions included Grignano.

Yet all was not entirely for the best, as Gianni (the Grand Duke's Minster) found during a trip through the province of Siena in 1786. *Laissez-faire* could — and did — lead to abuses. For one thing, deforestation (a particular evil in Tuscany, where it can so easily upset the water balance) was already having harmful effects. For another, the new laws played into the hands of the land-owing oligarchy who, by acquiring land that had hitherto been bound up in the royal estates or by ecclesiastical mortmain, were able to increase their power base and oppose any new measures of liberalisation that might challenge their position. Helped by one set of liberalising measures, they were able to stifle any others that might be to their disadvantage. If, from a reformer's point of view, the old enemy had been tariff controls and mortmain, now it was the entrenched economic position of the great landowners, as Gianni discovered when he attempted to replace the *mezzadria* system.

Gianni's general aim was to 'put the land in the hands of those who work it, above all . . . ' As a start, he suggested new methods of leasing out charitable land that would, he hoped, encourage the formation of a class of independent land-owning farmers (much as Stolypin attempted to do between 1905 and 1911 in Russia) and thus replace the *mezzadria* system. Simplistically speaking, as we have seen, *mezzadria* is a system whereby the landowner provides the capital and the tenant the labour, both splitting the harvest (and each believing that the other has done better than himself). But since rent was normally paid in kind, there was little opportunity for the *mezzadro* to improve his lot sufficiently to acquire an independent holding. Gianni proposed refurbishing a kind of half-tenancy, half-ownership contract that had been used off and on since the Middle Ages, particularly in land newly brought under cultivation: the *livello*. The recipient would make an initial payment equal to one year's estimated income and agree to pay a fixed annual rent thereafter. In return he would receive complete freedom to cultivate the land as he pleased, to sell it, or pass it to his heirs in perpetuity. Gianni applied such contracts to many royal estates and land belonging to the Conservatorio di San Bonifazio. His experiments promptly ran into the furious opposition of the Treasury, the local communes, the Georgofili, and the whole of the land-owning class. The Treasury wanted the sale, rather than the renting out, of royal property so that they could more quickly liquidate the state debt. The communes were usually in the pockets of the local squirearchy. (Part of Gianni's aim was to turn share-croppers into landowners and hence make them eligible for election to municipal councils, where they could protect their own interests.) And Georgofili experts like Pagnini and Serristori were horrified at such a veiled attack on the concept of private property.

For all this, the peasants were not entirely unchampioned. Bishop Ippoliti thundered to the effect that unless share-cropping contracts were modified, God would send the Assyrians to avenge the wrongs inflicted on the starving and humiliated peasantry. But the Assyrians didn't come. The system of *mezzadria* remained (not until 1967 were such contracts prohibited, and some of the old ones are still running). For the fact is that Gianni was ahead of his time. His proposals needed more than just the availability of land to make them work. Despite special concessions, the peasants simply didn't have the initial capital or the financial backing to buy up the contracts at auction. In 1779 only 25 per cent of the leaseholders' rents came from ex-*mezzadri*. By 1784 the proportion had dropped to 19 per cent. More and more, the land came to belong to the nobility and rich city folk who could buy out their poorer competitors.

Yet the experiment was significant, for it shows that the measures that are being taken today were already foreshadowed two centuries ago. Of course men like Gianni were exceptional at that time (and above all he was a bureaucrat who could afford to be indulgent towards the peasantry: they weren't a direct threat to his self-interest). And in any case people still felt that the division of the cake between proprietors and peasants — placing capital and labour on an equal footing — was eminently fair. For after all, there was still an enormous gap between the educated upper class and the illiterate worker, and Tuscan landowners were used to treating their horses better than their peasants. Paoletti, for one, described them as ignorant, slothful and stubborn, requiring vigilant supervision. It was this contemptuous attitude that Ricasoli was to find so prevalent and so vicious in his contemporaries.

When it came, though, to religious reform the roles of reformers and reactionaries were seemingly reversed. Basking as it had in privilege since the days of Cosimo III, the Tuscan Church had long been needing an overhaul — which Rucellai, along with Bishop Ricci, attempted to do. Strongly imbued with Jansenist ideas, the Grand-Ducal will imposed itself on ecclesiastic affairs. Textbooks for the clergy were prescribed, patronage rights of parishes and communes were seized, abuses were stifled, convents were closed and suggestions for a general reform of the Church raised questions of Papal prerogative. But when the showdown came, it was not through any challenge to the Bishop of Rome, but over Peter-Leopold's attack on image worship.

Adulation of the gory relics of martyrs and saints had always played a prominent role in Catholicism (it will be recalled that at one period of the Middle Ages there were five 'complete' and 'true' relics of Christ's circumcision circulating).[1] Nearer home in Chianti, the miraculous Madonna of Impruneta had been known to squeeze out a drop of milk, as in the plague of 1633. A young nun was said to have sucked liquid out of a painting of St Francis' stigmata. The appeal of such mystic events can be gauged by the response that the cult of the Sacred Heart met in Tuscany at the end of the eighteenth century. All of which went to show the deep roots of peasant piety. The products of the slow accretions of man's devotions over the centuries could not be easily overturned by an enlightened Grand Duke. To which must be added that Peter-Leopold's measures to suppress relics and images were embarked upon in a stupid and repressive manner. The use of police made it easy for reactionary clergy to appeal to their congregations. Public whippings and prison sentences in Prato made martyrs of his opponents. Resentment was nourished by anti-Riccian clergy and the Roman Curia. In 1790, disorders broke out all over Tuscany, even in the smallest localities. There was more or less serious trouble in Florence, Pistoia, Livorno, Chiusi, Colle Val d'Elsa, Montevarchi and the villages of Chianti. Peter-Leopold (or rather, his regency, since he became Emperor in September 1790) had to back down on the question of religious reform. The disturbances also brought about the fall of the two major architects of change: Gianni and Bishop Ricci. Secreted in a coal barrel, on a *barroccio*, the Bishop escaped to a refuge in Chianti. There he remained for several months 'in such carefully guarded hiding that even his visitors had to communicate with him through secret messengers'. (In fact he was at the Fattoria of Rignana, where his grave can still be seen in the chapel.)

But agricultural and religious reforms apart, there were other changes under Peter-Leopold which affected the structure of Chianti life. The 'terzieri' of the Lega del Chianti (Castellina, Radda and Gaiole) were suppressed: instead they were amalgamated into a single 'communità', thus ending a system of local government that had lasted since the thirteenth century. The taxation system was re-organised: Gianni abolished the tax-farm and made it the state's responsibility, streamlining it into a single land tax — with no exemptions. Civil law was revised by Pompeo Neri and special feudal jurisdictions (such as those exercised by the Ricasoli at Brolio) cancelled out. A new criminal code abolished torture and the death penalty. Censorship was reduced and the number of publishing houses multiplied. Periodicals flourished — such as the 'Giornale fiorentino di agricoltura, arti e commercio'. Expense was saved by disbanding the army (which was replaced by four civic companies) and the navy, that 'giant, useless expensive machine', as Gianni called it. (The French just marched in during the Napoleonic invasions.) There were attempts at public education through the 'Schools of San Leopoldo' and the free 'school for domestic education' of the Third Order Franciscans of Figline. Land reclamation projects were put under way in the Maremma and the Val di Chiana. There was large-scale house-building, and most of the late eighteenth-century farmhouses in Chianti, with their pigeon-lofts, their arches, their huge fireplaces and ovens, owe their existence, if only indirectly, to Peter-Leopold (who, sadly enough, authorised many ancient buildings to be knocked down and quarried for materials).

Hardly anyone gives a thought to Peter-Leopold today. And yet the 'model state' he tried to set up — before the whirlwind of the French Revolution had rent European society with its divisive questions about liberty and equality — set the pattern for life in Chianti that was to last until a few years ago. The history of Tuscany, if to a lesser extent that of Chianti, must account for sharp boundary lines drawn by the French invasion. New, heady, disruptive ideas swept in with it that led thinking people to concern themselves with political questions, and led ultimately to the Risorgimento. Peter-Leopold's achievements may seem small beer in comparison with subsequent events. But in Chianti they endured. His years of rule provided us with many of the distinctive farmhouses that characterise the Tuscan countryside, and (perhaps more by default than anything else) structured the agricultural system that was to continue for nearly two centuries until finally killed off — though still not entirely — by the car and the tractor, and other beguilements of the consumer society.

NOTE

1. A strange booklet published in Rome in 1890 is entitled 'Narrazione critico-storica della Reliquia del Sagrosanto Prepuzio de N.S. Gesù Cristo'; the relic was sheltered in the parish church of Calcata near Viterbo.

THREE

Dante and Petrarch had dreamt of a united Italy, and Machiavelli in *The Prince* had sought a liberator to deliver his compatriots from foreign bondage. But that was about all. For most Italians, fragmented as they were into independent principalities, the idea of unity was little more than an intellectual concept — or simply poetic skywriting. 'Occasionally we hear the word Italy,' wrote Pietro Giordani as late as 1814, 'but it finds little echo in people's hearts,' Yet barely a generation later the whole peninsula was knitted together into a single kingdom. What is more, by producing one of the key figures who helped to shape the country as we know it today, Chianti played its part in the Risorgimento. For without Bettino Ricasoli, things might have turned out very differently for both Tuscany and Italy.

If the precise parentage between the French Revolution and the Risorgimento has long been a matter of scholarly discussion, clearly the influence was there. In the wake of the Napoleonic invasions, a swarm of French agents appeared, bringing the challenging new ideas about liberty and equality that had shattered the *ancien régime* in France. (One of the reasons for the annexation of Tuscany was that of all the Italian principalities, it was thought to be the most similar to the French revolutionary state.) With the Restoration, these ideas lost their bite. But, if nothing else, they gave an incentive to political action — something Tuscans had not indulged in since the 1550s (excepting the religious riots of 1790 and disturbances during natural disasters).

Inevitably the arrival of the French and the forced exile of the Grand Duke brought conflicts of authority. Moreover a peasant, guerrilla resistance grew up against the French, whose depredations were not altogether in the spirit of fraternity, and whose suppression of ecclesiastic orders and confiscation of convent lands provoked great discontent. In 1799 there was something of a Vendée in Tuscany. Under Lorenzo Mori and the foreign agent Waugham (plus of course their shared mistress, Alessandra, the 'maid' of Valdarno) the army of Arezzo marched out to attack cities in Tuscany and Umbria, and massacre Jacobins and Jews to the tune of 'Viva Maria'. After

Napoleon's victory at Marengo in 1800, Arezzo was brutally sacked and the country put under military administration.

In due course the allied victories put an end to the French order in Italy. But, hated or not, it had lasting repercussions. The French might be vanquished, their ideas might have to go underground. But Pandora's box had been opened.

By the Congress of Vienna in 1814-15, the Austrians were re-established as the predominant power in Italy. Ferdinand III returned as Grand Duke to Tuscany, and was succeeded in 1824 by Leopold II. On the whole, their rule was more liberal than in most other Italian states. Vittorio Fossombroni, who led the Tuscan government during much of this period (on behalf of the Grand Dukes) realised that a total restoration was impossible, and that Tuscany could not return to what it had been in 1796. Too much had happened in the meantime. Liberals of one colour or another were far more numerous than they had been a generation previously. Of these there were two main groups: a moderate or right-wing element favouring some sort of constitutional monarchy and limited suffrage, and a left-wing element favouring republicanism and democracy. As the nineteenth century wore on, more and more intelligent Tuscans leaned at least towards the former. (This was, after all, a period of real intellectual revolution. An educated man's reading would include Locke, Voltaire, Rousseau and Bentham — hardly the stuff to sustain an absolutist grand duchy. Of course there was censorship of books in Tuscany. But there were ways of overcoming this problem — even Leopold II used to order from his booksellers books proscribed by his censors.)

Yet while the other states of Italy were saddled with restrictive economic practices, Fossombroni remained true to the free-trade principles of Peter-Leopold. Many of the convents that had been confiscated by the French were re-opened; reclamation work in the Val di Chiana recommenced along with some road-building and construction of bridges. By means of customs and banking reforms, industry was stimulated. The borax deposits found at Monte Rotondo in Peter Leopold's time and the copper mines at Montecatini helped to boost the revenues of the state. With a yearly surplus of 3 million lire, Leopold was able to reduce taxes. All of which added up to a positive balance sheet, though Fossombroni shrugged it off with the words, 'Il mondo va da sé' ('The world gets along by itself').

A happy little world, indeed, that quickly became the refuge of exiles from the more despotic and reactionary governments of the Restoration. Like Giordani from Piacenza who, in a fit of euphoria, called it 'the earthly paradise' (to which Gino Capponi drily commented what a pity it was that the earthly paradise lacked both the Tree of Knowledge and the Tree of Life). For clearly Leopold was a relatively enlightened ruler, and if from time to time he used a heavy hand, it was usually an inefficient one. The shadow of Austria was always there in the background, but the presence of these foreign exiles showed a certain tolerance of liberal ideas, if only through inaction.[1] As Gino Capponi summed it up: 'The people are tranquil and rich, and have happy ease, and that accursed, poisonous gift of tolerance.'

Epigrams apart, though, what were the real facts of Tuscan life in the long run-up to the revolution of 1848?

In 1837 the population was just under one and a half million, of whom less than a quarter of a million lived in towns (100,000 in Florence, 20,000 in Siena). The national revenue was 17 million francs, which in terms of *per capita* income compared favourably with the Papal states and the Kingdom of the two Sicilies but was considerably behind Piedmont and Austrian Italy (then by far the richest state in Italy, its five million inhabitants enjoying an income of 122 million francs). Only one in 69 children went to school, as against one in 12 in Lombardy and Venetia. But the first all-Italian Scientific Congress, which took place at Pisa in 1839, and was followed by a second in Florence two years later, pinpointed the growing awareness of *Italianità*. Both were only possible in a liberal atmosphere — an *ambiance* that allowed non-Catholics freely to attend university and made emigration virtually unknown.

Interestingly enough, the moving spirit of this liberalism was the prestigious Academy of the Georgofili, with its enlightened aristocrats like Cosimo Ridolfi (who, to the horror of the reactionaries, was made tutor to the heir to the throne). Yet, especially for Chianti, there were some negative aspects as well. Even if the most progressive agency was an agricultural institution, it was precisely in agriculture that the gravest problems arose. For, in contrast to the Georgofili's forward-looking experiments, the entrenched system of *mezzadria* was suspicious of scientific improvements, and incapable of standing up to sudden crises. While the agricultural areas remained quiet when the harvests were good (as in most of Leopold's early years), there was promise of trouble should things go wrong.

Which in due course they did. In 1848, 'the year of the revolutions', Tuscany was part of a general movement in Europe against restored and repressive régimes ('fare un quarantotto' has passed into the language as symptomatic of great disorder). There had already been premonitions: in 1847 d'Azeglio, the Piedmontese politician, had published his 'Programma', calling for the introduction of juries, legal reform and freedom of the press, which a group of Tuscan liberals led by Gino Capponi supported. That same year had seen some proposals by the white hope of all Italian liberals, Pius IX, and the Lorraine government had indeed abolished press censorship, thus allowing political journalism to start up. Anti-Austrian feeling was running high in Florence since part of Lucca, so recently reverted, was ceded to pro-Austrian Modena; and the activities of Guerrazzi, together with Mazzini's influence amongst the students of Pisa, could only spell trouble.[2] In fact in parts of the countryside some socialist and communist ideas had already taken hold.

More than anything, though, the Tuscan revolution was a reaction to the enormous gale of change that suddenly blew through Italy. As constitution after constitution was hurriedly granted, so demand after demand piled up. 'In the eyes of furious men,' commented Stendhal, 'concessions are nothing but a proof of the weakness of the government that makes them.' Maybe so. At any rate, under the leadership of Guerrazzi and Montanelli, Florence staged its revolt.

Openly voiced now, particularly by Montanelli, was the idea of an Italian Assembly elected by universal suffrage. After all, even Ferdinand of Naples had granted a constitution, and Charles Albert of Piedmont was waging what could be seen as a war of national liberation against the Austrians. Yet for Tuscans, the concept of unity held little appeal. What they sought was autonomy. That Charles Albert should be fighting the Austrians they were prepared to applaud: but no self-respecting Tuscan wished to be swallowed up in Piedmont. In 1848 Ricasoli was the only one who looked towards Turin — the others thought in terms of a federation or a balance of power to check what they saw as an octopus-like Piedmont. Capponi, who took over from Ridolfi as Minister in that bewildering year, was dominated by the fear of Piedmontese hegemony. Indeed Ricasoli's great achievement was to overcome these prejudices and convert Tuscany to his thinking twelve years later.

As it turned out, the fate of the 1848 revolutions was decided on the battlefield. Charles Albert's defeats meant that the Grand Duchy of Tuscany was bound to be restored. And if the problem of losing is an Italian trauma, it should be remembered that most of the Austrian fleet and a large part of the Austrian army were in fact composed of Italians. The Tuscan volunteers put up a good showing at Curtatone and Montanara, but then disintegrated into a rabble (weaving extravagant yarns about their own spectacular achievements). Many deserted, and the best — like Bettino Ricasoli's brother Vincenzo — signed up with the regular Piedmontese army. As King Ferdinand I of Naples remarked when his grandson 'Bomba' was designing some fetching new military uniforms: 'Dress them how you like; they will run away all the same.' (Though perhaps the British commentator, Hamilton, was nearer the mark when he commented: 'Love of war is not a quality of this amiable nation.')

17. Amerigo Vespucci gave an old name to the New World. The Vespucci crest, a wasp within the letter *V*, can still be seen on his house at Montefioralle, above Greve.

18. Niccolò Machiavelli head of a small estate in S. Andrea in Percussina where he wrote *The Prince* and later the *Histories*.

19. The first of the great British expatriates in ·Florence: Paolo Uccello's fresco of Sir John Hawkwood in the Duomo. Known to Tuscans as Giovanni Acuto, he was a *condottiere* who headed the Company of St George, a band of mercenaries who devasted the Sienese part of Chianti.

20. A self portrait (now in the Uffizi) by Michelangelo Buonarroti who bought his Chianti estate in 1549. He was proud of the wine, which he gave as a present to the Pope.

At all events, the Grand Duke Leopold II returned to Tuscany in 1849 with a body of Austrian troops in his wake. The character of the Restoration was now undisguised. Leopold was Grand Duke by virtue of the fact that he was an Austrian prince: so long as his house held the Grand Duchy, Tuscany would never be free of Austria. Yet even if the Grand Duke upset public opinion by his arrival at the head of Austrian troops, the Tuscan liberals were by no means unanimous in their opposition to him. The year 1848 had provoked a real and lasting split among them. Aristocratic and wealthy Tuscan liberals like Ricasoli, Capponi and Peruzzi discovered that they were much closer to the Grand Duke than to the 'socialist' left of Guerrazzi and Montanelli, who had come to exercise power in the aftermath of the revolt. Indeed from this time onwards the split between moderates, who at most wanted a constitutional monarchy and the expulsion of the Austrians, and radical democrats, who wanted anything from republicanism to Utopia, was the most striking factor of the Tuscan Risorgimento. It was this that kept the moderates and many of the leading aristocracy so loyal to Leopold in 1859. Nevertheless, when the crunch came, if Tuscany joined the new kingdom of Italy, it was above all through the actions of Bettino Ricasoli.

NOTES

1. Illustrated by the story of the Governor of Livorno, who was taken to task for not protesting against an inflammatory speech by Guerrazzi delivered before him. The Governor pleaded that he'd been fast asleep — against which the police contended that he'd been awake for at least part of the time.
2. Though Mazzini later admitted that Tuscany was not particularly receptive to his propaganda.

FOUR

Once Ricasoli took over the heavily encumbered family estates in 1829, he began devoting himself to what he called his 'apostolate' — that is, the education of his wife, his daughter and his peasants. By then the problems of agriculture were already getting serious, although they only grew to dangerous proportions during the lean years of the 1850s. *Mezzadria* was hidebound and often uneconomic. The peasants were usually in debt to their landlords, and there were the perennial problems about division of the spoils. Ridolfi, for one, declared that he only received a tenth of the produce from eight of his best farms. What incentive was there to invest money in agriculture, he asked, if one's efforts were dissipated by dishonesty and wasted through ignorance?

For it must be admitted that most of the Chianti *contadini* were unversed about the simplest modern methods of farming. The olive groves that had been so enthusiastically planted in the 1780s were being ruined by their inability to cope with either soil erosion, manuring or pruning. It was the same with livestock: they didn't even grow their own fodder. In many ways, thought Ricasoli, the Tuscan proprietors ought to answer for this: too often they only visited their estates for the *vendemmia* or to shoot small birds. He also blamed the priests, whom he considered over-numerous and slothful. But at least he didn't blame the *contadini* for their ignorance and indolence. He simply felt that it was his duty to instruct them.

And so in patriarchal fashion he got down to the job. (In many ways he was a feudal anachronism, looking backwards as well as forwards — to the point of trying on the armour of his medieval ancestors to recapture their spirit.) In his 'Regolamento Agrario della Fattoria di Brolio' he codified the laws of his domain, laying down the principles of right practice for everything from the care of implements to the problems of manuring or feeding of animals. The *Administration* threatened to *take steps against* those who failed to get up early in the morning, to take care of their tools, to keep their gardens in good shape, and to ensure that their family were instructed in Christianity. The *Master* would not concede the so-called right of dowry to any bride, unless he was satisfied that she was fit to be a good wife and a good mother. Obsessed with the moral education of his peasants, he gave religious instruction on Sundays, and read his own sermons. Moreover, this Puritan outlook was coupled with a desire to regulate even the minutest details — just as when he was in power in 1860. Bulletins were pasted on the walls of Brolio: 'The Master notifies the peasants that this is the time to put lime on corn; lime is a sure protection against the fox . . .' Like Gladstone, Ricasoli was possessed of a sure belief that his will most closely approximated to the divine intention. It was 'a happy thing to know that my will ought to be your will, since that which I will is to do you good in every way'.

In 1848 his work in Chianti was interrupted to play a part in Florentine public life. Besides, after the death of his wife, loneliness struck him and his apostolate lost its meaning. 'Agriculture pleased me; now it is insufferable,' he complained. (It was only when he was involved in reclamation work in the Maremma that his interest began to revive.) However, his carefully thought-out ideas for the future of Italy now began to mature. These were often framed in letters to his brother Vincenzo. Indeed Vincenzo, now an officer in the regular Piedmontese army, did much to convert Bettino to the cause of a united Italy under Piedmont. 'Piedmont today is all of Italy,' he claimed. To which Bettino replied: 'I abhor eunuch projects, and I consider eunuch all those which more or less leave Italy divided into parts.' Once his mind was made up, it was for the others to follow.

Some of them were already beginning to feel the same way: indeed the acceptance of the idea of a united Italy under the House of Savoy by activists of divergent leanings was the crux of the Risorgimento. Manin (the great defender of the Venetian Republic of 1848) renounced his republican convictions shortly before his death in 1857, and said to Turin: 'Make Italy and I am with you. If not — no.' Gioberti — the propagator of the neo-Guelph idea of an Italian federation under the Pope — also recanted and accepted Sardinian hegemony as the only hope. Garibaldi himself wrote to the Sicilian conspirators in 1859: 'Unite yourselves to our programme — Italy and Victor Emmanuel — indissolubly.' Even Mazzini finally surrendered his convictions before the altar of unity. Writing to the Sicilians in March 1860 he said: 'It is no longer a question of Republic or Monarchy; it is a question of National Unity, of existence or non-existence . . . If Italy wishes to be a monarchy under the House of Savoy, let it be so.' But the Tuscans felt differently. In opting for national unity under the Piedmontese, Ricasoli was at odds with virtually every other leading Tuscan. That he attained his object in the teeth of their opposition was his main achievement.

Clearly, time was not on his side. The growing discontent in Tuscany was all too evident. For one thing, the agricultural system was shaken by a series of disasters. From 1846, Chianti had a series of bad seasons: in 1854 severe frosts were accompanied by an outbreak of cholera — which returned again the following year, coupled with heavy flooding. On top of this there was a fair amount of rural disorder. Vagabonds were described as 'besieging' landlords for charity — a far cry from the traditional forms of alms-begging. By 1852 these vagabonds had organised themselves into sizeable groups and went about terrorising the peasantry with threats to destroy their crops and vineyards unless paid off. Ricasoli himself thought it unwise to leave his estates, and when warned that the country around was swarming with aggressive vagrants, replied that he wished to meet one face to face and fight it out. In some ways — from, for instance, the point of view of violence — Chianti in mid-nineteenth century was more like the Middle Ages than the peaceful area that we know today. And then, to add to the troubles, the grapes were hit by 'fungus crittogama', the dreaded white mould, which brought ruin to many farmers; Ricasoli only saved himself and his peasants by going in for silk-worms. The inadequacies of *mezzadria* were more than ever apparent, and some of the leading lights of the Georgofili began to question its usefulness. Ridolfi even urged a 'suspension' of *mezzadria*. Heresy in the Vatican! But there is little doubt that the economic discontent of the fifties (and the repercussions it had on the intellectually and politically aware in Florence), encouraged the growth of nationalism. The presence of Austrian troops, involving the Tuscan government in great expense, only fuelled it further. Incidents between Tuscans and Austrians created martyrs and fed anti-Austrian feeling. The Tuscan constitution was suspended, then abrogated, and the death penalty was restored. All of which began to bring a gradual, but decisive, change of opinion towards Piedmont. Vieusseux could write: 'Piedmont is considered, with reason, as the last anchor of Italy's salvation, and it is a notable thing how the Piedmontese party keeps growing even among those who were most averse to Charles Albert.' Basically the Tuscans still desired autonomy. But, as time wore on, they began to regard Piedmont with rather more goodwill.

In 1858 came the crucial meeting between Napoleon III and Cavour at Plombières, where the deal was done that settled the fate of Italy. While nothing was precisely fixed for Tuscany, Napoleon favoured an enlarged kingdom of Central Italy, to include Tuscany and parts of the Papal States. This would be based on Florence, and might, he suggested, be given to his cousin. Certainly he envisaged it as separate from the Piedmontese kingdom, which would incorporate

Lombardy and Venetia.

A number of conflicting interests were involved. The Austrians sought to preserve and tighten their control on what they already had. The French would have liked to see the lessening of Austrian influence and some sort of buffer state established: certainly they were not seeking a powerful and independent Italian state. The Italians themselves held a bewildering multiplicity of views from a federation to a unified nation. The English — whose negligent command of the seas made Garibaldi's crossing from Sicily to the mainland possible — were generally favourable to the idea of Italian unity, especially after Palmerston became Prime Minister and Lord John Russell Foreign Secretary in June 1859. After all, it was in the British interest to create a friendly independent Italian state as a Mediterranean counterpoise to either France or Austria. And, of course, there was Mrs Browning. Also, as Trevelyan put it: 'The fact that the Irish were on the side of the Pope, and occasionally disturbed the pro-Italian meetings, dispelled the last doubts of the average Englishman as to the propriety of the movement.'

By now, several distinct groups of Tuscan nationalists could be identified. There were the members of La Farina's National Society under Marchese Bartolommei, an ardent young nationalist and also a Georgofilo. There were unattached liberals who played a conservative role until after the revolution had been made by yet a third faction — the radical democrats under men like Dolfi, Cironi and Rubieri. From 1857 some members of the second group, including Ricasoli, Ridolfi and Peruzzi, had formed the 'Biblioteca Civile dell'Italiano', intending to publish monthly and educate their readers in *Italianità*. (Fellow Georgofili thought this rash. But gentlemen from Piedmont, such as d'Azeglio, began to make visits to Brolio to look at Ricasoli's silk-worms.) In March 1859 they came out into the open with 'Toscana e Austria' which put the Tuscan case against Austria, and was taken up as a nationalist manifesto. From now onwards such leading Tuscans as Peruzzi, Ricasoli, Cambray-Digny, Ginori, Landini, Corsini and Galeotti (at least three of whom had estates in Chianti) did all they could to bring Tuscany in on Piedmont's side in the war against Austria. But Leopold II and his Minister, Baldasseroni, clung to their policy of neutrality. Which placed his supporters in a dilemma. On the one hand they wanted to expel the Austrians from Italy, on the other to preserve the dynasty.

Yet what they feared above all was social revolution. As Giorgini put it: 'Let the people loose in the streets, and you will never get them back home again.'

So when Dolfi (the radical baker) and his friends successfully staged a revolution on 27 April and forced Leopold to quit, the moderates promptly joined in, if only to control it and stop what they feared might be 'the victory of the Reds'. But within a few days they were taking all the credit. Although Ricasoli had rushed off from Florence on the night of 26 April in an attempt to fetch troops from Turin to contain the uprising, his own secretary, Tabarrini, was soon referring to it as a revolution organised by aristocrats.

Yet in the end Tuscany's future was decided by two things: the influence of outside events on Tuscan opinion, and Ricasoli's dictatorship. The revolution of 1859 was not caused by any popular desire for Italian unity; far from it. Many rural communes remained faithful to the old order until they saw which way the wind was blowing. The Gonfaloniere of Firenzuola, for instance, hesitated ten days before confirming the support of his municipality.

Gradually, however, Ricasoli established himself at the helm in Florence with the same dictatorial style that he had shown with his Chianti peasants. Certainly his conversion of Tuscany from its tradition of autonomy to a fusion with Piedmont must rate as one of the most astute manipulations of propaganda on record. Though what now sounds like political brainwashing was to Ricasoli merely a form of moral education.

The existing press laws he kept. In his words, 'The time for free discussions will come. Now is the time for manly effort.' Or, as he put it, 'The government, faithful executor of the wisdom of the country, has left to the press in these times the liberty to help, and not to harm, the national cause.' Nationalists 'enlightened' ignorant people about Leopold and the Austrians, using myths — such as the alleged order to bombard Florence — to discredit the old Grand Duke. (Also that the tricolour flag meant religion in the hearts of men and a reduction in the price of salt.) 'The formation of a great kingdom of Italy under the constitutional sceptre of Victor Emmanuel is demanded by good sense, morality and civilisation,' preached Ricasoli. That Napoleon's antagonism frustrated the immediate achievement of this goal made no difference: Ricasoli refused to contemplate any other solution. Pasolini, a moderate from Romagna, was later to admit that but for Ricasoli's intransigence, a separate kingdom in central Italy would have been an accomplished fact. The 'Iron Baron' was completely inflexible. He would have no truck with any of the plans put forward as alternatives to fusion with Piedmont. 'Won't they understand,' he insisted, 'that the cause of Italy must be sustained openly, solemnly, on its merits, before Europe.' By the end of 1859 Napoleon was weakening and Ricasoli pushing through the Assembly a rash of unifying decrees concerned with weights and measures, money and the military code. And yet there was a touch of ambivalence about his politics. To the extent that he was nationalistic, he was a revolutionary; yet socially he was conservative. On the one hand he could write to Cavour in May 1860 that 'The Royal Government ought to . . . tolerate and even support and help the aid given by the Italians to the Sicilian insurrection, if this can be done covertly and at least without compromising ourselves too much.' On the other, he banned Mazzini from Tuscany — although he subsequently claimed that he would have been happy to have given him refuge at Brolio. (Would Mazzini, one wonders, have made many converts among the Chianti peasants?)

Eventually France backed down, but stipulated that plebiscites should be held on the issue of unification. Fairly conducted, these might well have proved a stumbling block — not so much through reaction as simply indifference. After all, the municipal elections of October 1859 were characterised by large-scale abstention. A clue to his fears can be found in Ricasoli's copy of his biography by Dall' Ongaro. Where the author asserted that the plebiscite was a spontaneous popular effusion, he noted drily in the margin: 'Ricasoli believes it possible to doubt this assertion as too absolute.' By which he meant, of course, that his government had done its utmost to arrange that the outcome of the vote should be in accordance with their desires.

To ensure that this happened he took every precaution. Reactionaries were put under close police supervision. A board of censors for the theatre was set up with instructions to 'aid the work of the National Risorgimento of Italy'. Teachers were told they must have and affection for the Fatherland and for Italy. 'Let youth,' pronounced Ricasoli, 'even in the penetralia of knowledge, find the Fatherland, and listen to the voice of liberty.' (Would he have agreed with Professor Pigli who, in the bad old days of the earthly paradise, used to turn his lectures on physiology into patriotic orations, and located Italy in the pineal gland?) Even priests were reported if they refused to pray for the king. For Ricasoli's struggle was in part with the clergy, who by no means all shared his view, and were just as inclined to be dictatorial themselves. In a sense, it was a battle between the government and the priests for the peasants' votes. The government vetoed certain pamphlets they were distributing among the faithful, and went so far as to threaten ecclesiastical property. 'We are at grips with the priests,' Ricasoli claimed. In his view, they should stick to their spiritual mission and not meddle in politics.

At all events, he set the government machinery working overtime. The Prefect of Arezzo received an increased expense allowance in December 1859 and by the following March was able to report that he was 'neglecting nothing so that the approaching vote should respond worthily to the cares of the government and the expectation of the country'. Florentine ladies wrote letters to their *fattori* and peasants expressing their views. Prince Strozzi lost no opportunity to advertise his desire for annexation in his social activities. In the final analysis it was a matter of active nationalists and the administration persuading an apathetic peasantry how to vote. A 'scruple for truth' forced Capponi to admit that the 'numerical majority' was not perhaps at one with Ricasoli. However, when the day finally came, an overwhelming percentage voted for the union (even if some of Ricasoli's own peasants tried to knock over the voting urns). We may never know whether the figures were cooked, but in March 1860 Tuscany was annexed to Piedmont. Against all the odds, Ricasoli had won.

NOTE

1. Even if the latter was still merely the desire of a few of the intelligentsia. Cavour's representative in Naples claimed that there were not one hundred believers in Italian unity in the kingdom's seven million inhabitants.

FIVE

On top of all this Bettino Ricasoli created Chianti — that is, the wine as we drink it today. The taste of the robust, dry, fruity liquid that emerges from a bottle of Chianti Classico (the really big wines from a jealously guarded area) is something that we owe chiefly to him.

Long before his time the Georgofili (which incidentally remains the senior agricultural association in Europe) had experimented with different sorts of Tuscan grapes, blending red Canaiolo, Malvasia, San Gioveto and white Trebbiano. At the end of the eighteenth century, in fact, exports of Chianti to London — then the principal overseas market — were higher than they are today. But gradually the business fell off. Tastes, in the Age of Elegance, became more demanding. The fragrant clarets of Bordeaux and the noble *cuvées* of Burgundy began to convert the mere act of eating into a symphony, even a philosophy; and with this the coarser wines of Chianti could no longer compete. Besides, a great deal of non-genuine wine was shipped over from Livorno, which brought the reputation of Chianti into disrepute. What is more, it simply didn't age. After three or four years even the best vintages turned into vinegar.

The trouble, of course, was that many of the cultivators were not up to the job. Grapes they could grow, but they had little experience in the subtleties of turning the juice into wine. Most of them just sloshed it around, making no attempt to sift out bad or unripe fruit, nor to strike any balance between the acidity and the sugar contents. When Ricasoli took over, he found that they were more interested in raising pigs. And the absentee landlords did little to help. Clearly, something had to be done. A good deal more control and blending were required.

In their experiments, the Georgofili had found that an equal blend of Canaiolo, San Gioveto, Roverusto and Mammolo produced a strong, richly coloured wine that could be relied on to age well, whereas a variation mixing Occhio di pernice, Trebbiano, Canaiolo and Mammolo, again in equal parts, gave a less brilliantly coloured wine but with a more delicate flavour.

Ricasoli noted these experiments and made some of his own. These, in the end, he wrote, confirm that Chianti wine draws most of its bouquet (which is what I aim for) as well as its vigour from Sangioveto; from Canaiolo a sweetness that tempers the harshness of the latter without detracting from the bouquet; whereas Malvasia (which could be used less in wines that are to be aged) tends to accentuate the taste while at the same time making it fresher and lighter and more suitable for daily use at the table.

On these criteria the basis for Chianti Classico wine was established and has remained more or less constant ever since. Pride of place goes to *Sangioveto* which accounts for between 60 and 70 per cent of production. But it needs to be blended with the others, for without them the wine would be too heavy and too hot. *Canaiolo*, once described as the grape of the Etruscans, has a greater sugar content, yet is far less juicy and tends to be unreliable: one year the plants will be full of fruit and the next year almost bare. *Malvasia* grapes are the most succulent, but of course they are white, and in any case they cannot stand up to frost. *Trebbiano* are the juiciest, but have too much acidity and not enough sugar — a little bit goes a long way and (in the words of my factor, Alvaro) is a soup without salt. However, blend them together and you get a balanced wine. In substance Chianti Classico has stuck faithfully to the recipe Ricasoli laid down well over a century ago.

Not, as it happens, that things went as smoothly as he had hoped. In 1835 he formed a company to propagate the wines of Chianti, offering 1,000 shares of 600 lire each to public subscription. But they were not taken up, and within a short time the enterprise foundered. Then during the 1850s, as we noted, the vineyards were hit by a virulent form of mildew or white mould which took seven years to get under control. Three-quarters of the Tuscan production was lost in 1853, and by 1855 the yield from the grand-ducal estates had fallen from an average (between 1830 and 1850) of 13,000 hectolitres to a bare 1,200. In desperation growers tried to deal with the trouble by washing the grapes with soap and water and even covering them with dust. Finally a remedy was found by spraying the vines with powdered sulphur. But by this time a good many of the *mezzadri* had given up in disgust, unable to cover their costs and meet the taxman's bills. (At which point Ricasoli stepped in and took over their holdings, to such an extent that in his heyday he owned over 300 farms.)

By 1860 the production of Italian wines was about 28 million hectolitres, most of it of poor quality and uneconomically made compared to the more sophisticated French production (which topped 68 million hectolitres in 1866). Vittorio degli Albizzi attributed this to the intercultivation of vines with olives and other plants, which in his view damaged the growth of the vine. Perhaps he was right. But at any rate, by advocating a 'coltura esclusiva' he anticipated the 'specialised vineyards' as we have them today.

However, when Florence became, for a brief five years, the capital of Italy in 1866, a host of bon viveurs moved in along with the Palace and the Ministers, and the old Tuscan city was suddenly swept up into the Piedmontese way of life. Traditional wine shops where previously one had been able to eat and drink the local wines to one's heart's content for 50 centesimi were transformed into smart restaurants and cafés purveying vermouth and *cappuccini*. The Bottegone on the Piazza del Duomo, for so long a favourite gathering place, blossomed out as the 'Gloria d'Italia', and the headquarters of the Melini firm in Via Calzaioli was so splendidly refurbished that a traditionist sighed: 'Oh my good old Florence, where have you gone?' And he might have said the same for Chianti wines. Both at court and in society, French vintages were exclusively served (this was, after all, *La Belle Epoque*) and Chianti was relegated to the humbler haunts with engaging names such as Beppe Sudicio, Cencio Porcheria and Gigi Porco — which can roughly be translated as Sweaty Joe's, Cencio's Pigsty, and Gigi the Pig. For all this, some discerning gourmets thought that Chianti was underrated. The Prince of Wales commented that the wines of Fiesole were most drinkable, while Queen Victoria, when staying at the Villa Palmieri, was full of praises for 'the excellent *vin santo* of the Chianti hills'.

It was at this point that the vineyards of Europe were hit by a disastrous disease. The *Encyclopedia Britannica* gives a graphic description of the *phylloxera*, or grape-louse, together with the alarming intelligence that the eggs from a single female can produce 25 million offspring within seven months. It appears to have originated among the wild vines in Colorado and to have been brought over to Europe through the importation of American plants for grafting purposes. At any rate the disease spread from France, and soon grew to gigantic proportions. In all parts of the world the vineyards were stricken. The vines became stunted and lost their leaves; such grapes as they bore were wrinkled and useless. Statistics from the commune of Graveson, to quote just one example, show the extent of the calamity. Whereas the annual production of wine there had been about 220,000 gallons in 1867, by 1873 it had fallen to 1,100 gallons.

There were three things that could be done. One was to kill the parasite itself. Another to destroy it along with the infected vines, and replace them with healthy plants; the third to graft American vines which, through long exposure to the *phylloxera*, were immune to its ravages. On the whole this proved best, and there is now not a single plant in Europe that has not been thus inoculated against the killing disease.

Needless to say, Chianti suffered like the rest. But the shortages caused by the wholesale drop in French production played in the favour of the Italian growers, and exports from Italy rose from 500,000 hectolitres in 1878 to two and a half million in 1883. There was a renewed demand for Chianti, though unhappily a good deal of poor-quality stuff from other regions was passed off by unscrupulous merchants in the famous straw flagons, which hardly helped its image, nor indeed the price that the genuine vintages could command. All the same, there was a concerted effort to market them.

That the wine should travel unharmed had always been a problem. No one realised this better than Laborel Melini, who had taken over his family firm that had been operating at Pontassieve since 1705, and among other things handled the shipping for the Marchese Albizzi's estate at Nipozzano.

The traditional way of sealing Chianti bottles had always been with a layer of oil between the cork and the wine. On the whole this was foolproof — were it not that people abroad, unaware that the oil must be removed, or not knowing how to do so (with a dab of cotton or a flick of the wrist) were inclined to drink it too, with disastrous reactions from the palate. So the problem, (to quote Melini) was as follows:

> Chianti does not find favour abroad if shipped in fiaschi with oil, because foreigners don't understand the function of the oil. But if shipped in ordinary bottles Chianti fails to please, because the overseas consumer likes the traditional Chianti fiasco. What is therefore needed is a container that combines the characteristic shape of the fiasco with the resistance of the bottle.

With the help of a glass firm in Pontassieve, he finally produced a flagon that was strong enough to stand up to automatic corking. So at least the outward aspect of Chianti as we know it was assured. There remained its content to be defined.

Once again, there was the old question of custom. Eighty or a hundred years ago (with the exception of a few big estates like Brolio or Antinori) the grower sold his produce soon after the *vendemmia* to a middleman for so much per barrel of fifty litres. It was collected on the spot in uncorked flagons sealed simply with half an inch of oil, which were then loaded on a special cart, from six to eight hundred at a time. The buyer paid cash on delivery, and the seller provided lunch for the carrier and food for the horses.

There were two grades of wine: top-quality Chianti which could not be marketed before the following June, that is, nine months after the vintage; and the second, more ordinary wine, dubbed 'half-Chianti', which could be sold as early as February. Apart from this restriction, what happened to the wine after it left the grower's premises was entirely the merchant's affair. Which led to a good deal of abuse. Some of it was mixed with inferior stuff but still sold as Chianti; some of it was sent as filler to France, and even appeared under a Burgundy label. Quite obviously a more effective control was needed for the protection of both producer and consumer.

In September 1895 the 'Association of Wine-growers of Gironde' was formed to safeguard the wines of Bordeaux, and the efforts of its 3,500 members proved so effective, both as vigilantes and as a pressure group with the authorities, that a similar association, known as the 'Sindacato Enologico Chiantigiano' was established in 1903. Its object was to ensure that only from grapes grown within the area could Chianti wine be produced.

The difficulty now was to define the area. What, after all, was Chianti? Historically speaking, the Lega del Chianti had been just the three communes of Castellina, Radda and Gaiole. Yet traditionally it meant the hills between Florence and Siena, which included the Val di Greve and the Val d'Ema, from which many of the best vintages came. In the interest of the great name itself, surely they must be part of Chianti? Against this was the fact that the hard rocky soil of the old Lega lands was quite different from the fatter earth in the valleys nearer Florence, imparting a distinctive flavour to the wines from each region.

Great were the arguments, vicious the polemics, ingenious the manoeuvres of those who feared to be excluded from the favoured zone. In 1904 the government turned the proposition down. In 1920 a Ministerial commission was appointed to study the matter, and eighteen months later a project was approved by the lower house of parliament. The Senate endorsed it on 12 May 1922, though with some modifications, which necessitated its return to the Camera; these changes were agreed by the parliamentary commission for agriculture the following March. The Council of Ministers then approved their revised text, but the law was never promulgated. Instead what Ricasoli would have called a eunuch piece of legislation emerged (No. 497 of 7 March 1924) which linked the concept of Chianti — and indeed of any other regional wine — not to the actual area in which it was produced, but to the 'special and constant characteristics' for which it was known. Another two years went by before even this law was published.

In the meantime the growers had taken steps of their own. On

14 May 1924 thirty of them from Castellina, Gaiole, Greve, Radda and part of Castelnuovo Berardenga met in the municipality at Radda and formed a 'Union to safeguard the genuine wine of Chianti and its provenance', which subsequently became known as the 'Consorzio del Vino Chianti Classico'. For its emblem they chose the ancient crest of the Lega del Chianti, a black cock on a golden background. Its area was defined by the boundaries of the communes in question, and (as a sop to certain influential producers) included part of the commune of San Casciano and a small bit of Poggibonsi.

Three years later, not to be outdone (and likewise to back up their products) the growers from Rufina, Montalbano and hills north of Florence, formed a second *Consorzio* with as their imprimatur a pink angel on a light blue background. From this hallmark the wines of that area — subsequently enlarged to take in most of the Florentine vineyards outside the boundaries of Chianti Classico — became known as Chianti 'Putto'.

In due course the producers from Siena, Arezzo and Pisa followed suit and formed their own local unions, so that in conclusion a Ministerial decree in July 1932 defined seven zones that were entitled to call their wines 'Chianti'. These were: Chianti Classico, Montalbano, Rufina, Colli Fiorentini, Colli Senesi, Colli Aretini and Colline Pisane. Which meant, in effect, the greater part of the Tuscan vineyards. But at the heart of them all (as a glance at the map will show) was the traditional, historic area that had always been the only real Chianti, now styled Chianti Classico, which still produced, if not better wine, at least the most prestigious vintages. ('There's no Chianti outside Chianti' still remains a bone of contention.) And when in the 1960s the wholesale programme of replanting specialised vineyards under the auspices of the Common Market got under way, the primacy of Chianti Classico became progressively clearer. In the last ten years, every suitable patch of land has been bulldozed and re-vined, and a bottle of Classico fetches a considerably higher price than its opposite numbers.

This is neither by accident nor design. In the hills of classic Chianti, the position of the land, the rocky nature of the soil, and the climate itself all combine, like in the Côte d'Or, to give the best possible conditions for the production of a full, dry, robust wine. It has always been so. Until World War Two a property in Chianti was greatly prized: if a Tuscan wanted to stress that a business or a deal was a solid, copper-bottomed proposition, he would exclaim 'Vale un podere nel Chianti.' ('As good as a farm in Chianti.') It was only in the 1950s, with the sudden spurt of light industry and the exodus of so many young farmers to take up work in the factories that the old *mezzadria* system collapsed and farms were abandoned. When I first drove down the Chiantigiana road I was astonished to see so few vineyards in the heart of Chianti. But this was in 1962 at the bottom of the recession. (At that time, I am told, there were some 60,000 empty farmhouses in Tuscany.) Arcadian in its seclusion, the little world of Chianti had cracked apart. The ancient way of agriculture had been destroyed, and had not yet been replaced by the new order we know today.

But, after all, to the eyes of the historian this was only a momentary aberration — just a wink in time.

SIX

In the summer of 1944, for the first time in four centuries, war returned to Chianti. For months the allied advance up Italy had been halted down by the Garigliano south of Rome, and up in Tuscany the peasants stolidly went on with the old rhythm of ploughing, planting and harvesting; milling, making cheese; pressing the grapes and the olives. Some of the men had been conscripted, but that was about all. The unvarying cycle of the natural year continued.

But then, in the spring, the Germans arrived to set up strongpoints and store depots for the defence of Florence. They began fortifying what was known as the 'Irmgard' line along the high ridge that stretched from Coltibuono through Radda and Castellina, and further back the 'Karen' line running westwards from San Giovanni Val d'Arno over the peak of San Michele and thence through Greve up to the hills beyond. At Grignano, I am told, like elsewhere, the peasants were turned out of their houses and the German troops moved in: the *torre* became a depot with self-propelling guns and lorries parked all the way up the old Roman road and a huge store of petrol drums was stacked under the concealing branches of the oak trees below. The partisans began to be active — lying in wait for the German supply trucks with anti-tyre mines and caltrops (devices that landed with a spike in the air whichever way thrown) and ambushing sentries or work parties, even though the reprisals were brutal. Alvaro relates, for instance, that when a German was picked off at the crossroads near Selvole, all the houses in the neighbourhood were burnt to the ground (including his own, near the fourteenth-century *torre* at Castiglione which, being full of hay, was completely destroyed) and that, on top of this, some of the villagers at Selvole were taken out and shot. Indeed an inscription on the church records their death 'through German barbarity'.

Yet sometimes the peasants contrived to have their revenge. Around this time a party of Germans drove up to Montagliari, the little group of houses below the *capella* of the Madonna della Neve, and told the male inhabitants that they were to be taken off to 'serve the Führer'. But first they must round up all the livestock and poultry. While the men set about this task, the women got busy, plying their unwanted guests with all the wine that they could find; once the Germans were ripe for the plucking, they signalled to their menfolk who returned from the woods and quietly cut their throats.

On 4 June, the Allies entered Rome, and soon after this the names in the radio communiqués began to have a familiar ring: Radicofani, Val d'Orcia, Val di Chiana. By the beginning of July, the 6th South African Division had reached Palazzuolo, to the east of Castelnuovo Berardenga, on the Siena-Arezzo highway, with the 4th British Division on their right, the 24th Guards Brigade on their left, and further to the west the French units. Opposing them were elements of the crack Hermann Goering Division, with to their east the 1st German Paratroop Division and to their west the 4th Paratroop Division — all élite troops. At this stage the German line of defence ran east from Monte Luco, with outposts and observation nests protected by infantry well forward of it. A particularly strong point was the Castello di Brolio, from which — as the South Africans later discovered — the German observation officers had a bird's-eye view of their positions. For a week fighting raged around Monte Benichi, which neither side could hold for long, as they were immediately shelled and mortared by the opposition. And then, on 14 July — the anniversary of the fall of the Bastille — came news that the French had entered Siena in time to hold an impressive ceremony in the Campo, bedecked for the occasion with tricolours. The Germans appeared to be thinning out, and the advance into Chianti began.

Ahead, as reconnaissance, went the Sherman tanks of the Natal Mounted Rifles. Close on their heels, and often alongside them, came two brigades of motorised infantry: the South Africans, and the 24th Guards Brigade, each of which was accompanied by a regiment of tanks. Intermingled with these troops were the guns of the divisional artillery, the signals units, the sappers, the supply services and the field ambulances. In country such as this, you could hardly speak of a line. It was more a matter of spearheads: infantry, tanks and all the supporting arms advancing along roads and tracks until they bumped into the enemy — whom they would then try to dislodge or out-flank.

The Germans were strongly entrenched along the strategic line of hills around Castellina, which changed hands three times before being finally taken by the New Zealand Division. On 18 July, the Royal Natal Carbineers entered Radda, and despite heavy shelling and mortaring, the Witwatersrand Rifles cum De La Rey took up positions to the north and west of the town — most uncomfortably too, since they were in full sight of the Germans across the valley at Volpaia. However, on the next day, helped by concentrations of fire from the entire divisional artillery, they fought their way up the wooded slopes to take Volpaia and the heights of Querciabella behind. To their right, the Guards Brigade moved forwards, turning the enemy's left flank; to their left the New Zealanders moved north along the high ground via Pietrafitta and Ricavo in the direction of San Donato (along the same route that the Florentine army had taken in a reverse direction 684 years before to Montaperti). On 20 July they were at Grignano, while the Royal Natal Carbineers, following the old Roman road past Monte Rotondo, La Balza, Bracciano and Le Stinche, occupied Panzano.

Now that the Irmgard line had been cracked, the Germans were withdrawing to their next area of defence — the Karen line that ran from Monte Maggio through Greve, and was manned by the 356th Infantry Division. But in the meantime, the German artillery and anti-tank guns hardly stopped for a minute. There was heavy fighting between Poggio alla Croce and Sillano, and the South Africans had a nasty time edging their way down the river towards Greve, over-looked as they were from both flanks. (The brigade headquarters was set up in a woodland glade just by the *cappella* of S. Maria della Neve.) But once the Guards had captured Monte San Michele to the west, they were able to force the enemy north of Greve and secure positions astride the Chiantigiana road.

From maps and aerial photographs, it was estimated that there were no less than twelve potential major demolitions, bridges and so forth, in the first three miles of road running north from the town. Predictably the Germans blew them all up. Nevertheless, working under intense and accurate fire, the bulldozers and bridging parties managed to put up Bailey-bridge substitutes. Meanwhile, the fighting was as heavy as ever: a company of Springboks that forced its way across the river bend and on to the high ground beyond lost all three platoon officers and all platoon sergeants. The Germans, clinging to their concealed machine-gun nests, poured a withering fire on them until the pressure of the attack became overwhelming. 'A note-worthy feature of the enemy's tactics at this time, was that he engaged his attackers from ranges as close as ten yards,' wrote a South African officer afterwards, 'He made full use of the cover provided by the vegetation and of the ideally defensive nature of the terrain. He stuck to his positions, in well camouflaged "nests" until the last moment.'[1]

Against the dogged German rear-guard action, the Allies could only creep slowly forwards, fighting for each bit of ground: it took the great circle of steel and manpower three weeks to make its way through Chianti and finally reach Florence. But one by one the strategic points fell: Strada to the Guards, San Casciano to the Kiwis, Impruneta to the Springboks. Here some of the heaviest fighting took place, and hereby hangs a story. In 1968, I revisited the battlefield with Colonel Anson Lloyd, who 24 years previously had been a troop commander in the 4/22 Field Artillery Regiment with the 6th South African Armoured Division. Inevitably the conversation led to the bombardment of Impruneta itself and above all, its exquisite church, S. Maria dell'Impruneta. Anson had been ordered to direct the fire, but he denied that his guns had ever been aimed at the church — in fact he was horrified by the notion. But as we entered the precincts our eyes were caught by a marble plaque which I had never previously noticed. It said: 'This church was destroyed by Allied bombardment on 28 July 1944.' Dramatically, the sacristan told us about the events of that day, but unfortunately for his peace of mind Anson had to leave without hearing the end of the story. For the priest concluded by saying,

> Before the bombardment the church was rather ugly inside. The bombs destroyed the baroque interior and disclosed the marvellous quattrocento building behind. Now the Belle Arte have restored it all to its former medieval beauty. Even the Della Robbias have been put back together so that you can hardly notice the damage. So in a way the bombing was a godsend. The church is far more beautiful now.

NOTE

1. W. L. Fielding, *With the 6th Div.*, Pietermaritzburg, 1946.

SEVEN

The four weeks of fighting took their toll. But once the front had passed, like a summer tornado — leaving fields littered with twisted guns and burnt-out, tenantless tanks — the country soon returned to its old rhythms and habits, just as it had been for the last fifty (or five hundred) years. Some Vespas brought new discordant sounds,[1] but it was not until the late fifties that the *miracolo italiano*, the post-war industrial surge, began to have a disruptive effect on Chianti, draining the peasants away to become factory workers in the brash new suburbs of Florence and Prato; tempting them to exchange the harsh traditional life of their hillside farms for the gleaming, soulless symbols of modern affluence that brought neither leisure nor peace of mind, but simply bills. For a few more years the old ways continued among the vineyards and the chestnut woods: the women baking flat round loaves over the wood-ash in the bread-ovens, slapping pasta into shape on the huge kitchen tables, gathering herbs in the fields (bitter sorrel, chicory or dandelion leaves for salad), turning the sheep's milk into soft, spongy *ricotta* — while the men went about their business of ploughing with white oxen, weeding between the vines, grafting and pruning. The shepherds still took their flocks up the stone-walled pathway, called la Maremmana, to graze them in the high Apennine pastures. Even then Grignano was one of their stopping places: up to eighty at a time would spend the night here, sleeping in the hay, their lambs in the courtyard.

This is how it was when we first motored through on a radiant June afternoon in 1962: special country, not unreal, yet not entirely removed from Arcadia. As we all lunched outside Nello's trattoria in the piazza at Greve (which, alas, no longer exists) my mother put our unspoken thoughts into words. 'I have travelled all over the world,' she said, 'but I've never found a place in which I'd rather live than this.'

Writing these lines now under a walnut tree that was only a sapling when I came, the memories crystallise into images like slides projected on a wall: but memory can play one tricks, and it is perhaps just as well that, riffling through the pages of an old leather-bound diary, I find that I have already scribbled down the story of how Chianti became my home.

The following year, after a cheerful month in St Moritz at the Chesa sur l'En — that cuckoo-clock castle which is more a club than a hotel — gathering material with Cornell Capa, René and Rosellina Burri for a series of skiing articles, I was heading back to Cairo (where we still lived and where I had some business activities). Rosellina had suggested that a country house in Chianti called the 'Tenuta di Ricavo', which had been turned into a hotel, might be a good spot for my mother to spend the summer, and since my route ran through Florence, it seemed a pity to pass so close without investigating the possibilities. Now let us switch to the diary:

1.4.63

To drift rather indolently down the Autostrade del Sole — the Bologna-Firenze stretch — was to reaffirm my impression that this most spectacular of roads is my favourite piece of motoring. Especially if the hood is down. Although William and Elaine Broadhead had given me the address of a notable eating place in Florence (the Trattoria Camillo, I think it was called) I'd made such a late start and driven with such a delicate right foot that it was past two o'clock when I reached the end of the autostrada, and rather than face the Vespas and Seicentos opted for lunch behind the plate-glass windows at the motel where one could keep an eye on the luggage on the rear seat. For a moment I felt sufficiently lazy to miss out Florence altogether, but a sense of the fitness of things prevailed and I made tracks, as undeviously as possible, for the Palazzo Pitti where dodging schools of sightseers took up more time than actually looking at the pictures. (It was the 'free week' for museums in Italy.) Then, after wandering over the Ponte Vecchio to the Palazzo della Signoria, I realised that time was passing and that Ricavo had to be discovered as well as somewhere to spend the night if it was closed. Out therefore past the Ugolino golf course and along the delectable Chianti road, through Greve and a reassuring sign directing one towards Ricavo. Even after only one previous trip in the opposite direction the soft and increasingly romantic scenery seemed fairly familiar. This was the part of the world, surely, that coming up from Rome last June, mother had said was the right place to live? There, looking over my right shoulder, was a medieval castello which had caught our eye, floating on an eminence in the valley. And there, a few minutes later, was the rather forbidding tower of Castellina in Chianti. Directed by the petrol pump attendant, I drove eagerly along a white-dusted byroad across the hills and down to Ricavo.

Just the welcome and the feel of the place — dark beams, brick arches, polished antiques and a huge log fire — convinced me immediately that here was another Chesa sur l'En. Without any ado, Signora Scotoni took me around and made me free of her domain. Of course I would stay the night? Of course I would. After a deliciously served dinner I pulled out the letter of introduction Rosellina had given me, to which for some reason or other she had attached details of a nearby estate that was for sale. (35 rooms, 1 bath, 65 million lire: hardly the place for me!) Everyone knew it. 'Are you interested in buying a property here?' asked some Swiss people who were sipping coffee and *grappa* round the fire. (As at the Chesa, everyone was introduced to each other.) I made mildly affirmative noises: why not? Mara Scotoni, it seemed, had some properties for sale. There was, for instance, a rather attractive *torre* . . . a photograph was produced, and I jumped with surprise. It was the castello I'd noticed on the way. 'Hasn't it got a small village below?' I asked, and Signora Scotoni nodded. She would take me down to see it the following morning. But I had a plane to catch at Rome in the evening! Never mind, we could get up an hour earlier.

2.4.63

Which is just what we did. After an early breakfast Mara took me in her Giulietta to see over it. (Nobody could have been less of a buyer, to be sure.) On the way she explained: she had just given first refusal to the young Swiss couple who were staying at Ricavo. But, if I were really interested, *if* I could make up my mind immediately . . .

Up the steep, bumpy drive we went in first gear, parked the car beside the massive tower, walked through an arch into a cobbled courtyard. The fat, rosy-cheeked farmer's wife showed us over. It was fabulously, breathtakingly romantic: such a place could be hardly real — it was more like a film set. Up to the top of the tower, two rooms per floor, all unused except the ground storey and over the arch to three rooms in a wing where the *contadini* lived. Cows and pigs underneath. A store which would make another perfect room. Barns, cellars, wine stores. Sixty acres, part of the tiny village at the foot of the hill, and healthily planted vines, producing some of the best wine in Chianti. And at a price equivalent to a thousand square metres in the Engadine.

Folly, of course. What on earth was I thinking of, saddling myself with the responsibility of running a farm in a remote part of Tuscany?

Yet some sort of devil prompted me to consider the venture. I was mulling it over on the way back when we met up with the Swiss couple. Mara stopped the car and asked them in *schwizerdütsch* if they would waive their option for 24 hours. They could have first refusal if I didn't decide on the spot. So I found myself asking, only half seriously, whether she would consider an offer? (Half of me asked: the other half washed its hands of the whole thing.) I then named a figure just over two-thirds of what she had mentioned. At that price, I reckoned, I could't go far wrong. And in any case (I rather hoped) the offer would not be accepted. She replied that she would think it over.

What would it cost to renovate the *torre*? A fortune, surely? By this time a cheerful character named Orlando Orlandi, who appeared to be Signora Scotoni's business manager, had been brought into the discussion. We called up Rome to postpone my flight and in the afternoon went back with the builder to make an estimate. Bemused by it all, I took rather less interest than I should have done in their deliberations: the feet were getting cold. But Orlandi was full of suggestions. It was proposed that the rooms in the tower itself should become bedrooms, each with a bath; the present three rooms used by the farmer would be knocked into a sitting-room; the stables would be turned into a kitchen and dining room; the store into a library. What an impossible project, I thought! However, by after dinner the builder had produced his estimate, a ridiculously low figure which included no less than four bathrooms . . .

3.4.63

Yet before taking the plunge, surely, one should see what else was around. So, this morning, armed with a large-scale map of the area, I went to have a look at the neighbourhood, driving down lanes along which the trees were just coming into leaf. Perhaps I would find some other *torres*? Bumping down a side-track, I thought I had spotted a twin — but it turned out to be the same one, from the other side. I made a long, detailed inspection of the property and then leant on the parapet of the bridge below and watched the farmer with his sturdy oxen tilling a nearby field. The vineyards stretched out in regular rows. The river ran placidly between the trees. What a feeling of permanence, tranquillity and ease! After a while I climbed up to the Torre and had a chat with Emilio, the *contadino*, who confirmed the figures that Orlandi had given me about the farm: four thousand litres had been produced the previous year. Bianca, his wife, still full of smiles, showed me over once again and then brought me six fat beautiful fresh brown eggs. For breakfast, she said. These eggs, I think, did the trick.

4.4.63

At Ricavo I found that several of the guests were Swiss people who had bought places here during the past year and were now busily renovating them. Mr and Mrs Schulthess of Basle were full of encouragement; both Mara Scotoni and Orlando Orlandi, they said, had arranged for everything they wanted to be done with a minimum of trouble. They knew the Torre well. In their opinion (and the opinion of a level-headed Swiss textile manufacturer is surely of value) I should buy it. Just after the war, said Schulthess, he had bought several hectares of land to the south of Locarno. 'You're crazy,' said his friends, 'that's the wrong side of the lake. Nobody wants to go there.' But he bought it just the same, at one franc a metre. Now it was worth a hundred. 'Of course,' he went on, 'I could buy some more there. I know the price will go to a hundred and fifty. But I'm not interested in that. I believe in buying at once franc a metre. And if you work it out, you'll see that what you're paying is a good deal less than that.' I think he had the grace to add that Chianti was a good deal more attractive than the Ticino. But it was excellent advice. I hesitated no longer. After working out some sums on the back of an envelope, I made up my mind. A preliminary contract was signed, and a cheque passed hands. Over a bottle of Italian champagne I was welcomed into the 'club'. Or rather, the Club that was to be. For Chianti was about to enter into a dramatic new era.

NOTE

1. Apparently there were only two motor-cycles in Panzano at the end of the war, belonging to two farm managers who, incredibly, managed to have a collision in the main street.

EIGHT

Remodelled Hideaway in Chianti is Europe's latest Vacation Chic.

A converted farmhouse in Chianti is Europe's current craze in secondary residences. During the last three years, fashionable British, Dutch, Americans, and even a few Italians have been snapping up properties in the area which produces Italy's most celebrated wines.

This triangle of vineyards and olive groves has for the first time in history, become easily accessible thanks to new autostradas linking Siena and Florence with Rome. Foreigners can now jet into Rome or Pisa and drive to Chianti in about two and a half hours. It is a neat paradox, however, that the previous lack of good roads is responsible for the current boom.

The region was so protected from the usual tourist track that the present landscape can still be recognised in the 12th and 13th century paintings of the Sienese primitives.

The pioneer was Englishman Raymond Flower who fell in love with a tower topping a Chianti hill while rambling through Tuscany a few years ago. He called on a former Oxford classmate, William Broadhead, an Anglo-American architect with an office on Rome's Piazza Navone.

Mr. Broadhead was so delighted with Flower's project that he later bought a crumbling castello for himself, and has since transformed a score of farms into stunning retreats for the new part time residents who generally come for a few weeks in spring or fall.

The young architect found the region a treasure for conversion. There were lots of competent workmen on the spot. The centuries-old limestone constructions were solid and pleasing. Vaulted pig-sties and threshing floors located on inner courtyards made a graceful transition to patios and charming living-rooms without disturbing the traditional rugged exterior architecture of the country-side.

The region has been given an addition fillip from an isolated luxury inn, the Tenuta di Ricavo, which has been installed with

taste in a complex of old Chianti buildings. It is an outpost affilia-
tion of the Relais de Campagne, a delightful fraternal grouping of
French country auberges.

The secondary residence has become the new sign of the times.
People may be stuck with the center where they have to make
their money, but where they live, entertain and decorate with
more lavishness than home base are the vacation centers of the
world. The luster places on the international circuit for lucky
house guests are Marbella near Malaga in Spain; Port Ercole on
Italy's Monte Argentario, and now Chianti. To keep the heavily
staked game on the move, house-swapping has become a norm
among proprietors who want to see the same people, but against
a different view.

New York Herald Tribune, Friday, 27 September 1968.

Archaeologists of the future may be perplexed, a thousand or so
years hence, to find distinctly non-Tuscan artefacts in the ruins of
our houses, and speculate about what sort of Nordic invasion it was
that took place in the latter part of the twentieth century. Signor
Orlandi (who was once registrar at both Gaiole and Castellina)
assures me that before World War Two there were no foreigners at
all in this region, not as residents at least, and this is borne out by the
communal archives. True, a German count lived for a while at
Passignano, but the first of the immigrants was probably Hugh
Hamilton, who came during the war, married the daughter of a local
landowner — and for the past thirty years has been noted as the
tallest man in the Siena market. Also, a bit later, an Italian lady,
Mrs Searle, and her English husband ran a girls' finishing school
near Greve. All the same, I don't think anyone will deny that Mara
Scotoni is the doyenne of Chianti's international community.

When in 1947 she and her husband bought Ricavo (which had
once been the estate of Duke Salviati, and during the war had been
used as a sort of *kibbutz* for Jewish refugees hoping to make their
way to Palestine) the big old house and its outbuildings were in
ruins as a result of the fighting around Castellina. But gradually they
restored the place, choosing marble from Carrara for the floors,
filling the rooms with fine antiques, and turning the garden into a
blaze of flowers, until the day when Mara's husband and daughter
were killed in a car crash outside Trieste.

It was then, rather than leave Ricavo, that she decided to turn
her family home into a guest house. 'We were always full of friends
and children,' she told me one evening as we sat around the fire, 'the
only difference was that they became paying guests.' Some of the

visitors followed in her steps and bought a cluster of nearby farms that came under the hammer at a bankruptcy sale — Montanino Vecchio, San Silvestro, Nittardi. The President of the Swiss Legal Association acquired the Villa Rosa estate, and an architect from Munich began converting a derelict little farmhouse known as La Piaggia.

From these modest beginnings the momentum developed, and, now on the spot, I had a ringside view of the sequence of events that transformed Chianti from what was officially styled a depressed area into one of the most sought-after chunks of real estate in the whole of Italy.

It happened quite gradually. Each new acquisition was a story in itself, and paved the way for the next. Thus, in the autumn of 1963 while I was staying at Ricavo watching my new home take shape, some Dutch fellow-guests lost their hearts to a farm called Navicuzzo, and evening by evening we shared their qualms and their hopes as Ruthy and Bas von Guens moved gradually towards the decision to exchange a bit of Holland for a piece of Chianti. Shortly afterwards, Denise and Georges de Uthemann stopped over from Geneva and fell for another of Mara's farmhouses. Others followed.

In those days I was still involved in the motor racing game, and nothing could be more pleasant, after blinding round Nurburgring or the Alpine Rally, than to amble through the olive groves and ginestra down to one's new domain and scratch the pigs' backs or watch a calf being born. Since the Torre itself was a working farm I began by doing up the small villa below, called La Cenerentola, which went with the property and was styled, with Tuscan panache, 'il palazetto padronale' — the owner's pad. It was certainly no palace, though the living room with its four big Florentine windows giving out over a lawn shaded by arches of vines made up for the scarcity of bedrooms (that is, until the pressure of family and friends made it expedient to move up to the Torre).

At one of these windows I was idly seated, some months later, when a car stopped, and some friends dropped in to see what was afoot. At that moment Pam and Andrew Crighton had no thought of settling in these parts. But that winter they borrowed my villa, and obviously the Chianti magic must have worked, because in February they wrote excitedly that they had bought a house near Panzano. Moreover by the time I got back they had already transformed what had been a nondescript building into an enchanting abode. So since Ted Slaughter (an American writer who had been consul in Florence) had already taken over part of the castello of Panzano, and Michael and Susan Rose, the musicologists, had also settled in that area, it was clear that a foreign community was beginning to emerge.

Yet as bits and pieces of the new mosaic, each of us was individually discovering the place — inventing, as it were, our own private notion of Chianti as we grappled with the problems of electric light and water, masons and carpenters, and the inevitable task of bulldozing a drive. There was a sort of Winnie-the-Pooh feel about it all as we stumped off, Pooh Bear fashion, to compare notes and sample each others' wines (some of which were drinkable and others rather less). But above all we were drawn together by the common interest of having a stake in the land. And there were still very few of us around.

It was all subtle and quiet in those salad days in Chianti, quite different from the sudden explosions in Sardinia or the Costa Brava. But then, in 1965, certain things happened that accelerated the rhythm. For one, my *mezzadro* farmer underwent a prostate operation, and could no longer work: a rickety van took the family and their possessions, amidst floods of tears, to life in the city, and I was left with the challenge, hitherto delayed, of restoring the Torre. So for technical and moral support I got on to my old friend William Broadhead, once captain of the Oxford University ski team, and now an architect in Rome. He and his wife Elaine turned up with two kids and four cats in a P1800 Volvo coupé, and instead of restyling the Torre bought a place of their own — not a crumbling castello, but a delightful little 'folly' that had originally been built a century previously by a local worth to house his *inamorata,* and was conveniently located so that he could keep his eye˙on her from his wife's bedroom window. (According to the villagers, moreover, it was haunted by the spirits of their unwanted children, who disappeared in the night and were allegedly buried in the vegetable garden.)

Around the same time, Richard and Souki de la Mare acquired another of Mara's farmhouses, and yet a further friend from my Oxford days, Michael Briggs, came to lunch announcing his desire to be 'seduced' by a house. The very first one he saw — a beautifully sited place called 'Le Case' — did the trick.

The cost varied, of course, but in those days for between six and ten million lire (or, say, the equivalent of £3,500 — £6000) you could pick up a good solid farmhouse with 20 or 30 acres of arable land and woods. And half of Chianti was for sale. Not surprisingly, therefore, the word got about. In the absence of any house agents we all enjoyed ourselves hunting for suitable properties for our friends. The Broadheads brought George d'Almeida (the artist) and his family from Rome. Richard and Michael chatted around White's and the Claremont Club circuit. In next to no time, Ronnie and Heather Grierson had acquired a complex of farms in the hills below Castellina; Teddy Goldsmith, in a flush of enthusiasm, had bought a valley behind Gaiole, Alistair Londonderry had plumped for a thirteenth-century fortified farmhouse near Radda; Barbara and Oliver Poole (then Chairman of the British Conservative party) had settled into a place at Cispiano. And so it went on: the one brought the other. Most of them bought their properties as holiday homes and restored the farmhouses in the rustic style of the region, with traditional tiled floors, whitewashed walls and beamed ceilings. Nearly all of these were to the south of the Pesa river, around Castellina and Radda in the province of Siena.

But north of the Pesa around Panzano (in the province of Florence) a parallel though slightly different development was also gathering pace. The English, as Christopher Pirie Gordon once remarked, have always lived thirty-five minutes from the centre of Florence. But whereas in the nineteenth century the expatriates settled in villas at Fiesole, Bellosguardo or Grassina, their motorised successors chose to congregate around Panzano, a twenty-mile drive from the bright city lights. Those who came here tended to live the whole year round, transforming their farmhouses into elegant, comfortable homes with the traditional appurtenances of an English country house. When you dined at Panzano, it was around a Jacobean table with silver candelabra, and you put on a tie: at Castellina you wore slacks and sat on a bench — though you were quite likely to have smoked salmon that your hostess had brought over from Fortnum's that morning.

For all this, some covert (and sometimes covetous) glances were given at each other's houses to see what solutions had been adopted — stables turned into living rooms, stairs moved indoors, barns become studios, and so forth — while tips were eagerly exchanged about builders, carpenters and plumbers and the prices they charged. On the whole I suspect that those of us in the province of Siena had less trouble, thanks to the efforts of Orlandi, and not quite such heavy bills to foot. Which, so far as I was concerned, was just as well. For, apart from the *torre*, I had Monte Rinaldi to fix.

If we had invested in a second property, it was because with the deteriorating situation in Egypt, my mother needed a substitute for her house on the Nile. And Monte Rinaldi was only a couple of miles upstream from Grignano. At that time I had no inkling of the historical connection between the two. But when the facts were uncovered, it was pleasant to reflect that after nearly a thousand years the same conjuncture — of the older generation at Monte Rinaldi and the younger at Grignano — should have again come about.

When we bought Monte Rinaldi in 1965, it was a *canonica,* or rectory, that had been abandoned since the church of S. Martino was deconsecrated in 1946 and moved down into the valley at Lucarelli after nine and a half centuries of documented existence. Shoulder-high weeds were growing in the living rooms, and as we trampled through the nettles on the terrace, I remember Orlandi muttering that he would't have it, not even as a gift. Yet even in this state, the atmosphere of the place was enthralling, and after three months of intensive work, which included replacing nearly 800 square metres of roof, the main floor of the house was ready and furnished for my mother's arrival.

Perhaps the most fascinating side of these restorations was that the mason's techniques were almost identical with those of the original builders. The wooden scaffolding lashed together with rope, the ladders, the bricks and the stones carried up by hand or in wheel-barrows, the cement mixed outside with long-handled shovels and then pulled up in buckets with ropes and pulleys, the masons themselves in their paper hats (to keep off the dust) carefully chipping stones into the right shape before slapping them into place with a wodge of cement: all this was exactly as depicted in the frescoes of Lorenzetti and others. Equally remarkable was the care with which Tassi, the builder, would search for precisely the right textured stone, sometimes hunting in the woods for one from the old castello to complete the jamb of a door, and his visible satisfaction as he fitted it into place. For just as they seemed to get a kick out of all the shovelling and chipping and hammering, it was clear that these masons were artists with a deep sense of commitment to their job. (William Broadhead maintains that you can sense their antennae turn, as it were, when the owner arrives on a tour of inspection. A jovial word of praise, and production goes up; but critical remarks and little more is done for the rest of the day.)

When at last the restoration is completed, it is always celebrated by a dinner *per coprire il tetto* (literally, the covering of the roof). Punctually at eight o'clock all those who have been concerned with the work — masons, plumbers, carpenters, electricians, lorry drivers — turn up in unfamiliar dark suits and roll-necked sweaters (but *sans* wives, for this is a strictly stag affair), and without further ado tuck into the time-honoured menu of antipasto (raw ham, olives and *crostini*, that is, pieces of bread spread with chickens' liver or anchovy butter), followed by *pasta al forno*, spaghetti or tortellini; and then in succession the boiled meats, roast chicken and pork, and elephantine steaks *alla fiorentina* accompanied by fried potatoes and salad. The feast ends up with *zuppa inglese* — a heavy concoction that no islander, alas, would recognise as trifle — along with Sienese *panforte,* fruit, coffee and an aniseed liqueur known as *Sambuca,* all of which is washed down with copious flagons of Chianti Classico. For most stomach linings it would be an ordeal. But the gusto with which the dishes are passed round, and the enjoyment with which everyone piles titbits on to his neighbour's plate (especially that of the host) makes up for this onslaught on the gastric juices. And — unlike some other places I could name — their manners are perfect: there are no dirty jokes, no horseplay, and no one gets drunk. Nor are there any speeches, though various little toasts are exchanged, and some friendly ribbing goes on — but all in such good humour that one instantly feels part of a large, happy family who are all on the best terms with one another. Here (you tell yourself) is a summation of the Chianti ethos, a legacy that goes deep into history, perhaps to the Etruscans themselves: by which I mean that when they are working, they work; and when they set out to enjoy themselves, they make sure that they do. Even if a more mercenary attitude is beginning to creep in along with the washing machines and TV sets, they seem to combine what is best of the serious-minded north and the easy-going south.

At the other end of the Chianti spectrum — as much a foreign import as the Etruscans or the Lombards — are the English, at whose headier (though equally relaxed) foregatherings almost anything can happen and practically anyone may turn up. And with them, a new 'swinging' dimension has come to Chianti, prompting *l'Espresso* magazine to suggest (with a chuckle) that it should be renamed Chiantishire. It is pleasant, after all, to visualise the chairman of Lazards sitting in the 'bar' at Castellina waiting for the telephone to call up England and settle the details of the merger between Leyland and the British Motor Corporation. It is intriguing to know that just before the 1970 election at which he was returned as Prime Minister, Edward Heath worked out his Cabinet with the chairman of the Conservative party under an olive tree of a farm that Margrave Ugo had made over to the Badia a thousand years before. It is fascinating, when one looks in for a drink, to find the heads of the Central Banks sitting in bathing costumes discussing the European economy.

Yet if such jet-set chatter smacks of the Riviera or the Costa Smeralda, it would be wrong to suppose that the foreign community is just a spurious film on top of a smiling landscape. Rather, it is an extension of the long, fruitful tradition of the English in Florence. What is more, Chianti is far more rugged than the traditional playgrounds of Europe. The seasonal changes are startling: in the winter it freezes, and in August you are scorched. Some years it rains with monsoon ferocity. Equally, there is the sudden explosion of spring towards the end of April, and an Indian summer in autumn, with warm, crisp October mornings as the *vendemmia* get under way.

Those who have come here have done so because they prefer the strong medicine of Italian country life, with its depth of tradition, to the commercialised beguilements of the coast. In what is neither a frenzy nor a void, but a deeply satisfying *ambiance,* they feel that they can put down roots. How successfully it works out depends on their ability to integrate with the curious un-xenophobic quality of the Tuscans, who are still prepared to welcome the invader so long as he has a smile on his face. In the end, I suppose, it depends on whether one is prepared to contribute, to add, to fit in.

Which most of us, I like to think, seem to do. Michael Rose, for example (whose father was Bishop of Dover), regularly plays the organ at the *pieve* of Panzano, sometimes accompanied by Charles Friedmann on the violin, so that different denominations participate in a Catholic service; Patrick Creagh and Matthew Spender play the trombone and the clarinet in the Radda village band, and even in the dead of winter I find myself turning out to coach the local lads at tennis or golf. Socially, too, one spends many pleasant hours not only in the superb villas of the neighbouring Italian landowners, but also in the equally hospitable homes of the postman and the grocer — who in turn seem to enjoy the change of scene that our own houses provide.

Yet if the British blazed the trail here, the other nationalities were not slow to follow, and the communal registers now include some 250 families from sixteen countries. Both the Swiss and the Dutch were in from the start, of course, and in due course celebrities began to arrive: Jan Brouwer, the chairman of Shell; Leon Ferre, the singer; Van Strycker, chairman of the Banque de Belgique; De Groot, a director of the World Bank, and recently Princess Beatrix of the Netherlands, who bought a farmhouse above Sambuca. Then, around 1970, the Germans discovered the charms of Chianti, forming what is almost a little colony of their own to the south of Castellina that includes Rolf Becker, the boss of *Die Welt*; Ernst Schroeder, the actor; Hans Lietzau, the film producer; and (near my brother Neville at Sicelle) Horst Antes, the artist. Unobtrusively, some Americans slipped in: Robert Cabot, the writer, to a wooded estate near Vagliagi; John Palmer of Yale to a modernised woodcutter's cottage in the landscape that Leonardo had drawn; and others here and there. Finally, moreover, the Italians themselves — not those who had always been here, but the autostrada set from Rome and Milan, who had hitherto spent July at the seaside and August in the mountains — began to be tempted by the countryside, and Chianti

21. Galileo Galilei lived in a villa near Arcetri, but he owned a farm at Grignano in the centre of Chianti and reckoned that its red wine 'put all others to shame'. When condemned by the Inquisition for his theory of terrestrial movement, he was given sanctuary by the Ricasoli family in their villa, La Torraccia, near Brolio.

22. 'Il Barone di Ferro', Bettino Ricasoli (1809-1880) laid down the principles which have governed the production of Chianti Classico wine. As Tuscan minister of the interior in 1859 he promoted the Union of Tuscany with Piedmont, and succeeded Cavour in the premiership of Italy in 1881.

23. The entrance to the villa of Monte Rinaldi after it was restored in 1966. One of the towers of the original Lombard Castle was converted into the campanile of the Church of S. Martino.

24. Eightieth birthday photograph of Count Bino Samminiatelli, the writer, on the lawn of Vignammagio, his lovely villa which was once the house of Monna Lisa.

25. The cellars in which Chianti Classico matures are often centuries old, as at the Castello di Meleto, which was in the hands of the Firidolfi-Ricasoli family for nearly a millenium.

26. Collecting olives in the old fashioned way. Nowadays a wide circular 'parachute' is laid round the tree and the fruit is raked off the branches into it.

27. (Top) A misty winter morning in Chianti. The traditional farm buildings of Monte Bernardi contrast with the new vineyards behind. The more distant farm, Terrarossa, once belonged to Galilei, and now forms part of the Melini wine complex.

28. (Bottom) A wine vat and press in a modern *Gallo Nero cantina*.

29. (Right) The traditional harvest and the ever-recurring question: how good will the wine be this year?

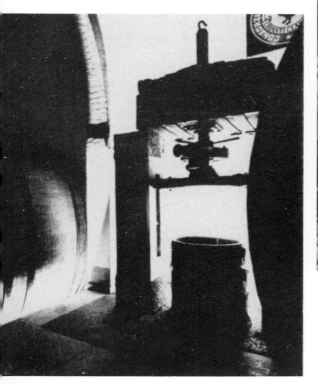

most of all. While many of them (including several Cabinet Ministers) bought large estates or carved out sleek weekend pads, others escaped from the hassle and violence of the towns to set up as working farmers. Thus the cycle had begun to close itself: the *contadini* were being replaced by the disappointed city-dweller.

Gradually, indeed, as life returned to one abandoned farm after another, and even derelict barns were converted into cosy retreats, one began to realise that the place was filling up. A turning-point came when the great Ricasoli estates of Meleto, Castagnoli and San Polo were put on the market, and to finance fresh vineyards the new owners sold off the farmhouses that were no longer required for salaried workers who preferred to live in the villages and commute in their cars.

For many folk, a house and a garden were all that was required. And so (helped by Swiss and London agents who were pricking up their ears, to say nothing of their prices) a new wave of 'permanent tourists' came in, with no commitment to the soil, but just as enamoured with the magic of Chianti for all that. Perhaps because of this detachment, they tended to bring a trendier style to the conversion of their houses, and to go in for activities less connected with agriculture — such as cordon bleu cuisine, and piano concerts in patios — while nevertheless turning gleefully up at an oenological binges.

Of these there are plenty, though the high spots are provided by the Lega del Chianti. Originally founded for the defence of the area (and suppressed by the Lorrainese in 1774) the Lega was re-constituted by Count Neri Capponi in 1970 — the five hundredth anniversary of its inception — to revive some of the ancient traditions and recapture the values of the past in a community that could all too easily brush them aside. And as such it has turned out to be an enormous success. One may smile at the sight of one's friends togged up in medieval robes, but somehow wine often tastes better with a bit of stage management in the cellars where it matured, and blind-tasting sessions in convivial surroundings, to get acquainted with each individual vintage, are surely preferable to hiding its light under a plastic bushel.

Who can doubt, indeed, that Chianti has benefited from all this? If these new romantics have come, it is because they feel that what-ever they want to do — be it to paint, compose, write, study, get to grips with nature with a spade, or simply take a holiday from the twentieth century — can be done better here than elsewhere. Cos-tumed masques by a mill-pool, summer dances in a courtyard, mid-night bathing parties, Oriana Fallaci's searing prose up at Lamole, Horst Antes' homuncular paintings at Sicille or George d'Almeida's abstracts at Selvole, Rudolph Baumgartner conducting a symphony orchestra in the church at Castellina, Denise de Utheman giving a conference on surrealism — all these are no murex-tinted illusions out of touch with the scenery. On the contrary, they tap deep into the springs of the place. And at least no one plays bridge.

The Etruscans, I'm sure, would have approved.

NINE

But in the end we come back to the wine, for this is the true signature of Chianti. In the days after World War Two and even in the early sixties when foreigners had already begun moving into deserted farmhouses, production was slowly dropping. Inefficient methods, high labour costs, and the relatively low price that it could command made the growing of wine a poor financial proposition: there was a glut on the market of stuff sold as 'Chianti' which had no connection with the genuine article, and not much with the grape either, by all accounts. But finally a particularly flagrant instance of this sort (exposed, if I remember rightly, by *Life* magazine) prompted the central authorities in Rome to introduce strict regulations to curtail such abuses, and at the same time a system of agricultural grants, which among other things offered subsidies for the planting of vines, was introduced by the European Economic Community. Protected in this way by *denominazione di origine controllata* and financed by FEOGA, it did not take long for big business interests, scenting a good thing, to look Chianti up on the map and buy all the land they could lay their hands on.

This smart money needed no accountants to explain that one did not cultivate vineyards just for fun. Genuine wine from the heart of Chianti Classico could fetch a good price, and bring in substantial profits, provided that it was efficiently produced. If the old vineyards showed a loss, it was because they were tended largely by hand: some 65 per cent of the cost went in labour, said the experts. So it was not just a question of sprucing up the existing plantations, but what was technically termed 're-conversion' — which meant, in fact, industrialisation.

Whereas only a few years previously there had hardly been a tractor in sight, and all the operations had been done with oxen or by hand, bulldozers and excavators were now let loose to flatten whole hillsides and rip away the stone terraces that had been so painstakingly built up over the centuries. These powerful machines produced a uniform surface, though as ecologists warned, the wholesale removal of the top soil meant that the land would be dead, despoiled of its substance like the forests that the Etruscans had bared, and unfit for agricultural use should any crop other than vines (whose roots go down deep) be required. And along with the old garlanded vines, entire olive groves were destroyed to make way for white concrete posts supporting rows of plants (between 45,000 and 50,000 per hectare) that were lined up with the precision of a drill sergeant. The human side of husbandry was swept aside in favour of these supermarket vineyards, which changed the aspect and the feel of the countryside in much the same way as High Street chain stores have done to so many ancient market towns in England. Over what has been lost, it is useless to shed tears: this is, after all, the ethos of our times, and if the landscape now looks as raw as a plucked fowl in wintertime, at least it is covered by a rich carpet of uniform foliage in the summer and the autumn — a wall-to-wall vesture that has an efficient beauty of its own: contemporary shall we say, rather than artistic. The *patina* has gone, but the land is used, which might not otherwise have been the case.

In contrast to the old scattered plants which had to be tended by individual farmers, the vast new vineyards can be ploughed by machines and sprayed by helicopters. For if untreated, the grapes fall prey to insects and mould ('la malattia', as it used to be called) and nowadays they are subjected to chemical sprays at least seven times a year, often more. The switch from organic nutriments to chemical substances, largely for reasons of cost, is a global trend, as disquieting here as anywhere else; yet it is encouraging to see that some producers (following cases of sickness among their workers) are moving back wherever possible to natural products, known locally as *pollina* (from chicken), *pecorino* (from sheep), *peluria* and *scarnicci*.

Yet, significantly enough, there has been little change in the actual types of plants that are used. As always, some 60-70 per cent of the vines are still 'Sangiovese', the balance being made up of red 'Canaiolo', the white 'Malvasia Toscana' which originated in Chianti, the juicy white 'Trebbiano', and in some cases a grape from the Valdarno, known as 'Colorino', is included to give extra colour and bouquet to the wine. These native Tuscan vines are all, of course, grafted with foreign imports.[1] But whereas normal practice had been to plant the vines and then subsequently graft on to the roots, the tendency now, as a labour-saving measure, is to use plants that have already been grafted.

Monarch of the vineyards though the machine may be, there is still one point at which human hands are needed. Technology may have reached as far as Mars, but it still has not come up with a device to pick grapes, which (unlike blackcurrants, that can be shaken off the bushes) have an awkward way of wrapping themselves around any twig or branch they can find. And so the *vendemmia* is still conducted in the traditional fashion. Come October, every man, woman and child is press-ganged into action, and each estate has its private reservoir of students and soldiers who are lured into the vineyards at so much per hour plus a midday meal. Picking grapes is harder work than one might think, but there are worse ways of spending an autumn day than moving companionably from vine to vine snipping the juicy bunches and tossing them into baskets, while the banter flows and one gets sticky all over. A tractor may now haul the tub into which the offering in one's basket is thrown, rather than the white oxen as before; but when the tub is full it disappears up the hill towards the big vat in the cellar, where the level of the grapes rises with each trip, and the pressure of the fruit itself crushes out most of the red liquid before whoever is in charge clambers in and begins trampling with his rubber boots. In the bigger *cantine* the grapes are brought in on lorries and machines take over, but for all this new mechanisation, we are not so far removed from all the generations of people who lived in this place and did almost precisely the same thing, as the Roman accounts show. They, too, were faced with the same problems of whether it would rain or not (which it so frequently does at just the worst moment) and how many tubfuls of grapes the vines are yielding as against the previous year. They followed the same motions, smelt the same pungent fragrance, and I'm sure got as purple under the finger nails as we still do to-day. And, I don't doubt, they all foregathered in the evening for *la cena della vendemmia*, the celebration dinner with great hunks of meat roasted in front of a roaring fire, indigestible cakes, and flagons of last year's vintage to ease it all down.

In February, as soon as the worst of the frosts are over, the preparations for the new crop begin again. First it is necessary to chop the dead wood off the plants, by this time gnarled and leafless, before ploughing round the roots and manuring the soil. The shoots, still bare, are bound up with willow-twine, so that each elbow of the vine is left with two or three points from which the first buds will emerge. As spring gets under way and the vines are suddenly covered with fresh, heraldic green leaves and tiny, embryonic bunches of grapes, the tractors creak up and down the verdant rows, covering them with a blue haze of copper sulphate. In summer the suckers are removed and the spraying continues, until by September the grapes have turned to a rich, plummy purple (or from green to pale gold) and it is time to wash out the barrels in anticipation of the harvest, and make a selection of special grapes to act as 'governo'. These are laid out to mature until they are almost rotten, and bursting with sugar.

If after ten days of fermentation in the vat, during which it is stirred every evening, the must, once pressed, is no longer sloshed around in pails but conveyed to the barrels by pump, it is still made — or rather, transforms itself — into wine in the same way as ever. But the special characteristic of Chianti is that it is given this extra fillip of *governo,* which apart from conferring more body causes a second fermentation in the barrel and eliminates the sediment.

To comply with the standards laid down by the Consorzio, all Chianti Classico sold under the imprimatur of the 'Black Cock' must have an alcoholic content of at least 12 degrees. While many of the vineyards in high, sunny locations reach this level quite naturally, others have to be boosted through the addition of *concentrati*, which may mean specially treated must from the strongest grapes from the estate itself, or the addition — to a prescribed amount — of the heavy wines from Naples and Puglia. (To add sugar would achieve the same effect. But in Italy this is illegal, not because it it harmful, but to stimulate the sale of the *mezzogiorno* must.) Sometimes, moreover, artificial concentrates are mixed in as well, to improve the colour and bouquet of the wine.

At Grignano, I must admit, we do not bother about such things. Our relatively low-lying vineyards produce a fresh dry tangy wine of around 11 degrees, with a hint of sparkle, or rather tingle, and if it is light at least you can taste the grape: too often in heavier wines the alcohol content tends to smother the fruitiness and give a strong, dead flavour. But we only produce about 5,000 litres a year (the equivalent of rather less than 7,000 bottles) which satisfies our own needs, as well as those of friends and neighbours, and so we do not put it on the market for sale. I don't think I want to get caught up in the struggle to achieve a high alcoholic content by the use of additives, although I fully sympathise with the desire of the Consorzio to maintain certain basic standards for each bottle that bears the famous 'black cock'.

For now these vast new vineyards are in full production, an integrated marketing drive must be launched to put their produce on the tables of the world. Chianti Classico may be, as Simon Frazer (of Harrod's fame) delightedly told me, 'the great undiscovered wine of Europe', but that is not quite what the growers are striving for. After all, the red wines of this area are among the most illustrious that Italy can offer. (The white wines are drinkable too, but they are never called Chianti.) The Consorzio — along with major producers such as Ricasoli, Folanari and Antinori — have already gone a long way to getting the message across, and are stepping up their efforts every day with increasing success, even though Europe is apparently swimming in a lake of wine. Classico may not yet have penetrated every home (like claret and Burgandy and hock) but at least you can now buy it at Marks and Spencer, and at a wide range of wine merchants in England and the Continent.

While the traditional straw-covered fiasco is still used, the Black Cock, or Gallo Nero wines are increasingly sold in a claret-type bottle known as the *bordolese*. For the most part they are bottled after about a year in the cellar, although some of the better ones — known as Riserva — are aged for a minimum of four years in oak casks. They have their own special flavour and their own characteristics: significantly, too, they are said to be among the few wines in the world that do not contain histamine — which, argues Charles Friedmann of the Institute of Pharmacology in Florence, is what tends to cause hangovers. Many of the unpleasant after-effects of drinking wine, in his view, are not so much caused by the alcohol content as the quantity of free histamine taken aboard. He reports in the *New Scientist*:

> We have documented many cases of people who have had to give up drinking red wine because this is nearly always followed by attacks of headaches, migraine, angina pains or skin itching, all characteristic symptoms of histamine ingestion, but who are able to drink Chianti Classico.

So, who knows, if French wine gives you a hangover, perhaps you should switch to Chianti Classico. (Conversely, if Chianti itself is too acid for comfort, swallow a histamine before pulling the cork.)

Whether this argument can be substantiated is open to debate. But there is no doubt that Chianti wines as a whole (and the Gallo Nero vintages in particular), should be judged on their own merits rather than being equated to the wines of France, as people tend to do.

There is, after all, a difference of concept — as different as the rasping rattle of a Ferrari is from the marbled murmur of a Rolls-Royce. A great claret, Maurice Healy once suggested, should be drunk on one's knees, with every sip consecrated as a libation to Heaven . . . With Chianti such genuflections are superfluous; you open your throat and gulp it down with an appreciative 'aah!' Yet increasingly Classico is acquiring an individuality of character that is worth studying in depth. If a good claret or Burgundy is almost a food in itself, to be sniffed, rolled around the palate and mused about afterwards, the same is now true of the best Gallo Nero vintages, so that it is becoming more and more rewarding to distinguish between well-groomed Classico and the lesser Tuscan breeds.

Generally speaking, Chianti is a good sound earthy wine with an aggressive, tannin tang: a full-bodied beverage that you take with food. For the most part it falls short of the sublime standards of the Gironde. But by the same token, it is less artificial, in the sense that less artifice has gone into its making. Simpler, earthier, more animal if you like, it is a straightforward wine to be drunk with a meal. And for many people the charm of Chianti lies elsewhere than in its rugged vinous taste. It is, they will tell you, as jolly a wine as you are likely to come across. It keeps winking at you over the straw covering of the flask and persuading you that it is time to fill your glass up again.

Yet this widespread image hardly does justice either to the delicious wines that certain dedicated vineyards have always produced, or to the efforts that are now going into the making of high-quality wine. New machinery, new techniques, and above all a new enthusiasm on the part of landowners are all playing their part. It may take another generation before wine-lovers come to appreciate the sharp accelerating taste of a fine Gallo Nero Riserva as much as the lingering grace of a Medoc or a Graves, or before hosts will uncork it with the same sense of pride. But the time will surely come. For there is no doubt that its acerbity — its *aggressività*, as my neighbours describe it — is sometimes magnificient, particularly in the company of game or a roast.

Apart from all else, the Gallo Neros tend to mature quicker than more northern wines, so there is less mystique about a venerable bottle. From the end of the fermentation the ageing curve of the wine lifts gradually in the course of three to five years: it then slowly levels off and maintains maturity for a dozen years or so before slowly fading into a tawny old age. Some people reckon that a good Classico can stay in its prime for as long as thirty years, and I recall a 1954 Le Barone that Franca Visconti gave us a little while ago which still flowed as clear as a ruby and caressed the gullet with a rich mellow bouquet. But on the whole such wines are now collector's pieces; and ideally Gallo Neros should be drunk after seven or eight years. (1971, a memorable year, is now at its best.)

The colour should be a clear, rich ruby, tending with age to what is known as *granato*, that is, a deeper ruby with golden tinges around the edge. Rarely strong to the nose, the bouquet should fill the palate with the scent of heavily ripe fruit and a touch of wild violets: sometimes it has a hint of the aroma of strawberries. Because they are so heavy in tannin and tartaric acids, the younger wines give what can best be described as a puckering sensation. But once they have matured they become rounder and smoother.

Soil, of course, plays a determining part: it is the difference in terrain between the valleys and the hills that distinguishes, for instance, the wines of Greve from those of Gaiole. On the whole the valley of Greve and the upper part of the commune of Radda — the area around Volpaia — produce the most harmonious wines with the best balance of colour, body and alcoholic content; these are the most typical of modern Chianti Classico and the yardstick against which the others can be judged. In contrast, those from Castellina have a more pronounced bouquet and a higher degree of alcohol. Heavily bodied, and of a rich deep colour, they need a certain amount of ageing. Castelnuovo Berardenga's offerings also require time; but they are softer, smoother and mellower, and have rather less body. Up in the hilly region of Gaiole, the *Monti del Chianti*, you find full rich wines that tend to have virtually no bouquet (though some will develop if you remove the cork an hour or two before drinking) but which age well in the bottle; they are softer, too, although very tannic, and of all the Gallo Neros are the nearest to claret. At San Donato and Mercatale, closer to Florence, the wine often seems more like *Putto* than the Classicos of Greve. Much depends, of course, on the location of the property, but they sometimes need to be vinified — that is, an alteration of the percentages of white and red grapes in the vineyard — to achieve the full Gallo Nero flavour.

Needless to say, a great deal depends on the weather, for nature can be as capricious in Chianti as everywhere else. In 1976 a wide sweep of the commune of Castellina and the Val di Pesa was hit by a freak hailstorm at the beginning of June which lasted only ten minutes but stripped the vines almost bare of both leaves and grapes. And on Easter Sunday this year (1977) there was a sudden snap of frost that played havoc with the budding fruit, especially in low-lying areas. For the grape needs protection from frost in its youth, and ideally a warming sun both in spring and late summer to fill it with sugar, along with periodic showers of rain to swell its bulk and give it plenty of juice. Too much sun in July and August can scorch the grapes; too much rain can induce mildew, and if it comes just before the *vendemmia*, will wash away the bloom and the minute particles of ferment without whose presence a good wine cannot be made. Most desirable of all is a warm sunny spell in October to give a final touch of ripeness and vigour; and there is always a last-minute gamble about choosing the right time in October for gathering in the grapes to make the most of the autumn sun yet escape the first frost which could ruin them all in a night. When all these elements come to pass in the right order you get a memorable vintage — such as in 1962, 1964, 1967, 1971 and 1975. (A score card giving overall quality for the last twenty years is given in appendix.)

Living as I do in these parts, it would be invidious for me to attempt to give a rating of individual wines: my friend Enrico Bosi, the Florentine journalist, published his private pecking order a year or two ago and raised an uproar among those producers who felt themselves slighted. At the blind tasting sessions that are held every year certain wines, such as Fonterutoli, Lilliano and Lodoline from Castellina. Riecine and Cacchiano from Gaiole; Vignamaggio, Uzzano, Calcinaia and Vicchiomaggio from Greve; Terciona and Poggiolino from Mercatale, regularly get the accolade; and there are of course the famous vintages from Brolio, Meleto and Antinori that have always been the standard-bearers of Chianti Classico. But many others are every bit as good, though perhaps not so well known. Try Verrazzano, or Coltibuono, or Pile e Lamole, or Monsanto or Nittardi or Montecastelli or Montefioralle, to name just a few.

You will be surprised and delighted at how good they can be.

NOTE

1. Most favoured of these are the Berlandieri, the Riparia, and the Rupestris (which are often mixed) though recently experiments have been made with Ruggeri 140 and 225.

POSTSCRIPT

It is curious to read as 'history' things you have experienced yourself. Yet today's daily life is tomorrow's social history; and so to round off our story I'll try to sum up briefly what has happened in the ten years since this book first appeared.

For one thing, the world has got smaller. You can now dial New Zealand or California from the remotest Tuscan farmhouse, or be back here for lunch after dining in Singapore. You can drive to Basel or Munich in rather less than six hours. Consequently the tourist traffic has accelerated, and Chianti is becoming a favourite destination for discriminating travellers. It is also increasingly a haven for disgruntled city-dwellers. So inevitably the old sense of idyllic seclusion is tending to diminish.

In compensation, the total amenities have improved greatly. Village shops now stock a wide range of groceries, and scores of excellent restaurants have appeared in Greve, Panzano, and even in small villages like Vagliagli and Querciagrossa. Villas or farmhouses have been converted into attractive hotels that retain a characteristic Tuscan flavour for all their swimming-pools and swanky tiled bathrooms (I am thinking of Le Barone at Panzano, Vignale at Radda, Salinvolpe at Castellina and S. Leonino off the Chiantigiana road near Fonterutoli, to say nothing of the venerable Tenuta di Ricavo, which started it all off.) Others, including grand places like Vicchiomaggio, S. Polo in Rosso, and Castelvecchi, have been partly turned into self-contained flats, or take in paying guests. Agri-Turismo is the name of this profitable game, which seems to be played with greater skill here than in other parts of Tuscany. (Another trend is the proliferation of 'rent-a-horse' stables.)

On the other hand, many of the earlier British and Dutch have departed, either because they were growing older and found it hard to get help, or because they chose to bale out once real estate values had risen so steeply. But their places have been taken by Germans and Swiss, so perhaps the old tag 'Chiantishire' should now be changed to 'Chianti-Land'. And while it would be quite wrong to suggest that Chianti is becoming a dormitory area for Florentines, the steadily rising flow of commutors (even by helicopter) emphasises the spread of urban cultural values. Now virtually indistinguishable from its suburban counterparts, the new well-educated genera-

229

tion of versatile youngsters, boys and girls alike, is tending to turn away from its rich agricultural heritage.

Of course this is an old story, what you might perhaps call a Euro-phenomenon. But it is nonetheless sad, for of all the developments in the last ten years, the improvement in the quality of Chianti Classico wine is the most spectacular. Thanks to the enthusiastic efforts of its producers, the massive investment in vineyards and equipment that was made in the Seventies is now bearing fruit. Moreover some distinguished newcomers have now appeared on the scene — such as Zonin from Venice — along with trend-setters like Paolo Panerai. Indeed the celebrated Ricasoli vintages are now operated by a British syndicate.

Not long ago there was a global overproduction of wine, to say nothing of the 'ski-wax' scandals in Austria and elsewhere, which seemed to bode ill for European vintners. But Chianti Classico was protected by its stringent DOCG regulations — not just controlled, but guaranteed. As a result, prices for the Gallo Nero vintages rocketted, and the higher they rose the more demand has increased. Today Chianti Classico is no longer cheap, but it is undeniably better.

I should add that part of its attraction lies in the fact that some of the producers have broken away from the time-honoured formula. Alongside their traditional Gallo Nero vintages they have been carrying out experiments with different types of grapes — more San Giovese and less white Malvasia or Trebbiano, for example. Such wines do not bear the Black Cockerell emblem. But they are equally delightful, and extend the range. Some quite drinkable white wines are also being produced.

Thus the future for our wine seems brighter than ever. And happily, for all the outward changes, the essences of Chianti life remain pure and strong. The human values still prevail. In these hills and valleys people still allow themselves to be happy, perhaps unfashionably happy, perhaps very happy indeed. It may not last; it probably will not. But at least it is so for the present. And this sense of contentment, so rare today, is the note on which I would like to conclude — along with a tribute to the spontaneous generosity of the people who live here, be they Tuscans by birth, or Tuscans by choice.

Many, out of sheer goodness of heart, have helped me put this book together. They are far too numerous to list, though it would be churlish not to slip in a special word of thanks to Neri Capponi, Captain-General of the Lega del Chianti; Bettino Ricasoli, heir to the most famous name in Chianti; and Lapo Mazzei, who heads the Consorzio del Vino Chianti Classico, and whose family have lived at Fonterutoli since the 15th century. Also to Franca Visconti, Piero Stucchi, Briano Castelbarco, and Dino Frescobaldi. Nor should I omit Dr Dario Lanzoni, the present director of the Consorzio, and his assistants Katerina Trauttmansdorff and Lucia Franciosi, as well as John Dunkley, Orlando Orlandi, Alessandro

Falassi, and Virgilio Pieralli, all of whom have contributed to my under-standing of the Chianti ethos. Moreover I continue to owe a great debt of gratitude to Sandro Boglione for having scrutinized my outpourings with a friendly but critical eye, and then most elegantly rendered the text, with some scholarly additions of his own, into Italian for publication by Bonec-chi under the title *Chianti, Storia e Cultura*.

I must also thank Peter Batty and Denis Rixson for having come out from Oxford to help with the research. It is a pleasant thought that Peter and his wife Sally met here, when she was working as my secretary. So if nothing else, this book served to bring them together. But that was ten years ago....

So Bless you, my friends! Let us fill our glasses high and drink a toast together: to the beauty of Chianti's landscape, the friendliness of its people, and the savour of its wine. Long may they endure....

Castellina in Chianti,
5 April 1988

LIST OF MEMBERS OF THE CONSORZIO VINO CLASSICO
(as at 20 November 1987)

BARBERINO VAL D'ELSA
(Firenze)

CANTAGALLI
propr. Eugenia Cantagalli

CASA EMMA
propr. Fiorella Lepri & C sas

CASA SOLA
propr. La Vela srl

FATTORIA LA RIPA
propr. S.A. Santa Brigida

IL CAMPINO DI MONDIGLIA
propr. Primo Benelli

ISOLE E OLENA
propr. SIAC SpA

MONSANTO
propr. Fabrizio Bianchi

PANERETTA
propr. Maria Carlo Musso

QUERCIA AL POGGIO
propr. Quercia al Poggio sas di
Ferri-Magnani & C

VILLA FRANCESCA
propr. Giovanni Mari

CASTELLINA IN CHIANTI
(Siena)

BARTALI
propr. Rivo Bartali

BIBBIANO
propr. Tenuta di Bibbiano srl

CAFAGGIO DI PESA
propr. Giacomo Castore

CAGGIOLO
propr. Il Caggio srl

CASANOVA DI PIETRAFITTA
propr. Roberto e Andrea Landi

CASANUOVA DI NITTARDI
propr. Anstald Nittardi

CASAVECCHIA DI NITTARDI
propr. Orlando Orlandi

CASINA DI CORNIA
propr. Luginbuhl e Fontani

CASTELLARE
propr. Paolo Panerai

CASTELLO DI FONTERUTOLI
propr. Lapo Mazzei

CASTELLO DI RENCINE
propr. F.lli Brandini Marcolini

CECCHI
propr. Casa Vin. Cecchi srl

CERASI
propr. Fattoria Concadoro srl

CISPIANO
propr. Cispiano SpA

FATTORIA SANTEDAME
propr. Alvaro Gaggelli

FATTORIA TREGOLE
propr. Bartolomeo Scalerandi

GRIGNANELLO
propr. Giorgio e Marcello Gori

IL VILLINO
propr. Il Villino srl

LA BRANCAIA
propr. Bruno e Brigitte Widmer

LA CAPRAIA
propr. Renato Della Valle

LA CASTELLINA
propr. La Castellina srl

LA PIAGGIA
propr. Piaggia sas

LE FIORAIE
propr. Gabriele e
Maria Grazia Neri

LE PIAZZE
propr. Pierangiolo Piccini

LILLIANO
propr. Eleonora Berlingieri Ruspoli

MONTESASSI
propr. Montesassi srl

POGGIO ALLA CROCE
propr. Luisa Masini Gozzi

ROCCA DELLE MACIE
propr. Rocca delle Macie SpA

RODANO
propr. Vittorio Pozzesi

SETRIOLO
propr. Desmond e Antoinette
Crawford

STRACCALI
propr. Giulio Straccali SpA

TENUTA CANALE
propr. Aiello srl

VILLA CERNA
propr. Luigi Cecchi & C sas

VILLA ROSA
propr. A. M. e G. Lucherini

CASTELNUOVA BERARDENGA
(Siena)

AIOLA
propr. Giovanni Malagodi

BERARDENGA FELSINA
propr. SIA Felsina SpA

BOSSI
propr. Fertiflora SpA

CAIANO
propr. Franco CECCHI

CALLENO
propr. Angelo Parodi & C

CASALGALLO
propr. Giuliano Redditi

CASA VOLTERRANI
propr. Paolo Benvenuti

CASTELL' IN VILLA
propr. Coralia Pignatelli della
Leonessa

CASTELLO DI BOSSI
propr. Casa Vin. Castello di
Bossi SpA

CASTELLO DI CERRETO
propr. Emilio Pucci

FATTORIA DELLE LODOLINE
propr. Maria Giuseppina Radicati
di Brozolo

FATTORIA DI MONACIANO
propr. Agricola Monaciano sas

FATTORIA DI PETROIO
propr. Gian Luigi Lenzi

FATTORIA DI SELVOLE
propr. Lanfredini e Tanzini

FATTORIA IL CASTAGNO
propr. Mary Manfrin Lamm
Rusconi

FATTORIA LE PICI
propr. Gunnar Lüneburg

FATTORIA LA CASACCIA
propr. Luigi Socini Guelfi

LO SPUGNACCIO
propr. Sergio Marchetti

MACIA
propr. Marcello e Patrizia Niccolini

MISCIANELLO E
TOMARECCHIO
propr. Angiolini e Pepi

MOCENNI
propr. Nicolò Casini

OLIVIERA
propr. Mario Bandini

PAGLIARESE
propr. Alma Biasiotto Sanguineti

PAGNI
propr. Casa Vin. Pagni srl

PODERE CAMPACCI
propr. Remo Migli

POGGIO BONELLI
propr. Poggio Bonelli srl

POGGIO DELL' OLIVIERA
propr. Brunaldo Bandini

QUERCIAVALLE
propr. Fratelli Losi

SAN COSMA
propr. Bent W. Myhre

SAN FELICE
propr. Agricola San Felice SpA

SAN PIERO
propr. Andrea Salvadori

SANTA VALERIA
propr. Alberto Procovio

VALIANO
propr. I.SV.A. SpA

VIGNA AL SOLE
propr. Ademo Bandini

VILLA A SESTA
propr. Guido Bertoni

VILLA LA PAGLIAIA
propr. Agrel SpA

VITIGNANO
propr. Vitignano srl

GAIOLE IN CHIANTI (Siena)

AGRICOLTORI CHIANTI
GEOGRAFICO
propr. Agricoltori Chianti
Geografico Soc. Coop. r.l.

BACCIO DA GAIUOLE
propr. Gianfranco Innocenti

BADIA A COLTIBUONO
propr. Tenuta di Coltibuono srl

CASA NOVA DELLA
CAPPELLA
propr. Aldina Noli Mosca

CASANUOVA DI AMA
propr. Ida Carli e Figli

CASTELLO DI AMA
propr. Fattoria di Ama SpA

CASTELLO DI CACCHIANO
propr. Elisabetta Ricasoli
Balbi Valier

CASTELLO DI MELETO
propr. Viticola Toscana SpA

CASTELLO DI SAN DONATO
IN PERANO
propr. S. Donato in Perano SpA

GIORGIO REGNI
propr. Giorgio e Giuseppina Regni

I SODI
propr. F.lli Casini

LA MONTANINA
propr. Oretta Leonini

LE MICCINE
propr. Le Miccine srl

MONTIVERDI
propr. Carmela Maisano

IL PALAZZINO
propr. Alessandro e Andrea Sderci

LA MANDRIA
propr. Vitis sas

POGGERINA
propr. Francesco Giorgi

RIECINE
propr. Palmina Abbagnano Dunkley

RIETINE
propr. Luigi Bazzani

SAN GIUSTO A RENTENNANO
propr. Enrico Martini di Cigala

SAN VINCENTI
propr. San Vincenti srl

SONNINO
propr. Sonnino e Taddei

TIORCIA
propr. Angelo Acconcia

VISTARENNI
propr. Fattoria di Vistarenni srl

GREVE IN CHIANTI (Firenze)

CANDIALLE
propr. Gerd von Bentheim

CARPINETO
propr. Casa Vin. Carpineto snc

CASTELLINUZZA
propr. Giuseppe Cinuzzi

CASTELLO DI MUGNANA
propr. Fattoria di Mugnana srl

CASTELLO DI QUERCETO
propr. Castello di Querceto SpA

CASTELLO DI TIZANNO
propr. Filippo Pandolfini

CASTELLO DI UZZANO
propr. Briano Castelbarco Albani Masetti

CASTELLO DI VERRAZZANO
propr. Luigi Cappellini

CASTELLO VICCHIOMAGGIO
propr. Tenuta di Vicchiomaggio srl

CASTEL RUGGERO
propr. Ilda Pecchioli d'Afflitto

CENNATOIO
propr. Leandro Alessi

FATTORIA CASENUOVE
propr. Pietro Pandolfini

FATTORIA LE CORTI ANICHINI
propr. Adriano e Giuseppe Anichini

FATTORIA QUERCIABELLA
propr. Ag. Campoverde di G. Mazzanti & C

FILETTA
propr. Guido Socci

FONTODI
propr. Domiziano e Dino Manetti

FOSSI
propr. Duilio, Gianfranco e
Andrea Fossi

IL GUERRINO
propr. Ornella Taddei Loretelli

LA COLOMBAIA
propr. Soc. Notorius sa

LA MADONNINA
propr. F.lli Triacca

LA MASSA
propr. Fattorie Vinicole Riunite La
Massa sas

LAMOLE
propr. Adele Carrara Toscano

LA PRESURA
propr. Carlo Bucciolini

LA QUERCIA
propr. So. Co. Vi. Ch.

LE BOCCE
propr. Le Bocce SpA

LE MASSE DI SAN LEOLINO
propr. Norman Bain

LUCA DELLA ROBBIA
propr. Gabriella e Leandro Alessi

MELAZZANO
propr. Piero Falciani

MEZZUOLA
propr. Assuntina Federigi Crispini

MONTAGLIARI
propr. Giovanni Cappelli

MONTORO
propr. Carafa di Roccella

MONTORO E SELVOLE
propr. Giovanni Matteuzzi

PODERUZZO
propr. Luisa Cappelli

PONETA
propr. Tenuta di Poneta SpA

RIGNANA
propr. Arminio Gericke

RIPERTOLI
propr. F.lli Gestri

SAGRONA E FAULE
propr. Nello Manetti e F.lli

SANTO STEFANO
propr. Mauro Bendinelli

SAVIGNOLA PAOLINA
propr. Carlo Fabbri

SUGAME
propr. Valerio Mazzuoli

VECCHIE TERRE DI
MONTEFILI
propr. Roccaldo Acuti

VIGNAMAGGIO
propr. Ranieri Sanminiatelli

VILLA CAFAGGIO
propr. Basilica Cafaggio srl

VILLA CALCINAIA
propr. Neri Capponi

VITIANO
propr. Ortensio e Marina Camagni

VITICCIO
propr. Lucio e Luciano Landini

POGGIBONSI (Siena)

FATTORIA DELLE FONTI
propr. Vito e Emma Imberti

FATTORIA DI CINCIANO
propr. Soc. SIA srl

GRANDUCATO
propr. Enopolio di Poggibonsi
SpA

MELINI
propr. Melini SpA

ORMANNI
propr. Francesco Brini

POGGIARELLO
propr. Piantella e Brini sdf

SAN FABIANO CALCINAIA
propr. San Fabiano Calcinaia SpA

RADDA IN CHIANTI (Siena)

CAMPOMAGGIO
propr. Luigi Sedelmayer

CASTELLO D'ALBOLA
propr. Fattoria di Albola SpA

CASTELLO DI
MONTERINALDI
propr. Agricola Monterinaldi srl

CASTELLO DI RADDA
propr. Giampaolo Bonechi

CASTELLO DI VOLPAIA
propr. Giovannella Stianti
Mascheroni

CASTELVECCHI
propr. Carmen e Isabel Gutierrez

COLLE BERETO
propr. Franca e Lorenzo Pinzauti

CROGNOLE
propr. Gian Paolo Sghembri

LA CASACCIA
propr. Nausika ltd

MONTEMAGGIO
propr. Giampaolo Bonechi

MONTERAPONI
propr. Maria Carla Tuci Braganti

PETROIO ALLA VIA DELLA
MALPENSATA
propr. Fausto Cammarata

PODERE CAPACCIA
propr. Giampaolo Pacini & C

PODERE TERRENO ALLA VIA
DELLA VOLPAIA
propr. Marie Sylvie Haniez

POGGERINO
propr. Floriana Ginori Conti

SALCETINO
propr. Adele Carrara Toscano

SAN FEDELE
propr. Alessandro Sampieri

VAL DELLE CORTI
propr. Giorgio Bianchi

VIGNALE
propr. Fattoria Vignale SpA

VIGNAVECCHIA
propr. Franco e Sisa Beccari

SAN CASCIANO VAL DI PESA
(Firenze)

CASTELGREVE
propr. Castelli del Grevepesa Soc.
Coop. a r.l.

FATTORIA BELVEDERE
propr. Campoli srl

FATTORIA DELLE CORTI
CORSINI
propr. Agricola Le Corti srl

FATTORIA DELLE
FORNACELLE
propr. Emilio e Paola Baroni

FATTORIA LA LOGGIA
propr. Giulio Baruffaldi

FATTORIA LE RIPE
propr. Eredi Bacci Croci

IL PALAGIO
propr. Goretti Miniati Eredi

ISPOLI
propr. Patrizia Landini

LA SALA
propr. Laura Baronti

LE LAME
propr. Mario Zanobini

LUIANO
propr. Fattoria di Luiano snc

MACHIAVELLI
propr. Serristori SpA

PALAZZO AL BOSCO
propr. Giovanna Querci

RIPANERA
propr. Maria Grazia Duranti

ROSSO DI MASSANERA
propr. Ambrogio e Carlo Cattaneo

SANTA LUCIA
propr. Villa Branca srl

TALENTE
propr. Ariberto Guidani

VILLA MONTEPALDI
propr. Villa Montepaldi srl

TAVARNELLE VAL DI PESA
(Firenze)

COLI
propr. Giampiero e Gianfranco
Coli

CONIO
propr. Imm. Conio sas di Godi
Umberto

FATTORIA MORROCCO
propr. Cosimo Fabri Guarini

IL POGGIOLINO
propr. Carlo Pacini

MARTRIOLO
propr. Federici e Moretta

MONTECCHIO
propr. Ivo Nuti

POGGIO Al SOLE
propr. Poggio al Sole srl

SANTA TRINITA
propr. Le Chiantigiane srl

CHIANTI WINE SCORE CARD: 1966–86

*****	a memorable year
****	a first-class vintage
***	a good year
**	an average year
*	a poor year

1966	***		1977	****
1967	*****		1978	****
1968	***		1979	***
1969	****		1980	****
1970	***		1981	****
1971	*****		1982	****
1972	**		1983	*****
1973	***		1984	**
1974	****		1985	*****
1975	*****		1986	****
1976	*			

SELECT BIBLIOGRAPHY

Over 200 publications have been consulted in the course of researching this book. But it would be pretentious, I feel, to fill up pages of bibliography for what is, after all, not an academic work. So I will confine myself to listing primary sources, and those publications which, in one way or another, are directly concerned with Chianti.

Sources

Appian: *Roman History*
Cassiodorus: *Variae*
Cato: *De Agri Cultura*
Catullus: *Poems*
Columella: *De Re Rustica*
Dio: *Roman History*
Horace: *Odes, Epodes and Satires*
Juvenal: *Satires*
Livy: *Histories*
Martial: *Epigrams*
Petronius: *Satyricon*
Plautus: *Plays*
Pliny the Elder: *Natural History*
Pliny the Younger: *Selected Letters*
Rutilius Namatianus: *De Reditu Suo*
Strabo: *Geography*
Suetonius: *Lives of the Caesars*
Tacitus: *Histories*
Varro: *Rerum Rusticarum*
      De Lingua Latina
Virgil: *Georgics*
      Eclogues
      Aeneid

Other Primary Sources

The registers of the Abbeys of Coltibuono and Passignano (in the State Archives at Florence)
The registers of the Badia di Ripoli
The Ricasoli Archives at Brolio
The Capponi Archives at Florence
The Datini papers, Prato
Il Libro di Montaperti, Cesare Paoli, Firenze, 1889
Liber Extimationum, Il Libro degli Estimi 1269, Olaf Brattö (ed.) Göteborg, 1956.
The Communal Archives of Radda and Gaiole (those of Castellina, unfortunately, have been destroyed)
Luca di Totto da Panzano: Cronaca (in Arch. Stor. Toscani, Vol. V)
Statuti delle Arti dei Fornai e dei Vinattieri di Firenze (F. Morandini, Firenze, 1956)
Tabula Peutingeriana, K. Miller (ed.), Ravensburg, 1888

General Works

Luigi Biadi, *Compendio storico politico religioso della Castellina del Chianti*, Firenze, 1867
Paolo Cammarosano, *La famiglia dei Berardenghi*, Spoleto, 1974
Gastone Canessa, *Guida del Chianti Classico*, Firenze, 1972
G. Canestrini, 'Documenti per servire alla Storia della Milizia Italiana del XIII secolo al XVI raccolti negli Archivi della Toscana' (in *Archivo Storico Italiano*)
Antonio Casabianca, *Guida Storica del Chianti*, Firenze, 1970
G. Cavalcanti, *Istorie fiorentine*
Consorzio Vino Chianti Classico, *Il Chianti Classico*, Firenze, 1974
Robert Davidsohn, *Storia di Firenze*, Firenze, 1956-66
Thomas Dempster, *De Etruria Regali*, Firenze, 1723-4
Alessandro Gherardi, *Le Consulte della Repubblica Fiorentina*, Firenze, 1896
T. Guarducci, *Guida illustrata della Val di Pesa*, San Casciano, 1904
Padre Ildefonso di S.Luigi, *Delizie degli Eruditi Toscani*, Firenze, 1700-89
Giovanni Lami, *S. Ecclesiae Florentinae Monumenta*, Firenze, 1758
M. Lopez Pegna, 'Castelli del Chianti', in *L'Universo*, 1954
O. Malavolti, *Historia de' fatti e guerre de' Senesi*, etc., Venezia, 1599
Ricordano Malespini, *Historie antica*, Firenze, 1568
Enzo Mazzeschi, *Cronache d'archeologia senese*, Siena, 1976

Italo Moretti and Renato Stopani: *I Castelli dell'antica Lega del Chianti*, Firenze 1972
  Chiese romaniche in Val di Pesa e Val di Greve, Firenze, 1972
  Chiese romaniche nel Chianti, Firenze, 1966
  La pieve di S. Maria Novella in Chianti, Firenze, 1971
  Volpaia: un castello fiorentina nel Chianti, San Casciano, 1972 (privately printed)
Alfredo Moroni, *Prime comunità cristiane e strade romane nei territori di Arezzo, Siena, Chiusi*, Siena 1973
Luigi Pagliai, *Regesto di Coltibuono* (Regesta Chararum Italiae), Rome, 1909
Lamberto Paronetto, *Il Magnifico Chianti*, Verona, 1967
Luigi Passerini, *Genealogia e storia della Famiglia Ricasoli*, Firenze, 1861
Silvio Pieri, *Toponomastica della Valle dell'Arno*, Rome, 1919
Johan Plesner, *L'emigration de la campagne à la ville libre de Florence au XIII siècle*, Copenhagen, 1934
Emmanuele Repetti, *Dizionario Geografico Fisico Storico della Toscana*, Firenze, 1833-48
Gaspero Righini, *Il Chianti Classico*, Pisa, 1972
Bino Sanminiatelli, *Vignamaggio e Montagliari dal secolo XIV ai giorni nostri*, Firenze, undated
Pietro Santini, 'Studi sull'antica costituzione del Comune di Firenze' in *Archivio Storico Italiano*, V.a serie, Tomo XXV and XXVI, 1900
Ferdinand Schevill, *Medieval and Renaissance Florence*, Harper Torch Books, 1957
  Siena, New York, 1907
Renato Stopani, *Panzano, un castello della Lega di Val di Greve*, Firenze, 1971
Giovanni Tarigioni Tozzetti, *Relazioni d'alcuni viaggi fatti in diverse parti della Toscana*, Firenze, 1768-79
Giugurta Tommasi, *Historie di Siena*, Venezia, 1625
Giovanni Villani, *Cronica*, Firenze, 1845
Lodovico Zdekauer, *La vita privata dei Senesi nel dugento. La vita pubblica dei Senesi nel dugento* (Ristampa anastatica, Bologna, undated)

INDEX